TOTAL RECALL

*Achieve and Succeed
in Business, School, and
Friendship* by mastering
simple techniques for
remembering *anything*

TOTAL RECALL

SUCCESSFULLY BOOST YOUR MEMORY POWER

Joan Minninger Ph.D.

THORSONS/RODALE
Wellingborough•Emmaus

First UK edition published 1987

Published by arrangement with Rodale Press Inc., Emmaus, PS, USA

British Library Cataloguing in Publication Data

Minninger, Joan
  Total recall : how to boost your memory power.
  1. Mnemonics
  I. Title
  153.1'4   BF385

  ISBN 0-7225-1505-7

Printed and bound in Great Britain

10 9 8 7 6 5 4 3 2

To Bob and Mary Goulding

Contents

Acknowledgements xi

Introduction xii

What Do You Want to Remember?

Part I

Why We Forget

1. How Much Can People Remember? 2

2. Emotional Blocks 4

Protecting Ourselves with Blocks/Blocks That Mean You Care/Blocks Because Nobody Cares/What Causes Emotional Blocks?/Resolving Emotional Blocks/When to Keep Your Blocks/What Does It Mean When You Always Forget?/Being in Therapy/Try This for a Fresh Attitude Toward Forgetting

3. Mechanical Blocks 18

Misfiled Information/What Do You See?/Creating Reality/How to Retrieve Misfiled Information/Distraction Before We "Remember"/Failure to Acquire and Record Information/Distraction during Retrieval/The Price of Remembering/When All Else Fails/Try This to See How Interference Thwarts Remembering

4. **Physical Blocks** **26**

Matter Over Mind/Diet/Illnesses/Injuries/Allergies/
Drugs/Alcohol/Smoking/Lack of Exercise/Fa-
tigue/Tension/Try This Defence Against Tension-
Induced Memory Blocks

5. **When It's OK to Forget** **48**

Forgetting for Self-Preservation/Forgetting Pain
and Sorrow/Forgetting for Attention and Support/
Using Negative Memories/Forgetting Because
We're Finished/Memory Misdemeanors/Learning
to Choose Your Memories/Try This Quiz to Assess
Your Ability to Forget Constructively

Part II

How We Remember

6. **The Seat of Memory—Theories through the Ages** **61**

Aristotle and the Ancients/Inventing the Brain/
Comparing Computers to the Human Brain/
Ebbinghaus and Nonsense/Bartlett and Meaning/
Twentieth-Century Debates/Freud and Memory/
Try This to See if You Forget for a Reason

7. **How the Brain Remembers** **70**

What We Remember With/A Brief History of the
Brain/How Much Will You Remember?/Where
Does the Brain Remember?/How Does the Brain
Remember?/Brain Size/Can Memories Be Swal-
lowed?/Memory Pills/Things to Come/Try This to
Evaluate Your Personal Potential for Remembering

8. **Three Stages of Memory** **82**

Immediate Memory/Short-Term Memory/Long-
Term Memory/Try This Exercise for Recognizing
Memory Stages

9. **Three Steps to Remembering** **90**

Registration/Retention/Retrieval/Which Lasts
Longer?/Why Learn Anything?/Try This to Compare Recall and Recognition

10. **Three Kinds of Memory** **99**

Are You Verbal, Visual, or Kinesthetic?/Which Is
Better?/Remembering Kinesthetically/Photo-
graphic Memory/Using Both Verbal and Visual
Memory/Where Does Kinesthetic Memory Come
In?/Try This to Determine Your Kind of Memory

11. **Four Ways to Remember** **110**

Episodic Memory—"Where Did I Put It?"/Seman-
tic Memory—Naming Things to Remember Them/
Skill Memory and Fact Memory/The Problem with
Theories/Try This to See How You Remember

12. **Remembering—Young vs. Old** **120**

How Older People Learn New Things/How Child-
ren Remember/Losing Synaptic Connections/
"Am I Getting Senile?"/Competing Memories/Try
This to Spot Abnormal Forgetfulness

13. **Does Anyone Have a Perfect Memory?** **128**

VP and Professor Aitken/Idiot Savants/Famous
People with Good Memories/Try This to Pinpoint
What You Remember Easily

Part III

How To

14. **How to Improve Your Memory** **135**

Rating Memory Capacity/The World's Digit-Span
Champion/Shortening the Trip from Short-Term
to Long-Term Memory/The Uphill Struggle from

Short to Long, or "How Scoop Flash Makes the Front Page"/The Mind as a Library/Using Retrieval Cues/"Depth of Processing"/Pleasant vs. Unpleasant/"We've Got to Get Organized"—Using Structures/Playing "Grown-up"/Reinforcement—Writing Things Down or Rehearsing/In the Mood to Remember/Recall through Hypnotism/"I've Got Rhythm . . ."/Misremembering/Making Structures for Remembering/Try This Exercise in Grouping to Remember

15. **How to Use Memory Systems** **151**

Numbering Things/A Foolproof Phone Number System/Abbreviations/Use Location to Help Remember/The Peg System/How to Remember 20 Things in Less than 2 Minutes/Using Pegs to Learn New Things/It's Okay Not to Love Systems/Try This to Impress Friends with Your Ability to Remember

16. **How to Study** **167**

Be Sure to Make Mistakes/The Bad News/Memorizing/To Understand or to Memorize?/Memorizing Techniques/Conjuring Your Own "Tricks"/How Long Should You Study?/Predicting Your Performance/Aural Repetition—An Inferior Study Aid/Forgetting and Restudying/Theories about Forgetting—Fading vs. Interference/Memories That Interfere with Memory/Studying Formulas/Studying History/Studying Music/Studying to Music/Some Laws for Learning/Experimenting with Rats, Cats, and College Students/Darwin's Law for Studying/Try This to Determine Your Best Studying Technique

17. **How to Remember Facts** **186**

Intelligence and Memory/Do You Understand?/Try This to Test and Enhance Your Power of Recall

18. **How to Remember What You Read** **192**

Structures for Nonfiction Books and Articles/Speed Reading—Good or Bad?/Misreading/The Patterns/A Need to Know/Try This to Test Your Memory of What You Read

19. How to Remember What You Hear **201**

Speed Listening/Mishearing/Analyzing What You Hear/Listening to Silence/Giving Directions/When Everyone Talks at Once/Inadmissible Evidence/ Structuring What You Hear/Try This to Sharpen Your Listening Memory

20. How to Remember Names and Faces **209**

Sharing a Common Weakness/Memorable Names/ "Naughty" Names/How to Remember Faces/How Well Do You Remember?/Divide and Conquer?/ Misnaming/Why Fictional Names Are Unforgettable/Stage Names/Strategies for Coping with Memory Lapses/Survival Kit/Try This Exercise for Remembering Names and Faces

21. How to Remember Dates and Numbers **229**

Using Your Life as a Calendar/The Easiest Way to Remembr/Reciting and Grouping/When Should You Try a Number System?/Don't Be Scared/ Exchanging Numbers for Letters/Try This if You Want to Learn a Number System

22. How to Rehearse **242**

Memorizing a Script/Should We Practice Memorizing?/Memorizing a Speech/Memorizing Movement/Even Professionals Can Goof/Rehearsing for Life?/Try This to Celebrate Memory

23. A Bag of Miscellaneous Memory Tricks **249**

24. How to Be Happy Though Forgetful **252**

Buy a Memory Insurance Policy/Three Things You Should Never Forget

Bibliography **255**

Index **262**

Acknowledgements

With special appreciation to Eleanor Knowles Dugan, whose humor, brilliance, and generosity are woven through the fabric of this book; to Mark Harrington, whose intelligence and tenacity make him the ideal researcher; to Robert L. Goulding, M.D., and Mary McClure Goulding, M.S.W., who taught me how to move my clients through memory blocks using Redecision Therapy; to all the conceptualizers and researchers from Aristotle to Alan Baddeley whose contributions to the understanding of memory have enriched this book; to Colgan Schlank, who foresaw the book; and to Charles Gerras, superlative editor, who said "Yes!"

Introduction: What Do You Want to Remember?

Students at a memory workshop were asked what they wanted to remember:

"Names and events."

"I want to connect names and faces."

"Remember what I read."

"Not to forget appointments."

"My mother-in-law's birthday."

"The key points and not get bogged down in detail."

"Where I put my shopping list."

Most people go around saying they have a terrible memory. They use their "bad memories" as a tool to protect, comfort, annoy, or sabotage themselves.

It may comfort you to think of your memory—what it is, how it works, what it retains, and what it loses—as something outside yourself that has nothing to do with what you do and who you are, but this just isn't so. Once you find out *why* you forget and *how* you remember, you can decide what you want to do about it.

The most important discovery you can make is to realize that *you* alone decide what you will remember. This discovery doesn't have to be threatening or involve drudgery either. It can be invigorating, liberating, and even pleasurable.

Remembering in new ways stretches the mind like a new exercise stretches the body. Imagine your mind togged out in a bright, new exercise suit, jogging in place, ready to try something new.

How do you want to remember differently when you finish this book? Make a statement.

"I want to _____

_____"

Part I

Why We Forget

1
How Much Can People Remember?

A typical adult's brain contains 15 billion to 100 billion neurons. If we accept the lower figure, this means that you can remember two-to-the-ten-billionth-power bits of information. Just to write out this number that represents the items your mind is capable of holding, you would have to write a zero a second for 90 years, says neurologist Richard M. Restak. Popular science writer Carl Sagan uses the higher figure, representing the equivalent of information in 10 billion encyclopedia pages. The brain, he says, is a very big place in a very small space.

The glory of the human mind centers in its ability to be bombarded with a million bits of diverse information every day and convert them to intelligent thought. It does this by evaluating, sorting, deciding and redeciding on sequences and relationships, discarding the irrelevant, filling in the blanks with bits of information from its files, and filing the new images for later use.

The key word here is *evaluating.* By placing a value on a bit of information we let it advance to the forefront or recede to form a part of a larger picture. We can do this temporarily or permanently, and we can convert the images later if we want to. No tape recorder, camera, or even computer can do all of this. Computers, in fact, are just very fast, efficient morons, with neither imagination nor common sense. It takes a computer four minutes to work out the right combination for a Rubik's Cube, considering every possible turn until all the correct ones have been made. An efficient teenager can do it in two minutes and the 16-year-old 1982 World Champion did it in 22.95 seconds!

Discarding information is essential for remembering. According to *Science Digest* (November, 1983), scientists estimate that we remember only 1 out of every 100 pieces we receive. If we remembered everything, they say, we would be "paralyzed by information overload." A good memory must be selective.

Imagine yourself strolling through a park. You hear the babble of children's voices, the twittering of birds, and the sound of traffic in a nearby street. The mother on the bench hears her own child's voice. The bird watcher hears the mating call of the yellow-breasted titmouse. The car enthusiast recognizes the familiar hum of his friend's souped-up T-bird. Each individual automatically tunes in the sounds that have value and blocks out the extraneous ones.

This blocking process is part of intelligence, but it can also lead to problems. What happens when our natural blocking process becomes a handicap? And what about blocks caused by illness, injury, fatigue, or misunderstanding? We are going to look at three kinds of memory blocks:

emotional, mechanical, physical.

We filter noise for information that interests us: a mother hears her child; a bird watcher hears the yellow-breasted titmouse's song; a teenage boy hears the hum of a friend's souped-up T-bird.

2
Emotional Blocks

People are upset when they forget what they want to or need to remember. The result of their memory "blocks" can be anything from a casual annoyance to a major inconvenience to a life-threatening disaster.

At the very least, memory blocks affect how we feel about ourselves. How do you feel when you forget? People at my memory workshops say:

"I go blank."
"I feel frustrated."
"Selfish."
"It embarrasses others and makes me look silly."
"Disappointed."
"Stupid."
"Guilty."
"It doesn't bother me at all."

How do you feel when someone forgets your name? "If one of my bosses forgets my name, I feel pretty worthless," said one of my students. "I assume others feel that way when I forget their names."

Memory blocks can even threaten how we live, our health, our personal relationships, and our income:

"I lose a lot of business contacts."
"My wife is furious with me."
"I waste so much time."
"I really mess things up at work. I may lose my job."
"My employees think I don't like them."
"My life is a wreck."

Protecting Ourselves with Blocks

Some memory blocks are curious, dramatic, and specific to the people who have them. These people are unconsciously protecting themselves in some way.

Gisela attended a workshop I did for the Civil Service Commission. She worked in a typing pool for 20 men, and her goal was to be able to walk down the hall at work and address her bosses by name: "Good morning, Mr. Thompson. Good morning, Mr. Harris." When her turn came to recount the names of those in the workshop, she remembered all the women's names but none of the men's.

My attempts to resolve this curious memory block ran up against a blank wall time after time. Finally, we re-created her office setting in the workshop and invited her to "walk down the hall," saying hello to the men as she passed them. She seemed embarrassed and didn't look them in the eye.

"What are you feeling when you look away?" I asked.

"Guilty," she replied.

"Why?" I asked.

"Well, I'm a married woman."

"Yes?"

"The Bible says that 'he who lusts after a woman in his own heart is guilty of adultery' and I think that applies to women, too. I get very excited when I see these men, and I don't want my mind and heart feeling that way about anyone but my husband."

In time I was able to convince Gisela that remembering the names of men she encounters socially or in business need not affect her morals. She had been confused. She really thought that having warm, happy feelings about a man and subconsciously acknowledging him by remembering his name was to betray her husband. She had no idea that much of the human race walks around having warm, happy feelings about much of the rest of the human race (both sexes!) without violating even the strictest moral code.

She decided to try looking men in the eye. When she risked it, she found she could remember the men's names as well as the women's.

Mary, a singer from San Diego, had trouble remembering song lyrics. "No matter what I do," she said, "I forget words to songs. I repeat them over and over in my head, but it doesn't help."

"What do you do when you're performing and you forget the words?" I asked.

Her face lit up. "I tell jokes and stories."

"Does the audience like them?"

"Oh, yes. People laugh and laugh." Mary had never really thought of laughter as the root of her problem. Now she understood. The positive response she got for burlesquing her forgetfulness was an incentive *not* to remember.

"If you cut out the jokes and stories, you'll be able to remember the lyrics," I said.

"Oh, I can't do that. That's the best part of the act."

Mary had developed this wonderful way to amuse, but part of her kept saying, "You should remember the lyrics to the songs." It was a happy block. She decided to stop arguing with herself and tell jokes.

Louise from Seattle could remember first names, but not last names. Several sessions in which we practiced techniques for remembering last names proved fruitless. "How do you feel about last names, Louise?" I asked one day.

She wasn't sure what I meant, thought a minute, then said flatly, "I hate them. Last names mean somebody owns you. First I had my father's last name. Then I had my first husband's last name. Then I had my second husband's last name. Then I had my third husband's last name. I'm so sick and tired of men's last names. Only my first name is really mine.

"When I was a little girl, I always had to call people 'Mr.' or 'Mrs.' so-and-so while they called each other by their first names and had a lot more fun."

She realized her inability to remember last names was entirely self-imposed. She had a choice: stay angry and refuse to learn last names or drop her anger and remember them.

Dan, a policeman, wanted help in remembering phone numbers. He was particularly annoyed at his inability to remember the number for police headquarters. For the past five years he had had to call headquarters every 90 minutes while on duty, and he had to look the number up each time.

This seemed incredible to me until I learned that Dan was a 20-year veteran of the force. His feelings soon came out. "For 15 years, they trusted me; and now I've got all these procedures like I'm a little kid. I resent it! My mind refuses to learn that number!"

"Well, who has to look it up each time?" I asked. He raved and ranted about unfairness and bureaucracy, but he finally recognized the connection and realized he had a choice.

Barbara wanted to remember addresses and telephone numbers. She could remember only three—those of her home, her office, and a close friend's. In one of their sessions Barbara's therapist wrote down his own phone number and asked her how she felt about it. She stared at it quietly for a long time.

Finally she said: "I haven't thought about this in years. When I was 12 years old, I read in the newspaper about people having numbers tattooed on their arms. Then they were taken off to concentration camps. I think I decided then that I'd never associate a number with a person. I don't think I want to give that up." This was her way of seeing people as individuals, and it gave her a sense of power.

Blocks That Mean You Care

Forgetting doesn't always mean you don't want to remember. Here is some news. Write it down. Embroider it on a tea towel. Chisel it in stone.

Caring Can Cause Memory Blocks

Sometimes we try so hard to remember that we end up defeating ourselves. Forgetting doesn't necessarily mean that we don't care. Sometimes it means just the opposite.

We can shut ourselves into a prison that denies us freedom to remember.

Much of this became clear to me while I was working on my own memory problem through several sessions with Arthur Rissman, a specialist in helping people break through creative blocks.

"What's the problem?" Art asked.

"I need to know how to remember students' names," I told him. "I sometimes have over 150 students a year in my university courses. I've resorted to taking their pictures, writing the names underneath, and covering each name as I look at the picture. But when I try to recall them, I wind up with a bunch I consistently forget or confuse."

"Tell me how you feel about the people whose names are in the bunch you forget."

Startled, I heard myself saying, "Why, those are the people I like best!"

Part of Art's genius is his uncanny ability to ask the right questions. This time he followed-up with: "Can you now see the playmates you had as a child?"

"No," I answered, "we didn't live near other children."

"Can you see the person who took care of you the most?"

"During the day I was with housekeepers."

"Did you like them?"

"Oh, yes," I told him.

"What were their names?"

"I can't remember. We moved a lot."

"What do your former housekeepers and your students whose names you can't remember have in common?" he asked.

"They both came and went," I said.

"My hunch," said Art, "is that missing people was less painful for you if you forgot their names."

"Of course!" I shouted.

"You are still protecting yourself in this way. Do you need to?"

"Obviously not. I know and enjoy a lot of people and see them when I want to."

"Is it okay for you to remember the names of the students you like?"

"Sure," I said.

"Will you?"

"Sure."

My block had been useful because it *protected* me from *caring*. I no longer needed it and could discard it. However, I had one more conflict. Sometimes I confused names.

"There are two students I like in my class whose names are Bill and John. I keep calling Bill 'John' and John 'Bill', and never remember which is which. Each has taken to writing his name in chalk on the sole of his shoe so he can hold it up when I call him by the other name."

"How are they alike?" Art asked.

"They both are warm and friendly."

"How are they different?"

"One talks more than the other."

"Got it?" he asked.

"Right," I agreed.

"Now, just notice which one talks more and you won't confuse them."

Blocks Because Nobody Cares

When my workshops meet, I usually canvas the room, asking the students what they hope to achieve in the class. An older woman in one group had a rather unusual request: "I want to remember my trip to China."

Several of the workshop members looked incredulous or stifled startled giggles. "You went to China and you don't remember it?" I asked.

"Very little. When I try to tell my friends about the highlights of the trip, my mind becomes a blank. They go to lots of exotic places. I want to impress them; but since I got back from China I can't remember much of what I saw."

I wondered if she had somehow failed to notice what was around her through preoccupation or some block. "Did you have experiences that delighted you?"

"Yes, of course."

"Then imagine you are where you usually talk to your friends. Start to tell them about your fascinating experiences and notice their responses."

Her face went blank and then looked sad. "My friends are very . . . animated. They have so many exciting things happening to them. They don't seem to want to listen when I talk unless I talk about them. Mostly they just want me to listen, and they sure don't want to hear about something they didn't do themselves."

I went to the blackboard and picked up a piece of chalk. "How many people here have ever been to China?" I asked. Several raised their hands and several more commented that they had read a lot about the country.

"Notice the attention you are getting here," I said. "Tell us about the first city you visited." As she talked, I wrote down the highlights of each remembrance on the blackboard. Slowly, she began to glow as she summoned up rich images of seven different places she had visited. Sometimes she couldn't recall the name of the city, but when people in the class called out suggested names, she was able to recognize it.

Obviously she had enjoyed her trip and remembered it in great detail. However, she had blocked the information because it had not served its purpose — to make her important in the eyes of her friends.

What Causes Emotional Blocks?

All these blocks grew out of conflict. Each of these people used memory blocks as protection from something. If you want an inscription for your thinking cap, here it is:

> A memory block is a mental barrier that we use to protect ourselves from what we perceive as harm, error, or ridicule.

Our blocks exist to protect us. When we forget some things and not others, there may be an internal conflict about the material that makes us anxious and prevents remembering. We sense that remembering may be dangerous, inconvenient, or embarrassing.

Forgetting may be protective, but it can also be a dreadful nuisance. We can eliminate some of these blocks when we understand the cause. Others may be easier to live with than to change. Still others are desirable and should be maintained.

Resolving Emotional Blocks

You've seen how several people came to terms with their emotional memory blocks. If you suspect that you may also have an emotional block, you have several choices:

- Discard your block because you no longer need it.
- Develop new strategies for dealing with your block.
- Make friends with your block.

When to Keep Your Blocks

It is important not to discard a block until you are sure you can live without it. Your block may be protecting you in ways that you don't fully understand or appreciate.

For most of us the ultimate fear is death. This sounds melodramatic, but in one bizarre case, I encountered a woman who was certain that she would die if she remembered. The woman was the mother of my friend, Florence Mischel, and her strange story began in Europe at the end of the last century. Florence's mother, Rose, was born in Russia in 1889, the ninth of 11 children in a Jewish family. During the pogroms, the family fled to Romania.

To fully understand the implications of this story, you must appreciate the great reverence and thirst for education possessed by all Jews. "Even the poorest Jewish family," recalled Rose, "had a little tin box on the mantle where they would put coins to send boys to study the Torah."

All the children in Rose's family were remarkably bright; but as they reached their teens, they died one by one, in the order of their birth. They may have succumbed to some genetic disorder or to the hardships and diseases common at the time, but Rose's mother began to wonder if there was a curse on her family.

One of Rose's older sisters was a brilliant scholar, and her parents were preparing to send her to the university, something unheard of for a female. Then the girl died. Rose was just nine and remembered that the entire village closed their shops and went into mourning for this remarkable young woman.

Rose's mother was desolate and frantic at the relentless toll death was taking on her children. She consulted the village rabbi (literally "teacher") to try to understand why God was punishing her in this way.

Now, the rabbi may have been a stupid man; or he may have been the product of an era in which men genuinely believed that women should not be educated; or he may have been misunderstood by Rose's mother. In any case, Rose's mother returned home with the rabbi's judgment: "God is angry because you worship education more than you worship Him." Rose's mother resolved that none of her surviving children would ever attend school.

Times were hard and Rose's father set out on foot to find a better life for his family. He walked across Europe, reached Glasgow, and took passage to the United States. After working in New York City for a year or two, he sent for his family. Rose was now 14 and went directly to work, but her younger sister, Leah, was required to attend school. After a year of education, Leah died.

Despite Rose's inability to read and write, she was very clever. It was common for sweatshop owners to cheat their uneducated workers, but Rose could figure the wages owed her in a few seconds – "I did 6 wool dresses at £0.27 each plus £0.04 a dress bonus for black-on-black, 8 silk dresses at £0.31 each, and 17 shirtwaisters at £0.12 each, you owe me £6.38." When the garment factories were unionized, she became a shop steward. Rose was beautiful and talented; but throughout her adult life, she maintained that she couldn't read a word. Despite the efforts of her children to teach her, she would cross her arms, press her lips together, and say, "I'm just a dummy."

Yet Rose was somewhat embarrassed by her illiteracy and made every effort to hide it from outsiders. Once, in her later years, she was going to travel cross-country on the luxury train, the Super Chief. It was customary for passengers to read the menu and write their meal orders on little cards, something Rose could not do. Florence discreetly contacted the waiters ahead of time. She told them her mother had very poor eyesight and was too vain to wear glasses. Florence would be so grateful if they would read her the menu and write her order for her. Well tipped, the waiters complied.

Still Rose disdained information from books. "What, you made it from a cookbook?" she would say to her daughters. "*I* never cook from books!" It was the ultimate dismissal.

When Rose was in her seventies and bored with inactivity, Florence hired a reading teacher to come three or four times a week. Still Rose would not learn to read. Florence began to speculate on what had happened. Rose had been nine and *must* have known how to read before her mother's fateful visit to the rabbi. After that, Florence suspected, Rose had been so terrified by the deaths of her beloved sisters that she blocked all memory of how to read. Her own life would be forfeit if she committed such a blasphemy. Remembering meant dying.

Florence tried a new approach. "Mother," she said, "you are very smart and have a fantastic memory. I know you're not a dummy and you have had to work very hard for many years *not* to learn to read. It must have been very difficult for you." To her surprise, her mother began to cry. "It's true," she admitted. For a long time they talked about Rose's dead sisters and whether God would really punish anyone for learning to read.

Then Florence said, "Mother, you are 75 years old. That's a good, long life. Suppose that God would strike you dead tomorrow if you learned to read? So what? Why not risk it?"

Somewhat reluctantly, Rose consented. Florence made flash cards for her with pictures and the English words. When Rose went to sound out a word like "cat" or "dog" she would say it backwards from right to left as Hebrew is written, showing that she really had learned Hebrew as a child!

Rose died at 95, still not fully literate, but almost convinced that God would not strike her dead for remembering how to read.

What Does It Mean When You Always Forget?

Much of this book will urge you not to harass yourself when you have good reasons for forgetting. But what happens when forgetting becomes a major disruption in your life?

Stop and ask yourself these questions:

- Do you frequently exceed an acceptable level for errors caused by forgetting? (This level will vary widely from person to person and situation to situation.)

- Are you forgetting more than you can emotionally and physically afford to forget? (This frequently depends on temperament, upbringing, and profession.)

- Has forgetting become physically or emotionally threatening? Is it even self-destructive?

If you answer yes to any or all of these questions, it may be time to get outside help. If you constantly forget, and if that forgetting is *constantly* distressing, destructive, or dangerous, then you need more help than this book can offer.

When the disasters of forgetting become the central issue in a person's life, when the stress of forgetting gets irreversibly bound up in the stress of social, financial, and personal failure, then it's time to look for fundamental causes. Extreme stress, in itself, can produce memory loss. Self-destructive urges can make us sabotage ourselves, and poor emotional health in general can create a climate in which "everything goes wrong."

If neither old nor new memory structures work, despite all our energies, and the everyday reasons for forgetting don't seem to be the cause, then it's time to seek professional help.

Being in Therapy

Many of us resist therapy as a resolution to our personal concerns including memory blocks. Therapy has a broad range of techniques and approaches, each has a particular strength or effectiveness with individual persons and psychological problems.

In my own practice I have found Redecision Therapy to be of particular value to clients who berate themselves over their poor memory. This is a short-term results-oriented therapy developed by Robert L. Goulding, M.D., and Mary McClure Goulding, M.S.W., that asks the client to make a contract to change something in his life—not to "work on it" or describe it or justify it, but *change* it. The contract can be for something as seemingly trivial as not biting your nails during the next week or as urgent as not committing suicide during the next 24 hours.

Redecision Therapy has proven successful with people who realize they are at an impasse and are willing to look for a different way to solve an old problem. Because logic and "ought to" have already failed, Redecision Therapy gets the client to experience his *feelings* and then decide if he is willing to trade "safe" old feelings, however unpleasant, for positive new feelings. As Eric Berne explained in *Games People Play* (Penguin, 1970), there is usually a "con" that we give ourselves to keep playing the game, even though we "lose" all the time. Redecision Therapy differs from traditional analysis in its emphasis on resisting the "con" or bad feeling payoff and on focusing on "what you want to change today." *You* do it, not the therapist. You can't just "work on"; you must change. Your goal is to change *now*.

Leslie, a divorced mother of three, was a very successful estate agent. To make more business contacts, she joined many civic and business associations and worked for the local Chamber of Commerce. Several times a week she made presentations to local businesses and to major corporations around the country to encourage them to move their plants to the area. She was a popular speaker and she self-published several travel guides which sold well to tourists. As her career expanded, she acquired a housekeeper, secretary, bookkeeper, accountant, and agent. Her busy life should have run very smoothly. . .but "should" doesn't always mean "did."

Leslie started her session by stating, "I want to find things more easily." When asked for an example, Leslie became a little tearful. "Last week, my daughter sent me a birthday present. It came four days before my birthday and on the wrapping it said, 'Do not open until Friday.' I was so excited, I wanted to open it right then, but I forced myself to put it away. Now I can't find it anywhere."

Going back to Leslie's original statement, I asked her, "What does 'find things' mean to you?"

"To be able to go right where I put it and enjoy it." She smiles ruefully. "I'm not losing things for fun. I really wanted that present. I know it's something she made herself. I wanted it so badly, I put it in a special place." I asked her what she would like her contract to be.

"I want to put things so I know where they will be when I want to get them back. There is so much stuff that comes in."

I quizzed her further and found out that she "loses everything, forgets everything." (This is a parental judgement and obviously not true.) The previous weekend Leslie had gone off to a much-anticipated vacation at the beach with her family and forgotten her suitcase. "There I was, trying to walk through the sand in tights, silk dress, and high heels."

I asked Leslie if she sometimes felt like a little girl when she lost things. A mischievous look came into her eye. I then asked her if she would be willing to think like the little girl who dropped things everywhere, and to talk to her adult self about how the little girl felt. "I'm going to ask you to switch places, to sit in that chair and be a little girl." Leslie agreed.

"Little girl Leslie, how do you feel about putting things away?"

Leslie the adult business woman and Leslie the child discussed the old "bad feelings" about being forced to remember to put things away. Leslie recalled that her father yelled at her and her mother threatened punishment when she lost or forgot things. In other words, she got lots of attention for forgetting. Her parents were preoccupied with their business. They were inclined not to give her attention unless she created a problem. Leslie learned to get negative attention rather than no attention. Now mum and dad are no longer around to punish little Leslie, so adult Leslie and little girl Leslie were able to strike a bargain: "I don't have to feel bad about forgetting where I put things."

Leslie can now *choose* to feel bad and continue to harass herself or she can solve the problems her forgetting sometimes creates and *choose* to feel all right about it.

"Imagine it's tomorrow, Leslie," I said. "You can't find your shoes and the phone number you need. How are you feeling?"

"Terrible. . .but I will stop it, stop feeling that way. I can make myself stop if I notice it."

"So when you start feeling terrible because you've lost something, you can make yourself feel better? You can stop harassing yourself?"

Leslie smiled. "Yes, I think so."

15

"So what is your decision?"

Leslie leans back in her chair. "My decision. . .is that when I notice I am making myself feel bad because I've lost something . . . I will choose to feel good anyway. I will solve the problem, instead of harassing myself, and feel good about solving it."

This conclusion may not sound like a solution to all of Leslie's problems, and it isn't. But she frees herself of her guilt long enough to see the cycle of self-harassment and self-sabotage that she has set up. She sees that, as an adult, she has choices about how to feel, as well as about where she puts things.

Once she deliberately chooses her feelings, it is a short step to deliberately choosing her actions, to *noticing* where she puts things and remembering where they are. In the past, the more she forgot, the more she harassed herself, and the more she harassed herself, the more she forgot. By removing her bad feeling payoff, Leslie is removing her unconscious reason for forgetting. Eventually she will stop losing things because there is no payoff.

Try This...

for a Fresh Attitude Toward Forgetting

Here are some options that you have about memory:

- I can remember and feel good.
- I can remember and feel miserable.
- I can forget and feel miserable.
- I can forget and feel good.

In this chapter, I told you some ways that people in my workshops said they felt about forgetting: "I feel frustrated," "Selfish," "It embarrasses others and makes me look silly," "Stupid," "Guilty," "It doesn't bother me at all."

Make a note of some ways *you* react when you forget something: _____

_____.

Don't decide which is "right." Don't even decide which option you usually choose. You are experimenting with new ways to do things and new ways to feel about what you do. Don't lock yourself into an old pattern by labeling it as yours.

3
Mechanical Blocks

"Quick, name a West Coast sound."

"Ah, er, the Grateful Dead."

"No, Puget."

When we can't remember something, the cause isn't always an emotional or physical block. A misperception or an interruption, either from outside or of our own making, can block memory just as effectively. For convenience we'll clump these together and call them "mechanical" blocks.

These blocks can take three forms. Sometimes we misunderstand something we see or hear and so we misfile the information. Sometimes we're distracted before we can file the information. And sometimes we're distracted during the retrieval process. We start hunting through a mental file drawer and find another captivating thought that diverts us or the phone rings or our bus comes. In all three instances, the result is the same. We "forget."

Misfiled Information

This happens when incoming signals aren't recorded properly. Your chances of summoning up Puget Sound from your memory file would be close to zero if you were searching for the name of a California-based rock group. Focusing on the word *sound* in one context makes it just about impossible to find the answer in another. This is called "the specificity of encoding."

Misfiled information, information that isn't coded properly before we tuck it away, is a major source of "forgetting." There are many homonyms and words of multiple meanings in English to add to our confusion. Jam—session or strawberry? Read/reed? Weak/week? Guilt/gilt?

What about English words that have opposite meanings?

- rent—pay for the use of and be paid for use
- fast—go fast or stick fast
- sanction—allow or prevent
- overlook—see or fail to see

And what does this sentence, taken from a newspaper article, actually mean? "He was shot at once."

When we don't give sufficient context—encoding—to a bit of information, we will forget it. This is one reason foreign languages can be so difficult to learn.

An example is the Frenchman who endeavored to remember the English phrase "Thank you" by rhyming it with "Saint Cloud" (pronounced "San Clue"), a suburb of Paris. When his American sweetheart next complimented him, he blushed and stammered, "Montmartre."

What Do You See?

Memory is complicated by how we perceive the sights, sounds, and sensations that surround us. The possibilities for variations in encoding are almost infinite. Some things that may affect how we evaluate information are our age, sex, intelligence, education, disposition, our nationality and social status, our political and religious beliefs, our physical appearance, income, the weather, the people around us, where we are, and the time of the day, month, and year.

Consider reading about a war in the history books of the opposing countries. Or the ununiversality of music—how the sound of bagpipes, rock and roll, or Chinese opera can enchant or torment different listeners.

What do people remember when they look at you? No two people see exactly the same thing. Depending on who is doing the looking, they may see a parent, a child, a spouse, a lover, a friend or a foe, a menacing foreigner or a kindred spirit, someone too fat or too thin, too young or too old, too rich or too poor, useful, lovable, or dangerous. Yet each viewer is looking at the same collection of atoms.

No two people see exactly the same thing. It depends on who is doing the looking.

Creating Reality

"Reality is not so much recorded as constructed," says neurologist Richard M. Restak. If we are walking down a sunny hallway and a figure suddenly appears ahead of us, we assume that he has stepped through a doorway. If we are walking down a spooky, dark hallway and a figure suddenly appears ahead of us, we might assume that he has stepped through a wall and is a ghost.

We shape the recorded information to our expectations, to our template of reality at that moment. We discard information that doesn't fit (Mrs. Throgbottom appeared to walk through a wall, so there must be a door in that alcove) and adapt information that is out of kilter (Mrs. Throgbottom appears to be nude, but that can't be true, so she must be wearing a beige dress). Tossing out bits and pieces that don't form patterns is essential to getting through life. The disadvantage is that sometimes the information we discard in this way is true. Many eccentrics have made great discoveries because they refused to ignore information that didn't fit.

Seeing with a Sound Track

Imagine that you are watching a piece of film with no sound. A young man is running across a field toward a grove of trees. Now replay the film and imagine lilting, bucolic music in the background. The film is obviously showing us a happy young man, full of exuberance on a sunny day. Now run the film again and, this time, the music is thunderingly romantic. He is now on his way to a rendezvous with his love in the trees. On our third replay of the film, imagine an agitated theme. This time he is being chased by something menacing. If only he can reach the trees, he may be safe. And finally, the music is ominous. He is unaware that something *terrible* is waiting for him in the woods. What you see is always the same, but your mood or expectation creates your perception.

The Effect of Language on Perception

"How fast were the cars going when they *crashed* into each other?" A group of people were shown a film of two cars bumping. Those who were asked the above question estimated the speed at an average of 40.8 mph, while those who were asked "How fast were they going when they *contacted* each other?" estimated 31.8 mph. Their perception had been altered by the language of the question. The same people were quizzed about damage. Those who were asked "Did you see *the* broken headlight?" were twice as likely to say yes as those who were asked if there was *a* broken headlight. (There wasn't any.)

Linguist Benjamin Lee Whorf noted this phenomenon in his work as a fire investigator. Men who were working with *full* petrol drums showed appropriate respect, but once the drums were *empty*, they were treated casually, even though the latter drums, now filled with petrol vapour, were much more likely to explode. In another case, some distillation vats were encased in "spun lime stone." The word *stone* implied "fireproof" to those working with the material, but it wasn't. Result—poof!

Advertising takes full advantage of word associations. I recently bought a set of "professional" cookware. The fine print in the accompanying brochure stated that it was "not for commercial use." Can one be a "professional" cook and not a "commercial" one? Products are touted as "natural" (arsenic is natural), and "fresh" (well, they're certainly not rotten when they have a shelf life of two years), or "pure" (pure what?). We like to think of ourselves as too sophisticated to be taken in by slick advertising, but many of our everyday perceptions are deliberately or accidentally affected by language.

How to Retrieve Misfiled Information

Is it any wonder that we file information and then can't find it later? We are looking under the wrong heading. Sometimes the information is hopelessly lost to us, but occasionally we can retrieve it by letting our mind float high over the landscape, looking for random free associations that might provide a clue to where we put it. We may come across it accidentally as we search through another file, a delightful bonus for giving ourselves exploratory time.

Distraction Before We "Remember"

Funk and Wagnall's Dictionary defines *distraction* as a diversion. This sounds like a playful, refreshing interlude, and it may well be, unless you are being diverted when you don't want to be. Distraction can keep you from recording information or stop you from recalling it if you're interrupted in the process. No wonder being easily distracted gets bad press. On the positive side, a distracted mind roves nimbly over a lot of territory or responds quickly to a variety of external stimuli. Just don't expect to remember much of it later.

Ironically, preoccupation can be just as effective in blocking memory. The mind is focusing totally on one thing and doesn't let other ideas get in the way. This is considered admirable if the thinker is concentrating on performing a heart transplant, less so if the thinker is absorbed in a fantasy about dating a movie star instead of listening to an economics lecture that is essential for the final exam. Whether our preoccupation is "good" or "bad," it is very effective at preventing us from noticing and storing new information.

Failure to Acquire and Record Information

A woman in one of my workshops wondered why she couldn't remember anything about the time she spent in Europe. As usual, I asked why she wanted to remember.

"Well, when I tell people I was there for two years, they want to know what I saw. I can't remember anything."

This seemed incredible until I dug a little deeper. I learned that she had lived on an army base, shopped only at the base PX, and associated only with other American army wives. The fact was that she *hadn't* seen Europe at all, only an army base identical to bases all over the United States. She couldn't remember Europe because she had never really been there.

Distraction during Retrieval

Another kind of mechanical loss is failure to complete the retrieval process. It frequently happens when we are juggling a lot of different activities instead of concentrating on one. A popular name for this is "overload."

Busy people are always wrestling with overload, trying to handle many unrelated activities without forgetting any of them. We may be thinking simultaneously about an important business letter, an errand we need to do on the way home from work, an upcoming social event, and an unpaid bill. Unless they are related in some way, they don't reinforce each other, and it is very easy for one to "slip through the cracks."

On the other hand, if a group of subjects are related—the many steps necessary to drive a car, cook an elaborate dinner, or run for president—we tend not to forget them because they represent progressive parts of a whole. Each step taken suggests another step, so we can remember an almost limitless number of bits.

The Price of Remembering

You probably could remember just about anything if you focused on it totally, excluding all other thoughts and activities. This can be effective, but it's not much fun.

An easier way is to build a structure, a kind of mental egg carton in which to arrange and count your odd bits. The simplest structure is, of course, the written list. The acts of conceiving, writing, and then reading back a list of objects or actions reinforces the information and gives us extra ways to retrieve it later, even if we lose the list. We'll talk about structures and reinforcement in part III, "How To."

Remembering Is Hard Work

Keeping track of lots of things is work. During his years at Princeton University, Albert Einstein could never remember his own unlisted phone number, and once he had to call the switchboard to ask which house he lived in. When Paul Erdos, one of the world's foremost mathematicians, was lecturing at Washington University in St. Louis, he couldn't tell them his Social Security number. Each of these men was keeping his mind free of clutter for the important work at hand.

As long as the discomfort of forgetting doesn't get in the way, it may be easier for certain people to keep several spare car keys and house keys hidden around the neighborhood or simply to pay for forgotten dentist appointments. Some of this kind of disorder may even be your way of being in control, of setting yourself apart from "ordinary" people by creating a personal environment so distinctive that no one else will try to violate it. It's a little like a dog marking his own favourite lamp post so that other dogs will know it is a part of his private territory.

Some people can get as much real pleasure from their personal disorder as others get from controlling and creating order in their environment. If that works for you, that's fine. There's nothing wrong with disorder caused by forgetting as long as

- You don't mind.
- Others don't mind.
- It's not dangerous.
- It doesn't scare the horses.

When All Else Fails

You try and try and still forget things? That's okay. When all else fails, give up. It may be easier and more rewarding for you to tolerate occasional lapses of memory in order to be available to all the pleasant notions that flit through your unconscious mind. One price for being unusually disciplined is less spontaneity. By making friends with the way you already use your memory, you will actually remember more of what you want to remember. Self-harassment rarely improves memory because it sets up a system of negative stimuli that is, at best, distracting and, at worst, destructive.

Try This...

to See How Interference Thwarts Remembering

Interference can prevent you from remembering correctly or remembering at all. Glance at the figure below and then "remember" what you saw.

You could have seen any of the following words:

bird   bans   bard   bind   find   fans

bins   band   bars   firs   fins

Much of the information you try to process each day is mixed with other information. Sometimes you will see it clearly because you're looking for it.

Other times it will be hopelessly muddled.

So keep your eyes open, maintain a sense of humor when information is garbled, and remember that self-harassment is optional.

4
Physical Blocks

Mental blocks are dramatic and frequently fascinating. Physical blocks are much less stylish, more common, and not nearly so arresting. In fact, the only nice thing to be said about them is that some of them are easier to overcome.

Matter Over Mind

Any physical condition that prevents our delightfully complex bodies from delivering information to the brain or storing it there qualifies as a physical block. Some physical conditions are permanent —blindness, color blindness, deafness, or tone deafness can effectively prevent a memory of colors or of melodies. Other conditions that interfere with memory may be temporary or reversible.

The pain of a stomachache or of hitting one's thumb with a hammer can effectively garble memory input or retrieval temporarily. These discomforts pass quickly enough, and you can probably postpone trying to remember the Table of Elements or your sister's address until you have recovered. (Of course, this is a good reason to have emergency phone numbers written down next to the telephone.)

Other physical memory blocks are long-term: nutritional deficiencies, some illnesses and/or the drugs used to treat them, recreational drugs, fatigue, tension, and lack of exercise. Some of these —poor nutrition, tension, and lack of exercise—we can correct ourselves. Other physical blocks, the ones caused by illness or prescribed drugs, may become less frustrating and frightening if we understand what is happening. The panic and depression that occur when strange things happen in our bodies and minds are effective memory blocks.

Let's look at some physical memory blocks.

Diet

You've heard the old joke about the elderly honeymooner who disparaged oysters as an aphrodisiac: "I ate twelve of the things and only six worked."

Food is seen as a universal remedy for what ails us. In our search for health and well-being, we consume everything from mother's chicken soup to brewer's yeast to a hundred different hangover cures. Most of us would love to find a food or a vitamin that would "cure" our bad memory.

The bad news is that it's not that simple. Memory is so incredibly complex that, so far, no one has been able to prove that any single nutritional element will improve it. We do know that the *absence* of certain substances, especially thiamine, from the diet may be accompanied by a memory loss, but we can only suppose that the opposite might be also true — that the presence of these substances in the diet would promote a good memory. We certainly have no proof that increasing the intake of any nutrient, or combination of nutrients, would proportionately increase our power to remember.

However, one recent study may finally establish a direct link between specific nutrients and mental efficiency. The Brain Aging and Neuronal Plasticity Research Group at Ohio State University Medical Center has just completed a major collaborative study in which 11-month-old mice (comparable in age to human adults) were fed any one of 11 different diets for 11 months. The diets varied combinations of three substances: dietary choline, lecithin, and phosphatidylcholine. The last is a substance found in lecithin itself and is also a crucial component of the neuronal membranes. (Neurons are the information-sending cells that make up the brain.)

While the mice were on their special diets, each group was given behavior tests to compare their mental efficiency and memory capacity with that of mice on an average laboratory diet. The research group found that three of the diets notably increased the number of synapses, the connections between neurons that are necessary for memory. The study covered more than a third of the mice's life span, far longer than most previous research on choline.

The Ohio State mice were put in a two-chambered box with a door between the lighted front compartment and the darkened back.

When a mouse walked into the dark section, the door dropped and the mouse was stuck in pitch darkness while getting a mild, but unpleasant electric shock for three seconds.

To test the mouse's long-term memory, it was put back in the box 24 hours later. The researchers then measured how long it took before the mouse forgot its previous unpleasant experience and returned to the darkened room. The mice who ate the standard laboratory diet waited an average of only 290 seconds before they wandered into the dark room. The mice fed the three most successful diets waited more than 400 seconds, indicating that they remembered their previous unpleasant experience longer.

The diets that resulted in this memory improvement were two rich in phosphatidylcholine and one rich in lecithin. On the basis of their study, Dr. Ronald Mervis says: "I would recommend lecithin or phosphatidylcholine [to enhance human memory]. Ingesting free choline itself produces no effect."

Does such a diet hold any hope for treating memory loss due to senility in later life? Dr. Mervis says that "lecithin or phosphatidylcholine, taken chronically, seems to be most effective when taken before the onset of memory loss. In other words, they have a prophylactic (preventative) effect. [But] we'll be running our tests on senile mice too, to see whether any improvement in synaptic connections can be induced."

Dr. Mervis suggests that previous testing of "precursor substances" (chemicals necessary for neurons to send out signals in the brain) may have been inconclusive because researchers were concentrating on choline. "Forty percent of the phospholipid found in neuronal membranes is phosphatidylcholine," he says, "so using its precursors on a long-term basis may preserve or help rebuild neuron membranes and thus offset or delay brain atrophy." (Alzheimer's disease, a cause of organic memory loss in older people, is known to attack the choline production of the brain.)

These findings are very exciting and may be a key to great advances in treating a variety of disorders. As with any scientific experiment, this one must be duplicated by other researchers who get similar results. When this happens, a theory becomes a fact.

While this lecithin/phosphatidylcholine theory still needs to be confirmed by further testing, it invites conjecture about possible applications. For instance, alcoholics are predisposed to early senility because their neuron membranes have become rigid. Lecithin therapy, suggests Dr. Mervis, might be able to improve brain functioning in reformed alcoholics. It might also aid children with certain nervous dysfunctions and forms of retardation by encouraging the development of more synaptic connections. Eventually even the common man might use it as a nutritional means to more efficient memory.

If you are tempted to start consuming quantities of lecithin, consider Dr. Mervis's warning: "It's important to emphasize that lecithin and phosphatidylcholine are most effective when used in low dosages. Larger amounts produce a bloating effect, among other undesirable ones."

What the Future Holds

In the past, scientists thought of the brain as a protected organ, unaffected by the diet of its owner. Now we know that the food we eat can cause profound changes in brain output, affecting behavior in drastic ways. But since no one is certain exactly how the brain records information—whether by molecular changes, chemical changes, electromagnetic changes, or on a holographic basis—we are just beginning to discover how diet affects memory.

Some comforting news is that our knowledge of biochemistry is now doubling about every seven years. Lecithin researcher Dr. Ralph G. Walton is optimistic about this progress. "I think we'll see a real knowledge explosion over the next ten years."

A summary of nutrients sources that may be related to memory appears on the following page.

How Food Affects Children's Memories

When children don't remember well, we worry that they have what is now called "a learning disability." In other words, we wonder, is my kid stupid? Since most people (particularly teachers) equate intelligence with the ability to recall information, poor memories in children can be alarming.

Children respond quickly to many things they eat. They are especially susceptible to imbalances in their diets because their bodies need nutrients for growing. A number of studies have shown that iron deficiency in the mother during pregnancy and in the child causes a noticeable slowdown in memory functions and learning. The iron-deficient child can still learn, but not as efficiently or effectively.

Dr. Ben F. Feingold has shown that many people, especially children, react dramatically to food additives which may in turn create a sensitivity to natural salicylates found in many nourishing foods. Some of the symptoms of this sensitivity are an inability to concentrate, a short attention span, fidgeting, aggressiveness, excitability, impulsiveness, a low frustration threshold, clumsiness, and insomnia. Children with these problems rarely do well in school. The Feingold diet, designed to avoid additives, has shown some success in treating this problem.

Children's diets have been subject to even more food fads than those of adults. At various times in recent history almost every food

continued on page 34

Summary of Selected Dietary Elements

Nutrient	General Functions	Good Food Sources	Relationship to Memory
Vitamin B₁ (thiamine)	Emotional stability. Energy. Memory.	brewer's yeast, dark-green leafy vegetables, lean meats, legumes,[1] nuts, sunflower seeds, variety meats,[2] wheat germ, whole grain products	Necessary for good memory.
Vitamin B₆ (pyridoxine)	Production of antibodies. Elimination of excess fluids in premenstrual women. Emotional stability. Healthy skin. Central nervous system regulation.	bananas, brewer's yeast, buckwheat flour (dark), hazelnuts, peanuts, poultry, rice, salmon, sunflower seeds, tomatoes, variety meats,[2] wheat germ, whole grain products	Gives emotional stability. Provides central nervous system regulation.
Vitamin B₁₂ (cyanocobalamin)	Normal growth. Healthy nervous system. Normal red blood cell formation.	eggs, fish, meats, milk, variety meats[2]	Deficiency may cause poor memory and inability to concentrate. An alert sensory motor system depends on a good supply.
Choline	Prevents buildup of fat in liver.	Widely distributed in foods that contain fat	Deficiency seems to lead to confusion and memory loss. Increased levels appear to lead to clearer thinking and improved memory in older people.

[1]Legumes include peas, beans, peanuts, and lentils.
[2]Variety meats include liver, heart, and kidney.

Nutrient	General Functions	Good Food Sources	Relationship to Memory
Folic Acid (folate)	New red blood cell production. Found in the most rapidly growing tissues, such as bone marrow, alimentary tract lining, or tumors.	asparagus, brewer's yeast, broccoli, dark-green leafy vegetables, legumes,[1] liver, nuts, onions, tempeh, wheat germ, whole grain products	Deficiency may seriously impair learning abilities.
Niacin	Reduced blood cholesterol levels. Mental and emotional health. Aids metabolism of carbohydrates, fats, and amino acids.	brewer's yeast, fish, legumes,[1] poultry, variety meats,[2] whole grain products	Reduced levels cause nervousness, confusion, depression, hallucinations.
Vitamin C (ascorbic acid)	Formation of teeth and bones. Bone-fracture healing. Wound and burn healing. Resistance to infection and other diseases. Collagen formation.	broccoli, brussels sprouts, cabbage, cantaloupes, cauliflower, citrus fruits and their juices, currants, dark-green leafy vegetables, green peppers, persimmons, pimentos, strawberries, tomatoes	Low levels can cause confusion, listlessness, depression.
Calcium	Blood clotting. Normal functioning of nerve tissues. Normal pulse and cardiac contraction. Formation and growth of bones and teeth.	almonds; brewer's yeast; broccoli; dark-green leafy vegetables; hazelnuts; milk, cheese, and most dairy products; salmon; soybeans; tempeh; tofu; watercress	Strengthens and stimulates neuronal growth and plays a crucial role in brain function. A severe deficiency may lead to memory loss.

continued

[1]Legumes include peas, beans, peanuts, and lentils.
[2]Variety meats include liver, heart, and kidney.

Summary of Selected Dietary Elements—*continued*

Nutrient	General Functions	Good Food Sources	Relationship to Memory
Copper	Builds proteins that give blood vessel walls strength and flexibility. Protects myelin sheath around nerve fibers.	avocado, banana, beef, cod, legumes, mushrooms, nuts and seeds, oysters, pork, poultry, whole grain products	Promotes calm nerves and clear thinking.
Iodine	Regulates growth and development. Important in thyroid function.	saltwater fish, seafood	Deficiency slows thought processes.
Iron	Blood formation. Transportation of oxygen within the body.	apricots, blackstrap molasses, brewer's yeast, dark-green leafy vegetables, eggs, legumes,[1] nuts, sunflower seeds, variety meats,[2] wheat germ, whole grain products	Deficiency leads to irritability, dizziness, headaches.
Magnesium	Biological reactions within the cell. Conduction of nerve impulses. Normal muscle contraction. Healthy heart, muscles, nerves, brain, kidneys, liver, and other organs. Maintenance of normal basic metabolism.	brown rice, dark-green leafy vegetables, molasses, nuts, peas, soybeans, tofu, whole grain products	Essential for transmitting nervous system impulses. Reduced levels bring about hallucinations, mental confusion, disorientation, memory loss.

[1]Legumes include peas, beans, peanuts, and lentils.
[2]Variety meats include liver, heart, and kidney.

Nutrient	General Functions	Good Food Sources	Relationship to Memory
Manganese	Necessary for skeletal and connective tissue development. Fatty acid metabolism.	bananas, corn, dark-green leafy vegetables, legumes, lettuce, nuts, whole grain products	Aids central nervous system and muscle coordination. Necessary for precision between mind and body.
Potassium	Biological reactions within the cell. Healthy kidneys, heart, and skeletal muscles.	apples, apricots, avocados, bananas, beef, blackstrap molasses, brewer's yeast, broccoli, chicken, halibut, oranges, peanuts, potatoes, raisins, sesame seeds, sunflower seeds, tomatoes, tuna, wheat germ	Deficiency affects nerve functions.
Zinc	Production and growth of new healing cells. Healthy skin. Numerous enzyme actions throughout the body. Carbon dioxide exchange. Normal maintenance of levels of vitamin A in blood.	beef, cheese, eggs, fish, green beans, lamb, lima beans, meats, nuts, wheat germ, whole grain products	Is essential for synthesis of DNA and brain function.

group has been considered harmful to them. In the 1920s and '30s, for instance, many American mothers fed their offspring a diet low in protein to prevent "aggressiveness." The listless, hollow-eyed youngster fostered by such a diet was rarely aggressive, but frequently peevish and petulant.

Your child deserves the most nourishing diet possible within the limits of your income, food availability, and the current knowledge about nutrition. Special problems, including slow or erratic learning patterns, should get professional attention.

Your forgetful child also deserves as much understanding as you give yourself when you "just forget." Compared with adults, children have far fewer landmarks to use when they file information. Their experiences in learning the use of memory are similar to those you would have if you found yourself in a strange country, dealing with an unfamiliar language or customs. Children's discoveries and the new ways they develop for remembering what they see can be a constant delight to understanding, encouraging, loving adults.

Effects of Reducing Diets on Memory

Most of the publicized reducing diets are deficient in nutrients. (The best thing to be said for many popular and bizarre diets is that they are so bizarre that very few people stay on them long enough to do permanent damage. Unfortunately this is not always the case.) While a person is dieting, the brain, like the body, has to make up any shortage of dietary nutrients by drawing on its reserves to function. When the reserves are used up, the dieter can become nervous and susceptible to suggestion, easily upset, and find it hard to make decisions — all conditions that can distort or block memory.

Experts warn that any diet providing fewer than 2100 calories a day for an adult is likely to be deficient in some vitamin, mineral, or trace element, unless the diet is carefully tailored by a doctor for the individual. In a study by Dr. Russell Wilder, Senior Physician at the Mayo Clinic, healthy subjects agreed to stay on a low-calorie reducing diet for an extended period of time. Within three months, they experienced a host of unpleasant symptoms: they became quarrelsome, hostile and anxious, felt persecuted, had nightmares and moments of extreme panic, became clumsy, had trouble paying attention, and *their memories became faulty.*

The Big Picture

Even the most unsophisticated person is likely to know about psychosomatic illness, but many well-educated people are totally unaware of its opposite, somatopsychic illness. These are simply two sides of the same coin. Psychosomatic illness is disease of the body that originates in the mind, and somatopsychic illness is disease of the mind that originates in the body. Sometimes mental problems, including forgetfulness, are caused by imbalances in the body's chemistry.

Many nutritionists are successful in treating illnesses with corrective diets and food supplements. Unfortunately, a few enthusiasts insist that almost every human illness is due solely to imbalances in nutrition, and they regularly encounter the scepticism of doctors and laymen. If you are feeling sceptical about this right now, just remember that a number of mental and physical conditions *are* caused by poor diet and *do* respond well to improved nutrition.

Well-Balanced Diets

Doctors are fond of advising their patients to "eat a well-balanced diet." Patients presume the doctor has something specific in mind. Yet a study reported by Dr. Jean Mayer of Harvard University showed that "the average doctor at Harvard knows a wee bit more about nutrition than his secretary, unless his secretary has a weight problem, in which case the average secretary knows a wee bit more about nutrition than the average doctor."

If you think you have a nutritional deficiency, practice Disraeli's advice: "Moderation even in excess."

- Read as much as you can about recent discoveries in nutrition.

- If you decide you may be lacking a particular vitamin or mineral, increase your intake of foods that are rich in that nutrient but eat a *variety* of foods.

- Take moderate doses of supplements.

- If you feel a simple moderate approach isn't sufficient, see a nutrition-oriented doctor to work out a dietary program.

Good health is a great plus to memory. When you feel good, look good, and are bouncing with energy, your mind can process information faster and better, and remembering is easier.

Illnesses

The ravages of ill health, stress, depression, and serious injuries can have an adverse effect on our ability to concentrate or remember.

In fact, memory loss and confusion are classic symptoms of some diseases. Here are some physical conditions that affect the memory.

Amnesia

We are all familiar with the soap-opera version of amnesia. The victim-heroine forgets her name, home, and loved ones but is still able to dress herself (elegantly), talk (eloquently), and walk (gracefully). The unbearable personal portion of the victim's life is erased by the subconscious, but language, motor skills, and general knowledge remain. Some people with this type of amnesia score just as well on I.Q. tests as they did before the illness struck. However, in other, more dramatic varieties of amnesia, the victim retains formerly learned language, motor skills, and knowledge, and is quite capable of acquiring new skills and knowledge, but doesn't know how these relate to activities of daily living.

Doctors generally categorize amnesia as either physically based or emotionally based. In a tragic example of the former type, pioneering brain surgeons erased the long-term memory of HM when they removed too much of the brain during an operation intended to control his epileptic seizures. Though he could reply to questions, he would forget the conversation within a few hours. He read the same newspapers over and over. The death of his father, which had occurred many years before, remained a fresh tragedy whenever it was mentioned.

Amnesia due to head injury can affect perception, language comprehension, and personality. Most patients of this type have a multitude of symptoms, and isolating memory loss from the other symptoms is difficult. Only in rare cases do amnesia victims have what laymen think of as "classic" amnesia, in which they experience memory loss but have no intellectual impairment.

Emotional amnesia is caused by stress, and memory usually returns in a few days. This pathological forgetting in response to emotional crisis is called "fugue." In a way, these amnesiacs design their own illness, but they have absolutely no voluntary control over it. They retain all memories except those of their personal lives. If they just ran away, they would have to bring their painful and overwhelming problems with them. Forgetting offers them the most complete escape short of death. But the release amnesia offers is only temporary. Once the person has forgotten those unbearable anxieties, a new anxiety soon appears—where is my memory?

Amnesia can erase memories imprinted either before or after the trauma. Physical injuries can result in either/or both kinds; however, amnesia due to emotional trauma is more likely to erase the causative events.

Arteriosclerosis

When the blood vessels supplying the brain narrow or harden, the amount of oxygen delivered to the brain is reduced, resulting in memory loss. One theory is that the diminished oxygen supply, combined with older and fewer neurons, inhibits the electrical circuitry of the brain.

The effect increased oxygen has on the brain is heartening. Under the direction of Dr. Edwin Boyle, Jr., research director of the Miami Heart Institute, patients suffering from memory loss caused by arteriosclerosis breathed concentrated oxygen at three times normal atmospheric pressure. These patients were then able to remember recent events and learn new things, and the improvement lasted six weeks to six months.

ICU (Intensive Care Unit) Psychosis

The trauma of injury or surgery can affect memory. About 25 percent of the patients in hospital intensive care units experience occasional bouts of confusion and forgetfulness which have been dubbed "intensive care unit psychosis." In the first weeks after receiving the first artificial heart, Dr. Barney Clark sometimes could not recall the surgery or why he was in the hospital. Doctors speculate that the initial trauma, plus the ongoing stress of the hospital routine — the constant beeping of electronic monitors and the necessary but exhausting routine of taking blood samples, giving medications, and changing intravenous tubes — caused this temporary memory loss.

Senility

Just as *consumption* was once used to describe any illness of the lungs, *senility* has become today's catchall term for a variety of physical and emotional conditions that can affect our memories adversely as we get older. Sometimes, the specific condition is recognized and treated, and the negative effect on memory is reversed.

Two professional men in their sixties who had similar symptoms — they forgot where they put things and had trouble remembering names, dates, faces, and recent events — were tested at the National Institute of Mental Health in Bethesda, Maryland. One man did poorly on the tests that required mental effort, but he could improve his overall memory when he was given clues for organizing material. The other worked very hard at the various tests, but when he was offered help in organizing, his score did not improve.

The first man was diagnosed as being depressed. When his depression cleared up, his memory problems disappeared. The other man, unfortunately, was diagnosed as being in the early stages of Alzheimer's disease, a degenerative illness that kept him from using his accumulated memories.

Commonly called "senile dementia," Alzheimer's disease produces loss of memory and is ultimately fatal. The exact cause is still unknown and much work is being done on this devastating disease. One interesting discovery—the degree of memory loss in Alzheimer patients is in direct proportion to the loss of cholinacetyltransferase (CAT) in the brain. CAT is an enzyme necessary for the formation of acetylcholine, the chemical that transmits nerve impulses from neuron to neuron. The less CAT, the fewer the transmissions.

Another preliminary finding is that women seem to lose brain material earlier than men. Two British pathologists say that most women lose two ounces of brain material between the ages of 40 and 50, while men don't experience this loss until their late 50s. After that, both sexes lose brain material at about the same rate.

Though senility, or the public image of senility, remains a problem, doctors and laymen both are beginning to recognize that memory loss in later years is rarely inevitable or irreversible when it occurs. Arteriosclerosis, malnutrition, depression, and the side effects of drugs taken for other conditions are a few potential contributors to memory loss, and they can happen at any age. (Huntington's chorea, similar to Alzheimer's disease, strikes young adults.)

The picture is bright for older people today, and most of them *won't* experience real senility. Though we may castigate ourselves more at 60 than at 20 when we forget something, we are probably no more forgetful than we were 40 years earlier, provided we stay active, have lots of interests, exercise, and keep the circuits open. The motto, says neurologist David Krech, is, "He who lives by his wits dies *with* his wits." In other words—use it or lose it! For more about senility and what to do about it, see chapter 12, "Remembering—Young vs. Old."

"He who lives by his wits dies with *his wits."*

Injuries

Most people experience a good, hard crack on the head at least once during their lifetimes and recover with no ill effects. A few will find later that their intellect and behavior have undergone small changes, changes that may be irritating, frightening, or even dangerous. Memory, attention span, concentration, and abstract thinking may be affected. These people may be easily fatigued, impulsive, irritable, and no longer want to be with friends or socialize. Even worse, they may think they are going crazy; after all, the doctor has pronounced them "fine" since the original accident.

A study was made of 424 people who had been hospitalized for a day or two at the University of Virginia Medical Center for head injuries and then released as neurologically "normal." Three months later, 79 percent experienced headaches, 59 percent had memory problems, and 34 percent had not returned to their former jobs. Many could not do maths problems, had short attention spans, and were tired all the time. Some had trouble organizing their days, got bogged down in doing one thing, and couldn't maintain a routine for tasks. Naturally, they also experienced trouble on the job, loss of self-esteem, and depression. Some just sat around, lost track of things, and had difficulty learning new things and maintaining family and sexual relationships.

The common neurological tests used today aren't sensitive enough to detect the problems of these minor head injuries, says Dr. Leonard Diller, codirector of the head trauma program of New York University's Institute of Rehabilitation Medicine. He suggests having detailed neuropsychological testing and evaluation done by a neurologist, neuropsychologist, or rehabilitation medicine specialist. Recovery from even a minor brain injury can take years, and patients need to learn how to compensate in the meantime.

Allergies

Allergies play a very small part in memory loss, but anything that disrupts our physical and emotional well-being can make us forgetful. We now recognize that allergies can go beyond hives and hay fever. A few people are so sensitive to our twentieth-century world that they have been forced to retreat to sealed cocoons, free from hydrocarbons, plastics, pollution, formaldehyde in plywood and plasterboard, chlorine in water, and dyes and preservatives in food.

Drugs

Every drug, medical students are told, has two kinds of effects: the ones we know about and the ones we don't. Some drugs that are beneficial or even essential for treating physical problems have an unwelcome and unwanted side effect on the memory. Nervous-system depressants such as sleeping pills, tranquillizers, muscle relaxers, and antianxiety drugs can cause confusion and memory loss. So can arthritis drugs and cortisone.

Any drug that affects mood, perception, or alertness affects how you process information. Any drug which has depression as a side effect (and there are an awful lot of them) is bound to affect your memory. When you are profoundly depressed, you remember less. Even mild depression can make you *think* you remember less, although you still score well on an objective memory test. Among the drugs that can cause depression are blood-pressure drugs, boric acid, and ironically, antianxiety drugs.

Medications that produce drowsiness, such as cold remedies with their antihistimines, will probably have a temporary effect on your ability to remember. If the label says "Don't drive or operate machinery . . . ," plan on passing up heavy memory tasks too.

Another potential memory block, mercury, is found in a number of nonprescription medications. Prolonged use of such a product by a sensitive person could result in mercury poisoning, characterized by mental depression, irritability, fatigue, loss of appetite, anemia, and insomnia.

If you are taking a drug now and want to know if confusion, depression, or memory loss are recognized as possible side effects, you can get up-to-date information. Start by asking your doctor to check on the drug or look at the *Physicians' Desk Reference* (Van Nost Reinhold, 1981). If the doctor is reluctant to detail the possible side effects of a prescribed medicine, and you are concerned that something you are taking may be fuddling your memory, talk to your pharmacist or read the fine-print brochure that may come packed with the medicine or the most recent edition of the more technical *Physicians' Desk Reference* (popularly called "PDR") which they may have at your local library.

What about drugs specifically prescribed to improve the memory? Much experimentation is being done on substances that might improve memory affected by disease or injury. One of these, physostigmine, can cause a temporary improvement in memory when given intravenously in low doses. It temporarily inhibits formation of cholinesterase, an enzyme which breaks down neurotransmitter substances.

However psychologist Richard C. Mohs of the Psychiatric Service at the Veterans' Administration Medical Center, the Bronx, New York, warns that "higher amounts overstimulate the brain and block memory. Physostigmine is potentially toxic and not safe for casual or nonprescription use."

"My guess," says Dr. Mohs, "is that within ten years there will be drugs approved for treating certain memory disorders. They won't necessarily be so benign that one would recommend them for anyone off the street, and they'd have to be carefully prescribed and administered, but in the longer run I do see a variety of treatments being made available to improve memory functions for the ageing."

Another prominent researcher that we spoke to is less certain. "If you knew mechanistically how the memory trace is laid down, you could then shoot something into the brain to enhance that trace; it would become a biochemical problem. But the work of Lashley showed that the brain does not localize memories in a mechanistic way. You end up with the holographic paradigm, which is much more evasive to approach medically. I don't see a research breakthrough as particularly likely."

Marijuana

Is marijuana a memory enhancer or a memory blocker?

Perceptions seem stronger and ideas seem to flow more freely when using marijuana. Sixty percent of American high school seniors have tried it, one-third use it at least once a month, and 7 percent smoke it every day.

Marijuana use is a highly controversial social and political issue. In this climate, test results, pro or con, about the physical effects of marijuana are easily politicized and dismissed by opponents as "propaganda."

The earliest experiments indicated that marijuana was harmless and had no effect on memory. An article by Lester Grinspoon in *Scientific American* (December, 1969) concluded, on the evidence available, that marijuana seemed to interrupt cognitive processes slightly, without affecting attention span or visual coordination, that it had no effect on long-term or short-term memory, and that it actually enhanced learning in regular users. Then there was a rush to *prove* that marijuana could cause everything from sore feet to senile dementia.

Recent experimenters have become more moderate in their assessments. The results, allowing for contributing factors, show that there is *usually* some memory loss with marijuana use. No recent tests show any memory improvement. The impression of memory enhancement appears to be only that—an impression.

As to how marijuana affects memory, one theory is that marijuana intoxication may make us process and remember different kinds of information in different ways. One group of experimenters predicted that marijuana would produce a greater loss of word recall than picture recall because marijuana is supposed to enhance imagery. However, they found just the opposite. As their cheerful volunteers became more and more stoned, they were less able to recall pictures than words.

Looking at words alone, a 1980 experiment indicated that marijuana use decreased the understanding and recall of all 42 types of linguistic information. In a different test, the volunteers lost their ability to recall information in a direct ratio to the strength of the joint they had smoked, and while their ability to recognize information, people, and things remained unchanged, it took them twice as long—an average of four seconds rather than the normal two seconds. One theory on why marijuana reduces memory is that it increases the number of intrusive thoughts—ideas that flit across the mind while the subject is trying to concentrate on a list of words or a group of pictures.

While I have said a lot about improving memory by expecting to remember, in this instance *feeling* you are remembering well doesn't help.

Alcohol

Few people think of alcohol as a memory booster, but how harmful to the mind is "social drinking?" Ernest P. Noble, professor of alcohol studies at the University of California School of Medicine, Los Angeles, says that even a few drinks—two to three drinks consumed four times a week—will lower our ability to accomplish various thinking tasks including remembering.

Dr. Noble's studies revealed that people over 40 were most affected by alcohol in terms of memory impairment, and even young people, 21 to 30, experienced some memory loss. Dr. Noble theorizes that alcohol can lead to premature aging of the brain.

Another study done in 1979 at the University of Oklahoma Health Sciences Center showed that both young and middle-aged women who drank moderately experienced memory impairment that became greater as they drank more and as they aged. This impairment remained even when they stopped drinking.

People who are alternately drunk and sober experience "state dependency" — things learned in one state are difficult to remember in the other. This is why alcohol has a reputation for interfering with memory. You may have no memory of what you did at the party last night when you sober up the next morning, but if you got drunk again, it would all come back to you. What you learn when you are drunk is best recalled when you are drunk.

But even this has limits. One group of experimenters advertised for volunteers who could drink a (free) pint of whiskey in a few hours. They chose ten eager applicants who consumed their pint and then took simple arithmetic tests, answered questions about their early life, and tried to recall objects and a film they were shown.

All ten subjects could remember the objects and the film 2 minutes later, and five were able to recognize them 30 minutes later. These same five were able to recall 60 percent of this information 24 hours later, while sober control subjects could recall 80 percent. The other five, although still drunk, could *not* recognize objects after 30 minutes. They were all alcoholics and all had experienced frequent blackouts when they drank. Their memory loss was related to general brain damage, not to state dependency.

Smoking

Nicotine may start the day for a lot of cigarette smokers, but it doesn't necessarily start the memory mechanisms going. In Los Angeles, 23 smokers were divided into two groups by researchers at the University of California. People in the first group smoked a regular cigarette while members of the second group smoked a nonnicotine cigarette. All the volunteers then took a memory test, trying to recall a list of 75 items. After three tests, the nonnicotine group scored an average of 24 percent higher than the nicotine group.

Smokers who want to improve their ability to remember names have another good reason to give up the tobacco habit. In a British study, 37 smokers and 37 nonsmokers were asked to remember a list of a dozen names. Ten minutes later, the nonsmokers were able to recall significantly more names from the list than the smokers could. The Scottish psychologist who conducted the study suggested that smoking may impair the blood supply carrying oxygen to the brain, and this lowered oxygen level results in decreased memory efficiency.

43

Lack of Exercise

The brain is the most sensitive bodily organ. Deprived of oxygen for even a few minutes, it may be irreversibly damaged. We know that exercise improves general physical health and that good health is a powerful aid to memory, but research into the relationship of exercise and memory is just beginning. These initial studies indicate that lack of exercise may not block memory, but it significantly slows down response time; that is, it takes longer to call up the information we want.

One study at the University of Georgia in 1982 was limited to older women. Forty-eight volunteers (average age 65) were divided into two groups. The first group was made up of active people who worked out three days a week in an adult exercise program; the second group rated themselves as sedentary. The volunteers were tested on their ability to judge and predict the speed of a sequence of flashing lights. The active women recalled previous sequences better after ten minutes than the women in the inactive group. The retention was the same later, after one week, and again after 40 days. The researchers concluded that there is "some enhancement of cognitive processes, based on previous and present levels of physical activity."

In another study at Bowling Green State University in Ohio, adult volunteers were divided into "fit" and "unfit" groups and asked to remember certain numbers. They then acted as contestants in a quiz-show-style game. The nonexercisers were beaten hands down by the exercisers on response time, although both had similar recall of the numbers. Members of the "unfit" group who participated in a ten-week exercise program were able to reduce the time it took them to perform memory tasks.

This indicates two things:

- If you are sedentary, you may be able to remember as much, but you won't be able to remember it as quickly as your active friends.

- If you become active, you can improve your speed of recall.

In other words, we increase our *speed* of reasoning and remembering when we increase our exercise level, even at an advanced age. We don't know exactly why yet, but certainly the extra oxygen for our brain cells and the extra awareness of our surroundings that exercise brings can't hurt.

Fatigue

When we're not talking, we're often hearing . . . but not always listening. Withdrawal is a very helpful and healthy activity, letting us shut out an overload of irrelevant information and renew ourselves in the midst of chaos. The trick is to be in control of when we withdraw so we can snap back into awareness when something important happens.

Fatigue has a strong effect on this process. Occasionally fatigue can be a friend to memory. We float in a rosy haze in which we can call up and idly cavort with an astounding variety of bits from our memory files. Scientists, philosophers, and artists have characterized this kind of dreamy state as the time when all the pieces of a lifetime puzzle come together in a few dazzling seconds.

"You Never Listen to Me"—Fatigue and Distraction

Fatigue can also numb us to a point where we perceive inaccurately, or don't consciously perceive at all. This depleted state of the body (a physical block) can easily combine with a self-protecting mechanism (an emotional block) to turn off anything that will frazzle us further. The tired child simply doesn't hear all the instructions of his bustling mother so he can't remember them. The exhausted student doesn't read the textbook correctly and therefore can't recall the information later during the test.

When people say, "You never listen to me," they may mean, "You never hear me" or, "You never do what I ask" or just, "I need your attention." Sometimes a minute of undivided attention is the best gift you can give anyone . . . and a valuable way to build happy memories.

Tension

We've all experienced this classic self-sabotage block, the frustrating "It's-on-the-tip-of-my tongue" syndrome. We desperately want to recall a familiar fact, but we go blank. Our desperation to remember sets off a chain of physical responses that produces the opposite effect; we end up jamming our retrieval system.

First our heart rate speeds up, our muscle tension increases, and our digestive system knots. Naturally we concentrate on these unpleasant sensations, so we don't weave the usual web of rich sensory associations that will either let us recall an information bit from the past or file what is happening now for future use. Then, the more we try to remember, the more anxious we become, and the more we forget. It is the classic vicious circle.

Overcoming the Tension Cycle

The hardest thing in the world to do at this point is to relax, but that is just what you need to do if you're going to remember. Eastern cultures have practiced body control for centuries, and now Western medicine is teaching conscious techniques to control everything from migraine headaches to high blood pressure. Actors routinely learn to control tension to overcome stage fright and improve their performance.

Everyone has blanked out on a name or fact, then remembered it spontaneously hours or days later. You started by digging furiously in the wrong mental file drawer. As soon as you relaxed, your unconscious could continue going through other drawers until it found a cross-reference to the thing you were trying to remember.

If you relax and then try to remember, you will be able to begin the unconscious free association that lets you retrieve the connections that were made at the time of the original event. In other words, you will remember. *Forcing* yourself to remember bypasses this unconscious process. Encourage yourself to relax instead.

How Can You Relax?

Telling someone to relax is easy. It's usually done at the precise moment that relaxation is most difficult—You're taking the bar exam; a doctor or dentist has just inserted an icy steel implement into some part of your quivering body; you are about to address 4,000 delegates at a convention, and you left your notes in the taxi, and your zipper just broke.

Some long-term relaxation techniques that people find helpful include biofeedback, meditating, yoga, visualization, hypnosis, and an unsinkable sense of humor. Only the latter offers instant relief without some preparation.

As you struggle with stress, remember that it can be useful. There is strong evidence that the natural hormones produced when you are excited or under stress work to lock memories into the brain permanently. Adrenaline definitely increases the durability of memory in laboratory rats and blocking their adrenaline production interferes with their memory.

Try This...

Defence Against Tension-Induced Memory Blocks

To diminish stress and accelerate remembering, choose appropriate first aid measures from this list.

Take a deep breath, tense all your muscles, then slowly relax and exhale as you collect your thoughts.

Jot down a quick list of what you want to remember, adding to it as things come to you.

Visualize the adrenaline rush you are experiencing as energy for the task ahead, instead of fear. (Both these emotions show up identically when charted by an EEG.)

Play "once-upon-a-time." Go back and start over, rebuilding positive images and circuits to replace the negative ones that brought you to this impasse.

Try to see the humor in it *now*. Relish the details while they're happening as you imagine retelling this story at parties for years to come. (No, it's not possible to manufacture a sense of humor where none exists — you're born with it or not — but you can *arouse* a dormant one and refine and polish it throughout your life. Five-year-olds adore bathroom jokes, adults, Noel Coward. It's the same ability to laugh at ourselves, only more refined.)

5
When It's OK
to Forget

In general, we forget what we don't use, don't like, or fear. Also, we forget what we have never really learned to remember. What most of the famous memory books and systems seem to overlook is that forgetting can have subtle, yet substantial, benefits. Some of these benefits may be relatively frivolous — harmless little vanities that make our lives smoother and more fun. Others protect our very existence.

Forgetting for Self-Preservation

Not all protective memory blocks need to be discarded. When we forget hurtful and negative things, we may be enhancing our lives. Sometimes it can even be dangerous to remember. Consider the experience of a colleague of mine, a psychologist, who had been treating an especially difficult psychotic patient who suddenly missed three consecutive appointments. The patient telephoned several months later to set up a new appointment schedule, but the psychologist kept forgetting to return the call. Upon analysing why he "forgot," the psychologist realized that he felt the patient was dangerous. He didn't want to see him because it might be unsafe to do so, but he was afraid of provoking the patient by being the one to terminate their relationship. His forgetting may have saved him from a risky situation.

A student who desperately wanted to go to art school had parents who insisted he attend law school. When he forgot to file some crucial forms for law school, his application was rejected. The young man's disappointed parents didn't know about the forms and assumed he had been passed over for other reasons. Forgetting enabled the son to pursue his real goal without facing his parents' anger.

Both of these people unconsciously used forgetting as a form of self-preservation, to get them out of a threatening situation. Forgetting actually made their lives better.

Sometimes we need help to accept the benefits of forgetting. A woman in her sixties came to me because she could not remember the details of an automobile accident 35 years earlier that had killed her husband, but left her unhurt. She had been pregnant at the time and a doctor on the scene had soothed her by saying: "You're alive, and your baby is alive. You're going to forget all this and have a happy, healthy baby." She had functioned very well ever since, and now, suddenly, she had an urge to relive the accident. Did she really need this knowledge to resolve her grief about her husband's death? If not, what was her purpose? She couldn't think of any positive results that would come from her remembering. I persuaded her that it was best to forget the experience, that it could only be a source of painful memories.

Forgetting Pain and Sorrow

Forgetting is a great pain killer. Watch a toddler learning to walk. He forgets the bump on his forehead, teeters forward, and falls again. A woman forgets the pain of giving birth and eagerly plans another child. A widow or widower forgets the pain of loss and decides to marry again.

To remember every pain clearly would immobilize us. To blot out everything unpleasant would condemn us to a life of burned fingers, picked pockets, and poison ivy. Choosing which pains to remember is an ongoing everyday task, accomplished by weighing each hurt against others in our memory bank. Many are better forgotten.

Romantic young men used to do it in droves. Laurel and Hardy did it in a film. Workaholics practice a socially acceptable form of it, and it can be a lifesaver for the recently bereaved. It's called "joining the French Foreign Legion" and it's a valuable forgetting technique. We all resort to it periodically, blocking out sad or disturbing memories by immersing ourselves totally in a mentally and physically exhausting regime. It can be a very valuable short-term solution to severe disappointment or sorrow.

Sometimes forgetting is essential. People faced with unbearable tragedy may block all memory by developing amnesia. Fortunately most of us can deal with painful memories in a less drastic way, by moving them from our short-term to our long-term memories. Once the raw and agonizing images are filed in our total mental filing cabinet, we can mix them with and evaluate them against other information. This way of "gaining perspective" is important to survival.

A good night's sleep is one way to transfer strong short-term memories to our long-term memory. Shakespeare understood this when he wrote about "sleep that knits up the ravel'd sleeve of care." Some people resort to alcohol or drugs to block painful memories, but this can have erratic results. (See chapter 4, "Physical Blocks.") Fortunately for humanity, the memory is adaptable, letting us keep what is good and relevant while we discard what hurts and diminishes us.

Forgetting for Attention and Support

Harry's memory problem was unusual, among the oddest ever presented at one of my workshops. He frequently forgot to shave in the morning, and said he felt embarrassed at work because his boss and colleagues sometimes commented on his stubble. He forgot this basic grooming ritual so often that he had to keep an electric shaver at the office.

"Do you occasionally remember to shave in the morning?" I asked.

"When my wife sleeps late, I shave and fix myself breakfast. But when we get up at the same time, she starts demanding things and I forget about shaving." He mimicked her and her demands until the entire workshop roared with laughter. He glowed with energy and enthusiasm as he described their morning routine and received a round of applause when he finished.

Slowly Harry began to see that he loved these morning dramas that deprived him of a shave. If he retired to the bathroom to shave in isolation, he would forfeit the stimulating encounter with his wife and miss out on some new incident to relate to his friends at the office. He also realized that on the mornings that he shaved, he missed the attention implicit in the teasing he got at work. For Harry the benefits of remembering to shave were far outweighed by those that came with forgetting.

When her husband died suddenly, 56-year-old Eunice had to take charge of paying the household bills. This new responsibility was terrifying to her. She frequently forgot to make the mortgage, insurance, and electricity bill, etc. and that resulted in serious trouble. Her children had to come to her rescue repeatedly and soothed the pain of her loss with this demonstration of their concern and devotion. Finally they were forced to take over her financial affairs, freeing her to return to her daily bridge-playing where her phenomenal memory for numbers and detail made her a steady winner.

Neither of these people was deliberately forgetting, but subconsciously, they needed and relished the results that forgetting brought. A one-time memory lapse was reinforced by the response it brought out in others until it became an essential part of their self-image.

The need to be noticed and nurtured is primary in all human beings. But whenever we begin a sentence with "I always forget . . ." or "I can never remember . . .," it's time to be wary. We are starting to form an image of ourselves as a forgetter. With enough of the right outside reinforcement, we can soon lose our motive to remember, and our self-enhancing forgetfulness turns into a self-destructive block.

Using Negative Memories

She: Darling, remember that quaint, inexpensive hotel we stayed at in Hawaii? The exotic food?

He: You mean that seedy, fleabag slum-within-a-slum? We had to walk two miles to the beach, and I got food poisoning.

We can choose to remember experiences in different ways.

He: Remember when my mother came to visit? I
haven't had so much fun in years.

She: Yes. She criticized my cooking, my decorating,
and my clothes. I cried for weeks.

Both Sigmund Freud and psychological researcher Edward
Thorndike suggested that people are likely to forget unpleasant things
more quickly than pleasant ones. Though tests have failed to prove
this, they do show that both pleasant and unpleasant things are
remembered better than ordinary things. Also, results showed that
some people tend to remember pleasant things more than unpleasant
ones, while for others the unpleasant memories are stronger.

Can we choose between happy and sad memories? We all know
an eternal optimist who sees only the bright side of a disaster, or
an eternal pessimist who can always find something wrong. These
people have a strong image of themselves and the world, and they
choose to remember only the events and information that reinforce
that image.

But most of us have a choice. Resourceful people can even use
negative memories in positive ways. Consider the woman who dated
three recently divorced men in a row and discovered that each was
still so immersed in the mourning process that he was a poor com-
panion. As a result, she decided to avoid dating recently divorced
men. A movie star trusted his business affairs to a close friend who,
though well intentioned, lost all the money due to poor decisions.
The actor decided that in the future he would employ a well-established
investment firm. Both these people used negative memories to
motivate positive future actions.

Painful memories can also be a source of delight and even
income. Paul went to dinner at a resort restaurant with a group of
old friends. They waited 45 minutes before their orders were taken,
then another hour for their food. The waitress dumped a plate of
spaghetti in Paul's lap and had forgotten to order one of the meals
at all. When they called her attention to the missing dinner, the waitress informed them that the kitchen was now closed. As they shared
their poorly cooked dinners with the forgotten member of the party,
a janitor appeared and began to mop around their feet. Instead of
becoming angry or depressed, the men began to play "how much
worse can this get?" Indeed they were overcharged by the waitress.
After they left, they discovered that one man had forgotten his wallet
at the restaurant so they had to return the next day.

A good raconteur, Paul told the story for years afterwards to
appreciative friends. Like many well-paid comedy writers and
performers, he was able to use negative memories positively for
humorous purposes.

Forgetting Because We're Finished

Our minds love to play "School's out!" and discard information we're sure (or strongly hope) we'll never need again. It may be our identification number at a company we'll never work for again or the way to work a machine gun or an ancient, balky copying machine that we couldn't stand. It could even be our doctoral thesis on a subject we didn't select and never fully understood. We don't like the information and chuck it out of our mental library as soon as we can.

This is known formally as the Zeigarnick effect. Dr. Bluma Zeigarnick of the University of Berlin gave her volunteers all kinds of simple tasks: stringing beads, learning poems, copying pictures. They were all allowed to finish half of these assigned tasks, but she prevented the volunteers from finishing the other 50 percent of the tasks, forcibly if necessary. Afterwards, her subjects could recall 68 percent of what they did or learned in the interrupted tasks, but only 42 percent of the substance of those they had been permitted to finish.

Not every experimenter has been able to duplicate this effect, but both Kurt Lewin and Alan Baddeley had similar results. Baddeley found that subjects who were given the answer to a puzzle before they had been able to solve it remembered the answer better later. Both he and Lewin reasoned that their subjects had unresolved tension because they had been frustrated in their task. (Since the obvious extension of this result would be to abolish most of our educational practices, let me add quickly that finding the answer yourself generally makes a thing more memorable—the attention, rehearsal, and pleasure of success lock it in your memory.)

Memory Misdemeanors

Learn that you needn't harass yourself when you forget something. If you need assurance that it is okay to forget, look over the true stories below. Do you think the people involved were successful in their chosen work?

> A. Mr. A went to New York on business. After checking in to his hotel, he went out for a stroll. Sometime later he realized that he was lost and that he did not know the name of the hotel where he was staying. The police phoned all the major hotels in the area and learned that he was registered at the Waldorf Astoria, a half block

from where he was found. He had simply been circling the block during his walk. Do you think Mr. A was successful and well regarded by his contemporaries?

B. Mr. B was a public official who went on a good will tour of South America. Greeting the representatives of one large city, he said how happy he was to be in "_____" and named the capital of another country. When he realized his error, he said, "Oh, that's where I'm going next." The second city was not on his itinerary at all. Did Mr. B. have a chance for advancement?

C. Miss C was a film actress who was always late and usually forgot her lines. Her lapses cost the studio lots of money and her colleagues many unhappy hours. Her director vowed never to work with her again. Did she make another movie?

D. The film director mentioned above expressed great affection for this lady. Miss D was always on time and always well prepared. She never forgot an appointment. Her life was one of neatness and order, exemplary in all respects. Did he make a picture with Miss D?

E. Efficiency was Mrs. E's middle name. Her home was spotless, and her closets had rows of neatly labeled containers holding all her possessions. At work her boss counted on her to remember where everything was, to recall the names of everyone he had contact with, and to remind him of every appointment, all of which she did without fail. What impact did Mrs. E have on the world?

I'll bet you have some pretty strong opinions on the relative successes of these people, but let's take a further look.

A. Albert Einstein *was* quite forgetful about ordinary things. There are numerous stories about his absentmindedness, but he possessed the two things necessary to do what he wanted to do.

Energy—enough physical or mental energy to accomplish his goals.

Focus—concentration on those goals, resistance to scattering energy in too many directions. (While good health is a definite asset for a high energy level, there are many examples of handicapped, chronically ill or elderly people who overcome their restrictions by focusing their limited energy.)

B. President Ronald Reagan, trying to remember a vast number of names, statistics, and places connected with his 1982 tour, forgot where he was. Interestingly, although he was well past 65, no one accused him of senility, and the media treated the incident as an amusing anecdote, not a precursor of major mental decline.

C. Marilyn Monroe exasperated many people who worked with her. After directing her in *Some Like It Hot,* Billy Wilder (*The Seven Year Itch, Sunset Boulevard, The Apartment*) swore that he would never work with her again. In one scene Miss Monroe had to remember a three-word line, "Where's the bourbon?" as she rummaged through drawers. The line came out "Where's the whisky?" – "Where's the bonbon?" – "Where's the bottle?" The frantic Wilder finally had the line written on the inside of the drawers.

Later he relented, saying: "She's not a parrot. Anyone can remember lines, but it takes a real artist to come on the set and not know her lines and give the performance she did." He suggested that Monroe play the title role in one of his later films, *Irma la Douce,* but the part eventually went to Shirley MacLaine.

D. Billy Wilder explained his change of heart about Marilyn Monroe by saying that he had an Aunt Ida in Vienna who was always on time and ready to do what was required, but he wouldn't put her in a movie.

E. Mrs. E was the aunt of a friend of mine. She lived a very useful, if unspectacular, life. Her chief contribution, a very necessary one, was to create order for people whose minds were hopping pell-mell past the details to the larger view of the project at hand.

This does *not* mean that you have to be disorganized to be creative. If you can remember how things worked in the past and can see how to make them work better in the future, you are way ahead:

remembering + evaluation = positive actions

positive actions + good luck = positive results

For instance, if you *remember* that you always underestimate the time it takes to do something, and then you *evaluate* this, you can take *positive action* by deliberately allowing more time than you think the project will take. With *luck,* your action will lead to a *positive result*—finishing the job on schedule. This is positive because you have saved time (for others who must mesh with your scheduled completion or arrival time), saved energy (less anguish and frustration), and probably saved money (yours and other people's).

Without lots of Mrs. E's, we would probably have to do without dependable electric service and running water, well-stocked supermarkets, brain surgery, air traffic control, and TV quiz programs. A memory for details is essential in all these things.

People who remember everything don't have any real advantage over those of us who *select* our memories. Recall the last time you did something that was important to you. What stands out in your mind? What were the *big* things? How can you use this information in planning for the future? If, as Ralph Waldo Emerson insisted, "a foolish consistency is the hobgoblin of little minds," then total recall without evaluation is the role of computers and the unfortunate few with perfect memories.

We use our memories to create a rich, meaningful landscape of information by *forgetting* some things. What is important steps forward. What is unimportant retreats or disappears. To remember everything equally would be to live in a flat, comic strip world without perspective.

Learning to Choose Your Memories

Selective forgetting is healthful. It's one of the big advantages that human beings have over computers. Instead of berating yourself over every memory lapse, learn to spot the ones that actually help you. Discover how to pick through your memories just as you pick through a bin of apples, looking for the crisp, unspotted nourishing ones that make your life better.

A healthy person doesn't need to eradicate unpleasant or tragic memories, but will choose more valuable memories in their place, "rehearsing" these other mental pictures until they are automatically called up in place of the negative ones.

Try This...

Quiz to Assess Your Ability to Forget Constructively

	Often	Usu-ally	Some-times	Never
1. I remember personal insults.	___	___	___	___
2. I fret about the inefficiency and pettiness of my colleagues.	___	___	___	___
3. When I am cheated or get poor service, I don't go back to that business if I can help it.	___	___	___	___
4. I get so mad at the crooked politi-cians that I don't vote anymore.	___	___	___	___
5. My motto is forgive but never forget.	___	___	___	___
6. When someone describes a situation in which someone I love was humiliated, I remember it clearly.	___	___	___	___
7. I forget to pay bills and to return library books.	___	___	___	___

	Often	Usu-ally	Some-times	Never
8. When I am depressed, it's impossible to think about anything cheerful.	___	___	___	___
9. You have to keep your eye open for pickpockets and purse snatchers.	___	___	___	___
10. All in all, the world is a pretty nice place.	___	___	___	___

Score yourself below.   My Score

				My Score
1. Often 0	Usually 2	Sometimes 6	Never 4	_____
2. Often 0	Usually 2	Sometimes 6	Never 4	_____
3. Often 6	Usually 4	Sometimes 4	Never 0	_____
4. Often 0	Usually 0	Sometimes 0	Never 6	_____
5. Often 0	Usually 0	Sometimes 2	Never 6	_____
6. Often 2	Usually 2	Sometimes 6	Never 0	_____
7. Often 0	Usually 0	Sometimes 2	Never 6	_____
8. Often 0	Usually 2	Sometimes 6	Never 2	_____
9. Often 6	Usually 6	Sometimes 6	Never 0	_____
10. Often 6	Usually 6	Sometimes 4	Never 2	_____

Total _____

Score

50-60   Excellent—you are appropriately cautious and have a pretty realistic evaluation of the world, but it doesn't get you down.

40-48   Good—but you may need to be more cynical.

30-38   So so—too many things bother you.

20-28   Only fair—you need to forget more.

0-18   Poor—give yourself permission to do a mental version of artificial respiration: "Out with the bad memories, in with the good memories."

Now, study the following motto. You may write it in colored ink on shiny vellum paper or embroider it on a sampler or set it to music—anything that will lock it into your memory.

It's okay to forget—
    When you have to,
    When you need to,
    When you want to,
As long as what you don't remember won't hurt you.

Part II

How We Remember

6
The Seat of Memory – Theories through the Ages

After a long journey hunting for saber-toothed tigers, the caveman snuggled down into his bearskin for a good night's sleep, while his mind prepared for another journey. As his leaden limbs sank into the soft fur, his brain filled with flickering images that soon carried his spirit to another place and another time.

Such experiences convinced ancient man that the mind could be quite separate from the body, free to wander during life and after death. He reasoned that memory, as one of the mind's major assets, must also be free to come and go. (When we recall something, we still say, "It came back to me.")

To their credit, ancient observers did notice that injuries to the head sometimes affected memory and personality. Fossilized human skulls have been found with small, neat holes cut into them, showing that their owners underwent repeated "trepanning," possibly to "let the devils out." The surgeons must have been skilled since many of these patients survived to undergo later surgery.

Aristotle and the Ancients

Aristotle, the Greek scientist and philosopher, concerned himself with the nature of memory more than 2,000 years ago. He concluded that thinking took place in the head, but that memory was stored in the heart.

Memory, said Aristotle, cannot occur in someone who is in a state of rapid transition. "It is like a seal stamped on running water."

That is why young and old have trouble remembering, he said. "The former are growing and the latter decaying."

Aristotle also divided memory into two parts: a type of remembering common to all animals that he called "memory"; and a superior human action, involving a sense of time, deliberation, and the relation of a chain of experiences to a present experience, which can be translated as "recall" or "reminiscence."

Aristotle's teacher, Plato, conceived of thought as "an ideal form, existing separately from the sensible world"—the body. The more practical Aristotle decided that both thought and memory needed a home. What better place than the home of the soul, the human heart?

Whether he knew it or not, Aristotle was repeating a Chinese concept, then already several thousands of years old. The Chinese ideograph for both *remember* and *memory* is the same as the ideograph for *heart*.

Both the cavemen and ancient Egyptians performed brain operations but their learning has been lost to us. In the millenia since, the strong taboos against surgery and autopsies helped maintain many erroneous concepts about the brain. Only in the last few hundred years have these taboos diminished, allowing doctors and scientists to reveal the true nature of the heart and the brain. We now know that the heart is an active, enthusiastic muscle, capable of pumping blood around our bodies, while the brain is a silent, grey blob capable of exploring the universe.

Many ancient beliefs about memory were surprisingly accurate. Plato saw how one memory can lead to another when he described a lyre that made him think of its owner and then his friends, until a whole, rich picture of events and associations was called up from a simple, stringed instrument.

Aristotle also considered the mechanics of memory. He listed four kinds of association that would stimulate memory.

1. Things near each other, like ocean and shore.

2. Things that happen at the same time, like adolescence and pimples.

3. Things that are similar, like roller skates and ice skates.

4. Things that show a contrast, like city and country.

Twentieth-century memory expert James D. Weinland adds to Aristotle's list.

5. Cause and effect, like fire and heat.

6. Part and whole, like nose and face.

7. Particular and general, like bee and insect.

8. Numerical contiguity, like five and six.

St. Augustine thought that Aristotle's four memory associations were unnecessary. Instead, he reasoned, the only thing necessary for one idea to suggest another is "coexistence," that the ideas must have been active in the mind at the same time, however unlikely the relationship. This two-ideas-at-once concept is now generally accepted —under the term *contiguity of experience*. Pavlov, the nineteenth-century Russian scientist, showed that even dogs could associate such unlikely things as bells and dinner.

Inventing the Brain

Let's invent a brain—or, at least, let's invent a model of how our minds work. Roger von Oech makes a sprightly analogy of man's continuing attempt to compare his mind to his most recent invention. In the seventeenth century, the mind was seen as a lens or a mirror, focusing thoughts and reflecting them back. In the Industrial Age, the mind became a vast factory, with Freud's image of the repressed, hidden unconscious occasionally bursting into the action-oriented

Man tends to compare his mind to his most recent inventions.

conscious like steam from an engine. With the invention of the telephone, the brain was conceived of as a vast switchboard, sending and receiving messages. Now the computer is our model, with computer jargon describing many of our human exchanges — input, output, feedback, and programming. Our next brain model will probably be the hologram, a concept of matter in which the most minute particle contains a code for reproducing the whole. Indeed, the work of Karl Pribam of Stanford University indicates that the brain has many similarities to the hologram. We'll discuss this exciting holographic model of the brain in the next chapter.

Comparing Computers to the Human Brain

The computer has some big advantages over the human brain — speed, volume, flexibility, and lack of eccentricities . . . most of the time — but the human brain has more advantages. For instance, a human can beat a computer at chess. This is because there are 10^{120} (10 to the 120th power) different possible chess games. If the computer checked every possible move at the speed of one million moves per minute, it would take billions of years to play a game. Therefore chess-playing computers are taught basic chess patterns and groupings so they can discard illogical moves and speed up the game. Even then, a good chess player can beat them.

Another task that man can do better and faster than a computer is to figure the most efficient route for a salesman to visit 20 cities. The computer must compare distances between 20 to the 20th power locations, a task taking days. A child with a ruler could do it in minutes.

But if you are using them for something other than playing chess or traveling, computers are terrific for sifting quickly through mountains of information to find the one fact you want. In doing this book, we saved months, even years, of library research by doing computer searches of recent scientific literature for the latest studies on memory.

However, the key words the computer needed to start on its way were *retrieval* and *retention* — the computer didn't recognize the word *memory*. Thus, we were sometimes referred to articles on retrieval of foreign objects from the ear or articles on urine retention. A person knows instantly that these have nothing to do with memory, but the computer doesn't.

Ebbinghaus and Nonsense

Aristotle took memory out of the world of the spirit and brought it into the world of the scientist. A nineteenth-century German named Hermann Ebbinghaus (1850–1909) married memory study to modern science. He proposed three basic questions about memory.

1. How much information can we store?
2. How fast can we acquire it?
3. How long can we keep it?

In the 1870s Ebbinghaus addressed the latter two. With Germanic thoroughness, he set about a systematic search for answers, using himself as a guinea pig.

First he invented strings of nonsense syllables (wux, caz, bij, zol, etc.). Then he recited sequences of them aloud to see how many repeats were necessary before he could memorize them. He tested himself at the same time every day under the same conditions but varied all other factors such as the length of the lists or the time between memorization and recall. He also discovered that he could remember much better if he studied first thing in the morning than if he studied at 4:00 P.M., and concluded that fatigue affected memory. Ebbinghaus described three possible ways that we forget.

1. Memories are buried (interference theory) — "the earlier images are more and more overlaid . . . and covered by the later ones."

2. Memories undergo changes (trace decay) — "the persisting images suffer changes which more and more affect their nature."

3. Memories fall apart — forgetting is caused by "crumbling into parts and the loss of separate components."

All of these theories seem to hold up in different situations, and forgetting is probably a complex combination of all of them.

Bartlett and Meaning

The next major studies of memory were done in the early part of this century by Sir Frederick Bartlett (1896–1969) in England. He felt that Ebbinghaus's pure approach was highly artificial. The brain stores information, he said, by using what it already knows, laying a new pattern over a similar old one. He designed experiments that were closer to how people usually use their memories.

Instead of memorizing nonsense, his subjects looked at pictures and read stories, summoning up their personal associations, prior experiences, and attitudes. He still needed strict controls to ensure a uniform basis of comparison, but at the time, many felt his work was too vague and complex. However, contemporary computers show that his theory is correct, at least as far as computers are concerned; using existing patterns *is* the most efficient way to store new information.

Twentieth-Century Debates

Memory research is subject to as many fashions and fads as any other science. Before the 1950s, memory was thought of as one system. Then a two-system theory became popular—a short-term memory for our immediate environment and a long-term memory for "facts": language, history, arithmetic, and the like.

In the 60s memory was regarded as a storage system. In the 70s it was looked on as a component in a larger information-processing system that included perception, comprehension, and reasoning. The 80s has brought new interest in nonverbal memory: visual, auditory, and kinesthetic.

Freud and Memory

Sigmund Freud (1856–1939) was a Viennese doctor who specialized in nerve and brain diseases. When some patients did not respond to physical treatment of their physical ailments, he found that treating their mental and emotional conditions—their *minds*— could result in a cure. Freud was not the first person to see this relationship between the body and the mind, but his theories about the powers of the human psyche were so forcefully described in his many books and papers that they became the basis of modern psychoanalysis and psychiatry.

The Conscious and Unconscious Minds
While Freud is probably best known for his theories on sexuality, he was fascinated with the concept of memory and why we forget things. According to his basic theory, people have conscious

and unconscious minds, and the unconscious mind can have a tremendous effect on a person's conscious actions.

Of course doctors can't dissect the brain and locate these separate systems, neatly labeled. This is just a theory that attempts to explain the various forces that affect us, and as a theory it works pretty well. Freud decided that there is nothing accidental or arbitrary in our psychic lives. (If accepted unconditionally, this theory can produce a lot of guilt, so it is fortunate that Freud also did extensive theorizing about guilt.)

Aside from major memory loss caused by neurosis, Freud offered explanations for many everyday incidents of forgetting. He decided that temporary forgetfulness could be divided into both "forgetfulness" and "false recollection" — the latter substituting another name or word for the actual one. The memory process that should have produced the actual memory was interrupted; the memory was "displaced" by another. Displacement, Freud concluded, wasn't an arbitrary quirk. Instead it followed a routine as logical as summoning up the actual memory.

Freud on Forgetting Names

In *The Psychopathology of Everyday Life* (Penguin, 1975), Freud analysed a number of his own "Freudian slips." In one case he couldn't remember the name of a sanatarium, although he could remember the location, the doctor in charge, and the name of a patient who had been there. When his wife reminded him that the name of the place was "Nervi," Freud concluded that, as a nerve doctor, he, himself, had become weary of nerves. On another occasion Freud could not remeber the name of a major railway station, Rosenheim, which translates as Rose-home. Upon tracing the associations, he decided that the name was lost because he had just come from visiting the home of his sister, Rose (Rose's home). "This name was taken away by my 'family complex'."

Freud concluded that forgotten names are associated, however indirectly, with something painful and unpleasant. If you accept Freud's theory, you can decide that forgetting the name of your dear friend, Sue, may mean you are secretly angry at her, but it can also mean that the name reminds you of a nasty experience you had in *Sioux* Falls when you were *sued* by a *sewer* worker.

Freud on Losing Things

Once Freud intended to order a book by a favorite author and could not find the book store catalogue. He concluded that this was because he had at one time written to this author of his admiration and received a cool reply.

Freud described another case in which a patient mislaid a book, a gift from his wife. The patient and his wife had been at odds for some time. Then about six months after he lost the book, they reconciled. He promptly found the book.

Freud on Forgetting Appointments

Neither lovers nor soldiers, Freud noted, can get away with saying "I forgot." Their preoccupation with the task at hand should be and is so overwhelming that there is no chance of forgetting. We can see many demonstrations of this in our own lives. If we are fleeing a burning building or rushing to present the winning raffle ticket, we rarely forget what we are about.

Freud explained his own lapses in everyday matters as a dislike of the task he had reluctantly agreed to do. He noticed with chagrin that he sometimes forgot to make calls on charity patients and colleagues, but never on paying clients. He saw the everyday forgetting of the many small promises we make as antagonism toward the demands placed upon us. (A reputation for forgetfulness can also discourage people from asking us to do things.)

Freud had no kind words for people who forget and then blame it on an organic defect ("poor memory"). "The motive is an unusually large amount of unavowed disregard for others which exploits a constitutional factor for its purpose."

Freud and You

If you are analytic by nature, you may want to explore some of your own common slips in a Freudian way. It's fun, usually harmless, and occasionally insightful.

But Freud was so successful at uncovering deep, psychological manifestations in what seemed to be utterly casual occurrences that you might find yourself ascribing every instance of forgetting or loss to some repressed hatred, latent psychosis, or psychic abnormality. Keep in mind that such all-pervasive self-analysis is usually erroneous and could be harmful to you and those around you. There *are* repressed hostilities, of course, but there are also holes in pockets, misunderstood instructions, mumbled introductions, and ringing phones that can interrupt a train of thought.

Once I fell down a flight of stairs. Afterwards I painfully contemplated all the psychological explanations for my accident. I decided that my life was in pretty good shape and I had had no subconscious reason to injure myself, so I went and measured the steps. They were several inches smaller than standard steps, actually illegally shallow. Sometimes there are very ordinary explanations for extraordinary events.

Remember, too, that Freud concluded that "no psychological theory has yet been able to explain the connection between remembering and forgetting; indeed, even the complete analysis of what we can actually observe has yet scarcely been grasped." After a hundred years of study, this is still true. Human memory is still slyly and shyly retaining its secrets.

Try This...

to See If You Forget for a Reason

Write down some things that you have forgotten recently that really bothered you: _____
_____.

Now go back and speculate on why you may have forgotten. _____
_____.

7
How the Brain Remembers

Imagine sending three explorers into a strange land. One returns with an exhaustive report of the topography: the rivers, mountains, and deserts. Another deciphers the various languages spoken. A third describes the architecture but makes no attempt to relate it to the natural environment and resources or to political, religious, and cultural influences.

Until recently, the brain has been explored this way. Psychologists, biologists, and chemists looked at the brain independently, from the viewpoint of their separate disciplines. Now at last they are beginning to combine their studies.

Just as florists sort through masses of flowers to produce bouquets, scientists must pick through masses of sometimes conflicting facts and select the ones they want to shape into theories. Each works with a large variety of raw materials, and no two florists or scientists are likely to come up with exactly the same result. Sphinx-like, the brain quietly retains most of its secrets.

What We Remember With

To discover how we remember, we have to examine *where* we remember—the brain. The brain is a rather dull-looking grey mass, weighing about 3 lbs (1.4 kg). Despite its mousy appearance, it contains the universe as each of us knows it. In fact, it contains everything we know. "If the brain were simple enough ever to understand," says Lyall Watson, "we would be so simple, we couldn't."

Scientists used to think that we use only a small percentage of our brain. This was because much of the brain remained uncharted.

We now know that we use *all* our brain with differing degrees of efficiency.

The brain demands one-fifth of the body's blood and oxygen supply, but its energy output is equivalent to that of a 25-watt bulb. The brain can continue to function in the face of severe adversity— with several bullets in it or (once) even a crowbar; however, a few tiny crystals of a drug like etorphin can knock it out. One man lived a full, mentally competent life with only *one* cerebrum—half a brain. This amazing fact was discovered only through an autopsy.

The brain has changed little throughout our known history. Humans today are no smarter than they were 10,000 years ago, but they have a greater storehouse of knowledge to draw on, to *remember.*

A Brief History of the Brain

Join us for a diverting detour through the richest, most inscrutable galaxy of the universe—the brain. Let's look closely at our three-layered treasure.

The Reptilian Brain

Once upon a time there was a lizard with a perfectly good lizard's brain. It told him how to do all the essential things: look for food, defend his home, be sociable with other lizards, and reproduce. This simple brain has survived for 200 million years in all animals. We humans have improved on it, of course, but that primitive core is still there, controlling much more of our behavior than we might realize. It is responsible for much of our interaction with our fellow creatures and our need to follow leaders, everything from "keeping up with the Joneses" to "making the world safe for democracy." Scientists call this the R-Complex brain.

The Limbic System

As soon as our lizard ancestor stopped lying around on hot rocks and developed his own heating system, he added a more sophisticated brain to control it. One of the nice features of this new brain was love. While the old-style creatures ate (and continue to eat) their nearest and dearest without compunction, the new limbic-brained creatures were capable of all sorts of romantic notions. They could also smell and experience fear, pain, and pleasure.

You'll notice that we refer to this new, 150-million-year-old brain as a "system." That's because it consists of several parts including the *hypothalamus*, an inch-square organ that regulates sex drive, orders extra adrenalin during stressful situations, monitors body temperature, and lets us know when we're thirsty and hungry; the *pituitary gland*, our master producer of sex and growth hormones; and the *hippocampus* — shaped like a seahorse, it controls fear and rage, probably converts short-term memories into long term, and regulates memories about place.

The Neocortex

The newest and largest addition to the brain is the part that makes us human. The neocortex is rational and lets us store logic, language, mathematics, and speculation about the future. (Dolphins, monkeys, and dogs also have large neocortexes.) The neocortex lets us consciously change the behavior patterns dictated by our more primitive brains.

This three-layer-brain theory is relatively new. It was first set forth in 1972 by Dr. Paul MacLean of the Laboratory of Brain Evolution and Behavior of the National Institute of Mental Health in Maryland. Research and experiments since then seem to support it, and it is now generally accepted. This illustrates the process by which human imaginings, ideas, and speculations make the journey from fancy to demonstrable fact.

Could we add yet another more sophisticated layer? Maybe, in time. One basic problem — a larger brain would require a larger skull.

Since the current size of a baby's head just fits (usually) through the circle of its mother's pelvic bones, we would either have to evolve bigger women or smaller babies or perhaps grow babies outside their mother's bodies. Ah, brave new world!

How Much Will You Remember?

How much you remember is determined by

- Your inborn capacity to remember.

- Your training for efficient collection, intelligent interpretation, and maximum storage of information (sometimes called "education").

- Your enthusiasm for remembering a particular thing.

- The effect of things you learned before (proactive interference) and things you learned after (retroactive interference) on the particular thing you want to remember.

- The effect of physical, mechanical, and emotional blocks.

Where Does the Brain Remember?

Is the brain a big library, with different subjects stored on different shelves? One way to test this is to study people who have lost part of their memory because of head injuries. If several people have suffered damage in the same part of the brain and they all experience similar memory loss, then presumably the affected part controlled that kind of memory. However, attempts to catalogue such relationships or to duplicate memory loss in animals have been unsuccessful.

Amazingly, people who have had large portions of their brain damaged can frequently remember most of what they knew before they were injured, although they may no longer be able to remember newly acquired information. In another type of injury—damage to the medial temporal cortex—the person can still learn readily on a short-term basis, but forgets the information almost immediately.

How Does the Brain Remember?

The brain is full of information-holding nerve cells called neurons. Neurons are all over the body, but the ones in the brain are especially sophisticated. We have billions of these brain cells (estimates range from 10 billion to 100 billion) and more than 20,000 of them will fit on the head of a pin.

Neurons come in different shapes, depending on their function. On one side, each neuron has a long tail (axon) ending in a brush. On the other side, the neuron has a set of short tails called dendrites. When the axon of one cell shyly reaches out and touches the dendrite of another cell, the connection is called a synapse. The synapse is actually a gap or open space, but it acts like a bridge between two towns or a street between two houses. Like a bridge or a public street, the synapse has a lot of traffic and this is where information exchange takes place. Synapses are found almost exclusively in the memory portions of the brain.

There are three major theories on how these synapses work.

- Information is physically coded on the neurons.

- Information is transmitted and stored as electrical signals.

- Information changes the chemical structure of the neurons.

It is also possible that memories are stored in the patterns of connections between neurons, rather than in the neurons themselves. Dr. Mark Rosenzwieg, psychologist and memory expert at the University of California, Berkeley, suggests that whenever a person learns something new the neurons alter their areas of contact so that messages can get across the synapses more easily. New connections form, and old ones are removed.

To prove this, he put one group of rats in a dull, dreary cage. He put a second group in a veritable Disneyland for mice, with toys, mazes, ferris wheels, and merry-go-rounds. The brains of the stimulated mice grew larger and showed denser concentrations of neuronal connections. While there is no proof that fat, healthy neurons remember better than skinny, pale ones, we suspect they do.

The Holographic Theory

Scientists once believed that memories were stored in neat little pigeonholes in different parts of the brain. If only we could find out which memory goes where, they reasoned, we would be able to fix defective memories and improve healthy ones.

They located parts of the brain that control sight, smell, taste, and hearing, but memory eluded them. Now we know that, even though certain parts of the brain let us remember certain things, they don't *store* the memory itself. They are just receivers for certain signals. Because memory can't be pinpointed in any one part of the brain, more and more experts are turning to a holographic concept of memory formulated by Dr. Karl Pribam of Stanford — that all memories are stored in all parts of the brain. In a holograph, any fragment can reproduce the whole.

Profile of a Receptor

To record a memory, the recording agent must be able to do two difficult things: respond within a fraction of a second to a stimulus and then keep the information indefinitely. Scientists at the University of California, Irvine, have tracked down such a wonder in the synapses found in the hippocampus.

Electrically stimulating this part of the brain or treating it with calpain, a protein-digesting enzyme, uncovers receptors and makes synapses in this region more active for months. Once these receptors are uncovered, they stay that way, passing information back and forth and keeping their neighbor neurons healthy and functioning throughout the life of the brain.

It's possible that some older people lose their memory abilities because their bodies have stopped producing the enzymes that keep their receptors receptive. Some laboratory work has already been done, showing that blocking norepinephrine production in animals keeps them from remembering new information — possibly why some people can clearly remember events from years before, but not what happened this morning. Stimulation of enzyme production in humans may (or may not) prove to be an incredible new way to enhance and extend memory throughout our lives.

Receptors are also "binding sites" for chemicals that affect mood and behavior. Sharks are one of the few animals that lack these receptors, which may explain why they have such boring personalities.

Brain Chemicals

When nerve signals are passed from cell to cell over the network of synapse bridges, they are helped by chemicals called neurotransmitters. There are four significant brain chemicals currently being studied in America: calpain, norepinephrine, Deamino-D-Arginine Vasopressin (DDAVP), and serotonin.

Calpain has the ability to digest protein and appears to clean up blocked receptors and let the neurons communicate more easily with their neighbors. Calpain is naturally released by calcium in the cells, and one possibility being studied right now is that calcium deficiency may decrease enzyme activity in older people, leading to memory loss.

Norepinephrine triggers long-term memory. Fearful memories are essential for survival, and we hang onto such memories unless production of norepinephrine is blocked. This was demonstrated by Dr. Larry Stein at the University of California, Irvine, who conducted an experiment in which he gave rats a shock whenever they stepped off a shelf. Weeks later they were put back in the same cage, and they still remembered not to step off the shelf. But when their production of norepinephrine was blocked, they forgot and got repeated shocks. Conclusion: norepinephrine is a trigger to long-term memory. When we have a strong experience, norepinephrine tells the brain to "print it."

DDAVP is used by the body to balance water content, but it can also temporarily improve the ability to recall in normal humans and some animals.

Serotonin is the fourth significant neurotransmitter. Changing the diet of laboratory rats can affect their production of serotonin, but so far this has not been demonstrated in humans. A 1983 study at U.C.L.A. made the intriguing discovery that very high levels of serotonin are present in dominant male vervet monkeys and in officers of college fraternities.

The Role of Adrenalin

Adrenalin may be a key to locking memories in place. Psycho-biologist James McGaugh of the University of California, Irvine, reports that rats that can't produce adrenalin have poorer recall ability than their normal adrenalin-producing kin. Rats that get a booster shot of adrenalin after learning something can remember it better. He and his colleagues theorize that hormones such as adrenalin act as "fixatives," locking memories of exciting, stimulating, or shocking events in the brain.

This fixing is a valuable sorting tool, a filter that lets us discard the trivial while retaining the important impressions in our lives. "If you were going to build a brain that emphasized thinking functions," McGaugh says, ". . . you would need a system that can tell exactly what is important to keep and what is not."

One of their most interesting discoveries was that injecting adrenalin into older rats after they had learned a maze improved their memory of the maze. This may support the theory that hormone deficiency in older people contributes to memory loss and senility.

Hormones may act directly on the brain, McGaugh says, or they may alter body chemistry so that some other substance can reach the brain and lock in the memory. Brain research is barely beginning, but someday we may be able to maintain and improve memory through subtle reinforcement of our body's natural memory-storing processes.

Brain Size

When it comes to brains, bigger is not necessarily better. The average brain is 2.97 lbs (1,349g). Nineteenth-century scientists, seeking a correlation between size and intelligence, actually weighed the brains of famous men. Two writers, Jonathan Swift and Ivan Turgenev, weighed in as heavyweights, 4.4 lbs (2,000g) each. But Anatole France, no slouch as an author, had a brain weighing only 2.24 lbs (1,017g). The largest brain ever studied weighed 4.51 lbs (2,049g) — and belonged to an idiot! Brain size is no measurement of intelligence, at least in humans.

Relative brain size in animals can be confusing too. Many animals have larger brains than man. The elephant's brain weighs more than three times what a human brain weighs, but it represents only 0.2 percent of an elephant's body-weight. Spider monkeys, mice, porpoises, tree shrews, and sparrows have a higher brain/body-weight ratio than people do, yet only porpoises could claim similar intelligence. A horse's brain is only half the size of a human brain, yet a horse weighs ten times what a man weighs.

Between the time we are born and the time we reach adulthood, brain weight more than triples. From then on it decreases slightly, about 0.035 oz (1g) a year. Tall people have heavier brains than short people, but short people have a higher brain/body-weight ratio. Eskimos generally have the largest brains of any ethnic group.

Can Memories Be Swallowed?

We can't leave the fascinating intricacies of the brain without mentioning one memory experiment that involved lowly worms. These little fellows, called planaria, were kept in a dark place by a scientist who periodically flashed a light and gave the poor things an electric shock. Whenever they got a shock, their bodies would naturally scrunch up. After a while, they would scrunch up whenever the light flashed, shock or no shock. Then the scientist ground up his unhappy worms, made a slurry, and fed them to a new group of planaria. After their cannibalistic breakfast, the new worms were placed in the darkened worm tanks, and a light was flashed. You guessed it; the new worms scrunched up.

Memory Pills

Is there a pill or medicine that we can take to improve our memories? Not yet, but experts are working on it. One candidate would be an "enhancer" that would increase the brain's protein synthesis or slow the synapse breakdowns, preventing or reversing memory loss. A kidney drug called Vasopressin (not available in the UK) may turn out to be such a natural substance. It's a pituitary hormone that constricts the blood vessels, raises blood pressure, and regulates the body's water content.

In experiments in the Netherlands and at the National Institute of Mental Health in Washington, D.C., both people and animals experienced enhanced memories after taking the Vasopressin. Human memory improved between 20 percent and 100 percent in different types of tests. Patients who had undergone electric shock therapy, which is frequently followed by temporary amnesia, improved by an astonishing 300 percent. The effects lasted about three weeks. However, Vasopressin has dangerous side effects on the body's circulation and water retention, so its use is still in the early experimental stages.

Another potential memory drug, adrenocorticotropic hormone/melanocyte-stimulating hormone (ACTH/MSH), is a combination of two pituitary hormones. Injections of ACTH/MSH seem to increase the power of concentration and may be helpful in treating some forms of retardation that result in inattention. Its effects on hyperactive children and adults with senile dementia are also being tested. But, like Vasopressin, it has dangerous side effects.

Another element that may improve fading memory is choline, a dietary substance that is the forerunner of acetylcholine, a brain compound necessary for transmitting nerve impulses. The major dietary source of choline is lecithin.

In one study conducted by the National Institute of Mental Health, a single 0.35 oz (10g) dose of choline significantly improved both memory and recall in normal, healthy volunteers. After taking the choline, the volunteers were able to memorize a sequence of unrelated words more quickly. Interestingly, those with the poorest memory at the start of the study were the ones helped the most by choline.

Other studies suggest that choline may also help persons with Alzheimer's disease. In numerous cases, the memory of patients increased significantly although it did not quite return to normal. The improvement lasted for up to 18 months.

Unlike the powerful drugs, choline appears to be completely safe even when as much as 0.7 to 0.87 oz (20-25g) is taken daily. Scientists stress that research on choline's effectiveness has just begun, but so far the results are very encouraging.

Things to Come

Most of the brain's chemistry has yet to be explored. One prominent chemist estimates that we understand less than one percent of the chemistry of the brain's nerve cells. He anticipates that chemical pathways for the major emotions will be mapped within the next 20 years. Of course, knowing where and how still won't tell us *why.*

Try This...

to Evaluate Your Personal Potential for Remembering

Here are five major factors that determine how much you can remember. Which can you develop?

1. *Your inborn capacity to remember.*
   You can't change your parents at this point, so you have to accept your inherited capacity as a fixed part of your memory equation. (Don't underrate it!)

2. *Your training for efficient collection, intelligent interpretation, and maximum storage of information (sometimes called "education").*

79

Are you pretty good at this already, or would some practice help? The exercises in this book may show you where you need to do more work.

3. *Your enthusiasm for remembering a particular thing.*
   Think of three types of things that you rarely forget:
   _____
   _____
   _____.
   Are you enthusiastic about them, or have they become habits (like getting dressed in the morning)? Now think of three types of things you frequently forget: _____
   _____
   _____
   _____.
   Is there any way you could be more enthusiastic about them, or convert them to habits, or are they subject to the problems of number four and number five below?

4. *The effect of things you learned before
   and things you learned after
   the particular thing you want to remember.*
   Something that you learned earlier can keep you from recognizing or learning new things that are very similar. Imagine meeting people named Minninger, Benjanin, or Collingrood. You would probably convert them to the more familiar Menninger, Benjamin, and Collingwood. If something is very similar to something you already know, it is easier — and harder — to remember.

   The caveman spent much of his time noticing when things changed. His survival instinct constantly evaluated his shifting surroundings — can I eat it or will it eat me? When you encounter something that seems familiar, try playing caveman. What is the same? What is different?

   Learning something new is a good reason to review related things you already knew. That incredibly boring school task was also a very useful way to lock into our memory things that might have been replaced by newer information.

   Try playing "student" and give yourself lots of mental gold stars as you go over old information that you don't want to lose.

5. *The effect of physical, mechanical, and emotional blocks.*

   As a practise task for number four above, review the information in earlier chapters on physical, mechanical, and emotional blocks. Do you see new ways that you can improve how you remember things? Do you see memory blocks that have no immediate solution? Which blocks (such as ill health, fatigue, confused input) will you probably have to cope with throughout your life?

8
Three Stages
of Memory

For generations scholars argued this classic question about memory: Is memory one system that is used in different ways at different depths, *or* is it two systems, one for what has just happened and another for the big picture of life—culture, language, science, mathematics, and the universe?

Memory goes through three stages: immediate memory (seconds), short-term memory (hours or days), and long-term memory (months or years).

Today scientists speculate that memory goes through not two, but *three* stages:

- immediate memory
- short-term memory
- long-term memory

We are constantly redrawing the "map" of how memory works, but here is the way most experts see it right now. Immediate memory lasts about two seconds and lets us do continuous activities — walk across a room or read a sentence.

Short-term memory is recent — the last few minutes, hours, days. You could probably say what you ate for breakfast yesterday and, just maybe, the day before, but asking you a week or a month from now would be fairly useless, unless it was a very special breakfast, or you always ate the same thing.

Long-term memory is the select filing cabinet where we would like all those pesky names, dates, and numbers to end up. When we talk about remembering, we are usually talking about long-term memory (although occasionally short-term memories like "Where did I put my glasses?" are more vexing).

All memory stages have two characteristics.

Capacity: how many bits of information can be held?

Duration: how long can they be held?

Each memory expert has slightly different figures for these categories, and some aren't sure that short-term memory must precede long-term memory. They argue that some information can go directly into our long-term memories.

Immediate Memory

Capacity: thousands, in terms of generalities (thousands of leaves on a tree, thousands of ants at the picnic)

Duration: two seconds or less

Instinct plays a big part in immediate memory (also called the sensory memory). Simple comparisons are made between pictures: is this different than it was a second ago? Immediate memory notices a potential change and puts our short-term memories on standby.

Short-Term Memory

Capacity: seven things
Duration: 30 seconds to 2 days

The language of the Australian aborigine contains only eight words for numbers: one, two, three, four, five, six, seven, many. Seven seems to be the largest number of separate things we can remember. After that, things turn into groups, crowds, schools, herds, or congresses.

Seven is a mystical and popular number — seven days of the week, seven seas, the Seven Hills of Rome, the Seven Wonders of the World, even the seven dwarfs. Seven seems to be the one real biological limitation on short-term memory. If there are more than seven digits in a phone number, most people won't remember it from the time they look it up to the time they dial it. They will have to read it off the page as they dial. When more than seven things are needed from the supermarket, you write a list. And yet you can remember thousands of things by grouping them for storage in long-term memory. You remember more by remembering less.

Short-term memory lets us link things together, create contexts, assign meanings. Short-term memory is an active process. Reciting a phone number over and over until you can get to a phone is one example.

How long does short-term memory last? How easily are we distracted from remembering?

How long does short-term memory last? Again, the experts disagree. Some say only a few seconds; some say as long as two years. While the time period is probably several days for most things, you may find that a monthly event like a meeting brings back clear memories of the previous event, where you sat, what you heard and said, maybe even what you wore. An annual event, a holiday or birthday for example, may let you recall some surprising things: "Wow, Aunt Tootsie sent me this same card last year" or "I spilled gravy on my green shirt last Christmas." This information has survived one year, but probably wouldn't last another, unless the Aunt Tootsie or the green shirt was very important to you.

Was this information still in your short-term memory? Or did it make it to long-term and then fade with time? Right now we don't know, but let's assume that you made no effort to remember it and that it was reconstructed from a quirky, lingering scrap of short-term memory.

During the entire time that something is in your short-term memory, bits and pieces are being transferred to long-term memory. Everyone agrees that anything in your short-term memory *can* get into your long-term memory. Studying is one way to do this. When you study, you also create a context for remembering by deciding what the information means and clustering it with similar information. It's the "handles" you build onto an information bit that help you retrieve it later. If you meet a charming fellow named Harry and associate him with an event coming up in two years and also with a dear friend whom you see regularly, you have a much better chance of remembering him than if you simply think of him as tall and dark haired.

It is important not to try to do too much in short-term memory. Remember, your capacity is seven things. Elementary school teachers are careful about this when working with students. They create learning structures with no more than four to seven units. Some classic learning structures are North, South, East, West; the four seasons; the four elements (air, fire, earth, and water); and animal, vegetable, mineral.

Long-Term Memory

Capacity: infinite
Duration: forever
Canadian psychologist Endel Tulving divides long-term memory into two kinds: episodic and semantic.

Episodic: remembering incidents, like what you had for breakfast, a parliamentary election, a book you read

Semantic: remembering knowledge—meanings of words and numbers, locations

Neurosurgeon Wilder Penfield probed areas of the human brain during surgery and discovered that patients vividly re-experienced events that happened as much as 50 years earlier. There seems to be no limit to how much we can remember and how long we can remember it.

But the transfer of information from short- to long-term memory can be blocked by any number of things. When rats find their way through a maze and are rewarded, they remember the route. When they find their way through and get an electric shock, they forget the route. It is not profitable for them to remember, so they discard the information. Similarly we choose our memories. The person who spots a newcomer across the room and asks, "Is he anybody?" really means, "Is he worth remembering?"

Most people think of long-term memory as a large dresser drawer that has to be emptied periodically to make room for new things. Wrong. There are no known limits to the storage in your memory. You can learn and remember new things all your life.

Try
This...

Exercise for Recognizing Memory Stages

	Short	Long
Are the following examples of short-term or long-term memory loss?		
1. You lose your glasses.	_____	_____
2. You can't remember when Lady Diana and Prince Charles were married.	_____	_____
3. You forget to put money in the parking meter.	_____	_____
4. There's a word starting with *m* that means some kind of road, "Mac . . ." something, but you can't think of it.	_____	_____
5. You get lost trying to find a restaurant in your old neighborhood.	_____	_____

Now consider whether these same incidents are also examples of episodic or semantic memory, as defined by Tulving.

	Episodic	Semantic
6. You lose your glasses.	_____	_____
7. You can't remember when Lady Diana and Price Charles were married.	_____	_____
8. You forget to put money in the parking meter.	_____	_____

	Epi-sodic	Se-mantic
9. There's a word starting with *m* that means some kind of road, "Mac . . ." something, but you can't think of it.	_____	_____
10. You get lost trying to find a restaurant in your old neighborhood.	_____	_____

Here are three actions that can help you convert information from short-term memory to long-term memory.

Intend to remember.

Rehearse the information.

File the information in several ways.

Decide which is represented by the following actions:

	Intention	Rehearsal	Multiple Filing
11. You recite a phone number over and over until you can dial it or write it down.	_____	_____	_____
12. You set aside a time and place for studying and see that you aren't interrupted.	_____	_____	_____
13. You want to remember that your child's new teacher is Mr. Post so you imagine him standing near the fence post on the school playground and also posting a sign on the class door with his name.	_____	_____	_____

	Intention	Rehearsal	Multiple Filing
14. You see yourself as a competent person who rarely loses things or forgets appointments.	_____	_____	_____
15. You repeat a name when you are introduced.	_____	_____	_____
16. You tie a big red ribbon on your keys, always hang them in the same place, and have duplicates at the home of a neighbor and at the office.	_____	_____	_____

Answers

1. short-term
2. long-term
3. short-term
4. long-term
5. long-term
6. episodic
7. semantic
8. episodic
9. semantic
10. episodic
11. rehearsal
12. intention
13. multiple filing
14. intention
15. rehearsal
16. multiple filing

9
Three Steps To Remembering

As a child you learned your "three Rs"—Readin', 'Ritin', and 'Rithmetic, an illiterate but alliterative trio. Remembering also can be thought of as a "three Rs" process:

- Registration—you get the information.
- Retention—you file the information.
- Retrieval (recall/recognition)—you can find the information later, *or* it is familiar when you run into it again.

The three Rs of remembering.

Registration

You can't forget what you didn't get in the first place. We've already talked about overload and other distractions that prevent or confuse input. Trying to register information while the television is on, several conversations are taking place in the same room, the kettle is whistling in the kitchen, the phone is ringing, your head is aching, and the dog is barking at the door may be difficult or impossible.

Of course, if the information is *really* important, if the phone call is to tell you you've just won one thousand pounds, you will probably remember it. And some people thrive in just such an environment, letting the conflicting demands for attention cancel each other out until they blend into a soothing background noise like that of a waterfall. There are people who actually seek out crowded restaurants or bus terminals as ideal places to study.

Retention

Retention is "potential recall." You have noticed something and, hallelujah, it has made the trip from your short-term memory to your long-term memory, joining a billion other bits of information. You have filed it in your mental filing cabinet, put the book on the shelf of your mental library, and sent the box off to your mental warehouse, or however else you want to envision the process. Now the fun begins.

Retrieval

There are two different ways to get the information back: recall and recognition. In recall, the memory returns to your consciousness. This can be either voluntary or involuntary. The face of a friend or the lyric of a song or an algebra formula is right there, center stage, for your use. You may have summoned it up or it may have drifted there unexpectedly, but it is there.

In recognition, you either haven't tried or haven't been able to summon up that memory, but when you run into the information again — the clerk who waited on you last week, a place you haven't visited in years, a taste long forgotten — you know you are re-experiencing it. You recognize it.

You can play a parlor game to illustrate this. Most of us have seen the back of a five pound note or a picture of the Eiffel Tower or a can of Campbell's Soup many, many times. We would all recognize them instantly. However, ask people to draw or describe them, to actively recall them, and few will come even close. (Interestingly, people are usually more accurate in recalling the Statue of Liberty, the Jolly Green Giant, or the Mona Lisa—perhaps because they are representations of people and therefore more worthy of recall.)

I'll Know It When I See It

If you've ever worked as a salesperson, you know the frustration of trying to help a customer who won't know what he's looking for until he finds it. "Why," you grumble, "can't he just describe it."

Most of memory is recognition. We can recognize a lot more than we can recall.

Recognition sometimes seems like a weak substitute for the more vigorous recall, but most of memory *is* recognition. This is fortunate because we can recognize a lot more than we can recall.

You know those random lists of unrelated words that memory experts are so fond of: pizza, aardvark, espadrilles, etc.? Most of us asked to reproduce such a list would score only fair, but if we're shown a similar list, we would probably recognize most or all of the words that were on the original list. You can choose to think of your recall "failure" as a serious defect in your character, or you can be elated that you recognize so many millions of things. Much of the forgetting that people fret about is failure to recall, not failure to recognize.

Which Lasts Longer?

Here's a puzzlement: If we really never forget anything in our long-term memory as most scientists believe, then how can we talk about the length of memories? Some studies of learning retention seem to show that memory can fade.

According to these studies, we lose our ability to recall information much sooner than we lose our ability to recognize it. In one study, students who were tested a year after they completed algebra had forgotten two-thirds of the equations they had learned. Another study showed that half the psychology, zoology, and biochemistry learned in one school year was forgotten by the following October, although losses in recognition were less. A conflicting study showed that students never completely forgot what they had learned in elementary psychology classes during a five-year period. This study also showed slower losses in recognition than in recall.

Does this mean that we *do* lose things from long-term memory? Not necessarily. Much of the information that the students poured onto test pages in June may have been in their short-term memories, crammed there in the day or so before finals. The information that showed up as "recognition" five years later was certainly in long-term memory. If we think of our memory as a huge library, we can visualize these bits as books on high, dark shelves. We know where they are and can put our hands on them, but we haven't dusted them off yet and started to turn the pages. Numerous experiments show that we can re-learn what we have once learned in less time than was required for the original learning, even after many year's disuse.

Why Learn Anything?

"Ah ha!" some of you are muttering, "If I don't really remember all that dull stuff I had to learn in school, why did I bother?" If we broaden the definition of memory to "retained learning" or even "education," there are three good reasons.

First, you need to know something to learn something. All learning is comparing what's new to what's old. To make a simile, life is like a metaphor. A baby decides that its toes are like its fingers, except. . . . An adult decides that Einstein's theory of relativity is like riding a bicycle at the speed of light, except. . . .

Memory expert Alan Baddeley says:

> When we attempt to learn something new, we base our learning on already existing schemata. When these conflict with what is being remembered, distortions occur . . .

In other words, the more structure we already have to compare new information to, the less new information we are likely to discard because it is meaningless or to distort because we are trying to compare it to the wrong thing.

A second reason is that re-learning something you have already studied takes much less time. One doctor read his small son passages in ancient Greek every day when the boy was between the ages of 18 and 36 months. When the boy was 8, he phonetically memorized these selections plus some new ones. The previously heard passages took only 70 percent as long to memorize as did the new passages.

Once you have learned something, you can reactivate it much more easily than you can learn new material. With all the challenges that the world presents, would you really want to have to start from scratch at every turn? In our complex society, *knowledge* has come to mean knowing where and how to find out, not just knowing.

The final reason to learn is because *everything* you experience shapes your view of the world in some way. When you see order and purpose in even the most transitory experience, you come to expect order and purpose in life. Order is essential for people to function physically, and purpose is essential for people to function spiritually.

Try This...

to Compare Recall and Recognition

Try to *recall* the information on the quiz below. Then turn the page and take the multiple choice quiz with the same questions. Compare your score.

1. The heroine of *Gone with the Wind* is _____.

2. Lady Diana and Prince Charles were married in _____.

3. A kind of road starting with Mac is _____.

4. The "tail" sticking out from a neuron is the _____.

5. Abbey Road is _____.

Identify the following:

6. Hubert Horatio Humphrey _____.

7. Edwin Booth _____.

8. Elizabeth Bennett _____.

9. Bruno Hauptmann _____.

10. Kaiser-Fraser _____.

Now, without looking at the answers, try the same test for *recognition.*

1. The heroine of *Gone with the Wind* is (a) Melanie Hamilton, (b) Ashley Wilkes, (c) Scarlett O'Hara, (d) Prissy, or (e) Aunt Pitty Pat.

2. Lady Diana and Prince Charles were married in (a) 1982, (b) 1981, (c) 1972, (d) 1971, or (e) 1970.

3. A kind of road starting with Mac is (a) macadamia, (b) macadam, (c) macaque, (d) Macassar, or (e) Macruran.

4. The "tail" sticking out from a neuron is the (a) axon, (b) axiom, (c) axila, (d) axillary, or (e) axum.

95

5. Abbey Road is (a) the site of Westminster Abbey, (b) an alley in lower Manhattan, near Wall Street, (c) prison slang for visiting the chaplain, (d) an Australian pop singer who lost her vocal chords to cancer, or (e) the site of the Beatles' recording studio.

6. Hubert Horatio Humphrey was/is (a) the whaling captain who chases Moby Dick, (b) a nineteenth-century novelist, (c) a Minnesota senator and presidential candidate, (d) a brand of chewing tobacco, or (e) the secretary of labor under Franklin Delano Roosevelt.

7. Edwin Booth was/is (a) an actor and brother of John Wilkes Booth, (b) the designer of the first motion picture camera, (c) the first doctor to do a heart transplant, (d) a golf professional, or (e) the hero in Thornton Wilder's *Our Town*.

8. Elizabeth Bennett was/is (a) the heroine in Jane Austen's *Pride and Prejudice,* (b) the villainess in Donizetti's opera *Lucia de Lammermoor,* (c) the first woman secretary of the treasury, (d) the sister of actresses Joan and Constance Bennett, or (e) a tennis champion.

9. Bruno Hauptmann was/is (a) one of the founders of the Bauhaus movement, (b) a noted writer on psychiatry, (c) a Hollywood film director, (d) the man convicted of the 1932 kidnapping of the Lindbergh baby, or (e) the man convicted of running the World War II Auschwitz death camp.

10. Kaiser-Fraser was (a) a car company of the 1950s, (b) a pact between Germany and Switzerland in the 1880s, (c) a popular vitamin tonic in the 1920s, containing 60 percent alcohol, (d) a much-publicized society wedding in the late 1930s, or (e) the first company to patent a gene-splicing process.

Answers

Check your answers here and record your scores for recall and recognition.

1. The heroine of *Gone with the Wind* is (c) Scarlett O'Hara.

2. Lady Diana and Prince Charles were married in (b) 1981.

3. A kind of road starting with Mac is (b) macadam.

4. The "tail" sticking out from a neuron is the (a) axon.

5. Abbey Road is (e) the site of the Beatles' recording studio.

6. Hubert Horatio Humphrey was (c) a Minnesota senator and presidential candidate.

7. Edwin Booth was (a) an actor and brother of John Wilkes Booth.

8. Elizabeth Bennet is (a) the heroine in Jane Austen's *Pride and Prejudice.*

9. Bruno Hauptmann was (d) the man convicted of the 1932 kidnapping of the Lindbergh baby.

10. Kaiser-Fraser was (a) a car company of the 1950s.

Recall: _____ correct Recognition: _____ correct

Most people do significantly better on recognition than recall. When a group of volunteers were shown a list of 100 words five times, they could recall about 38 percent of them. But when they were shown the same 100 words mixed with 100 new words, they were able to recognize 96 percent of the original words.

Count the number of correct answers for each of the two parts of the test and enter the percentages below.

1 correct—10 percent	6 correct—60 percent
2 correct—20 percent	7 correct—70 percent
3 correct—30 percent	8 correct—80 percent
4 correct—40 percent	9 correct—90 percent
5 correct—50 percent	10 correct—100 percent

Recall: _____ percent correct
Recognition: _____ percent correct

Subtract your Recall score from your Recognition score for your Recall Quotient: _____ percent difference.

Score:

0 percent difference— superb recall

10 percent to 20 percent difference—very good recall

30 percent to 40 percent difference—good recall

50 percent difference— average recall

60 percent to 70 percent difference—fair recall

80 percent to 90 percent difference—poor recall

10
Three Kinds
of Memory

There are three principle kinds of memory:

- verbal
- visual
- kinesthetic

In our literate culture, it is often difficult to separate verbal and visual memories from each other and from the memories provided by our other senses. Does the sound of the world *lion* call up the image? Does the image suggest the letters l-i-o-n written on a sheet of paper? Does the memory of the taste of strawberries make us name the taste, or does the word *strawberries* cause us to re-experience the sweet, gritty sensation on our tongue? Which is the lock and which the key?

Few of us worry about the third kind of memory, kinesthetic, unless we're trying to master tennis or a piano concerto. However, kinesthetic memory is essential to our everyday functioning and a valuable aid to reinforcing verbal and visual memory. Kinesthetic memory means remembering with our muscles, the sense of space around our bodies. Tying our shoes, walking down stairs, driving a car, and playing a piano are all the results of kinesthetic memories. But when we play the piano are we remembering just the placement of the keys, or are we also affected by the sound of the tones, the sight of the notes on the sheet music, the melody in our head, or a complex combination of any or all of these?

Taste, touch, and smell are potent tools for locking in or summoning other memories. We've all caught a whiff of an old, familiar smell and been flooded with nostalgic memories. Some people remember these sensations more powerfully than verbal or visual patterns. Even emotional states, whether we are happy, fearful, angry, or sad, are another access to things we experienced when we were in that state.

Are You Verbal, Visual, or Kinesthetic?

The average person tends to remember things better in one of two ways, either verbally or visually. If you get to the store and find you've forgotten your shopping list, do you recall it by hearing and seeing the names of the objects that you wrote down, or do you see the images of the objects themselves?

If you name things to remember them, if the sight or sound of the word conjures up the sight or sound of the object, you have a good verbal memory. You probably form rich images as you read and can come up with quotes for every occasion: "I do desire we may be better strangers," "Tis safest in matrimony to begin with a little aversion," "I decline to accept the end of man," "I shall be irreproachably tender, /Not a man but a cloud in pants!"

Some people are better visualizers than others. Close your eyes and picture an orange. If that's easy for you to do, if you can see the texture and color vividly, then you're a visualizer. Another way to check on your visualizing ability is to recall the house you lived in as a child. Can you remember the furniture and how it was arranged? The wallpaper? The rug? If you can, you have strong visual recall. How about the address and phone number? If you remember those, you have good verbal memory. If you do well on both, congratulations, you have twice as many chances of finding things in your mental library.

Children usually remember visually until their language skills develop. Then they shift to verbal encoding. This is one reason that most of our earliest memories resemble snapshots rather than movies with sustained scenarios. We didn't have the verbal skills yet to write the script about what was happening. When we add both auditory and visual forms of verbal memory, we're able to start building our mental library, responding to all kinds of information around us.

There is even a communications theory that says you should listen to the imagery of someone you want to influence and respond in the same way. If the person says, "That doesn't look good," they are in a visual mood, and you can reply, "Let's see how we can improve it." If they say, "That doesn't sound quite right," they are being aural and you reply, "I hear it differently." And if they say, "That doesn't feel right," they are favoring their kinesthetic sensations and you can say, "I sense that we've touched on the problem but haven't come to grips with it."

One analyst, Ole Anderson, calls this "predicate usage." He classifies former President Jimmy Carter as auditory: "Those listening to my voice will have to make that decision," while Ronald Reagan is kinesthetic: "Do you feel that our security is as strong as it was four years ago?" Winston Churchill, says Anderson, used highly visual images, Gerald Ford was probably kinesthetic, while John F. Kennedy balanced all three well. Anderson estimates that about 20 percent of Americans are primarily auditory and about 15 percent are primarily kinesthetic. The rest are visual or a mixture. This, reasons Anderson, is why visual imagery is the most powerful.

Which Is Better?

The English memory researcher Sir Frederick Bartlett decided that visualizers tend to learn more quickly and be more confident about what they have learned. Visualizers are more direct, visualizing the whole without doing as much grouping or making comparisons as auditory learners do. Sound good?

He *also* found that visualizers tended to get the order of information mixed up more often, changed the information more often, and introduced more new, irrelevent material than did verbal learners. But they remained confident, despite their inaccuracy.

Verbal learners, on the other hand, captured more clues and signposts as they went along, and gave them names. They used more associations and comparisons than did visual learners. They were less certain about the accuracy of their memories, even when they were correct.

Another experiment tested the verbal and visual ability of subjects to remember long lists of numbers. One group heard the numbers and the other read them; then both groups had to say the numbers back. People who heard the numbers could repeat the latter numbers with more accuracy, while the people who read them could remember the earlier numbers better. The earliest numbers seen made the strongest memory traces, but the last numbers heard are still in the *echoic memory,* a device that seems to let us remember the last thing we heard. ("Yes, yes, I heard what you said, dear, you said 'right now'!") Echoic memory seems to be limited to speech, because a random comment such as "Now . . ." will help block the memory of the number that went before, while a musical tone won't.

Even if your natural memory ability favors verbal over visual or vice versa, you can develop the other with practise and motivation. Airplane spotters during World War II had a powerful motivation for differentiating visually between friendly and enemy airplanes flying overhead. Chemistry students have little desire to confuse a bottle of water with a bottle of sulfuric acid:

> Johnny was a chemist.
>
> Johnny is no more.
>
> For what he thought was H_2O
>
> Was H_2SO_4.

Remembering Kinesthetically

Are you a good dancer, typist, pianist, or football player? Then you have good kinesthetic memory. The movement of your muscles is stored in your brain. Many blind people routinely use kinesthetic memory to do complex tasks and negotiate complex routes for which sighted people would require instructions or maps.

How many times have you flailed your hands in the air, shaping an object you're trying to describe while you search for the word to name it? How many times has someone asked you for a key or other object and it seemed easier to get it yourself than to describe where it was? You were remembering kinesthetically.

Most people remember muscle skills longer and better than verbal or visual skills. The classic example is riding a bicycle. You may not have ridden one for 20 or 40 or 60 years, but you'll be able to wobble right off once you're back in the saddle.

Photographic Memory

The fabled photographic memory, popular in vaudeville and detective fiction, is strongest in childhood, and some people are able to retain it as adults. An example is the noted mathematician, John von Neumann, who could memorize and repeat the information in a column of the phonebook on sight when he was eight years old. As an adult, he was able to do complex maths problems in his head.

A photographic memory almost got one young law student in serious trouble when his exam paper contained lengthy quotes verbatim from his textbooks. He was accused of cheating, but proved his innocence by quickly memorizing pages verbatim in the presence of school officials.

Even if you have just a highly accurate visual memory, you may not be the best eyewitness. According to a Canadian study, witnesses who could remember all sorts of minute details such as the color of the suspect's socks were the least accurate in identifying the suspect himself. On the other hand, witnesses who could recall the main details were inaccurate on the trivia. Ironically jurors tended to discount the testimony of the latter group who were actually the most reliable witnesses.

Using Both Verbal and Visual Memory

Most visual memory uses the right half of the brain and most verbal memory uses the left half. When you use both verbal and visual cues to remember something, you are using your entire brain.

Since you are probably not reading this book in order to remember the Highland fling or the skin of an orange, it is safe to say that most of what you want to remember can be verbally coded. Here are two rules about verbal memory.

- Naming something increases your chance of remembering it.

- *But* naming something can limit it.

If, like most people, you find that either your verbal or visual memory is dominant, you can improve your ability to remember by calling on the other system. For instance, actively picture what you just read. We do this all the time with fiction, but try it now with nonfiction. If you are primarily visual, play "Adam" and run around naming all the new things in the world. Let the image summon up the name, the sound, the printed word. Invent a word if none exists—a new name for a sensation, quirk, odd situation, or thing-a-ma-whatsit. Either the dictionary name will come later, or you may create a useful new term.

Where Does Kinesthetic Memory Come In?

Learning physical skills seems to follow the same patterns as learning verbal or visual things. Fortunately, once learned, we tend to remember muscular/spatial skills better and longer, as in the bicycle example. Kinesthetic memory can reinforce verbal and visual memory in valuable ways. Recently, schools that teach people test-taking techniques for bar exams, college-admissions tests, and the like, have become popular. One reason for their effectiveness may be that they use a classroom setting similar to the one in which the student will take the real test. Sitting in the same position, feeling the same type of pencil between his fingers, seeing a familiar test sheet, he may find the needed memories tumbling onto the paper.

Kinesthetic memories are frequently responsible for déjà vu, the sense of having already experienced something. If you have been comforted or frightened when you were in a particular position, you may re-experience the same sensations when you assume that position later. (This may account for the popularity of the fetal position for sleep.)

Take a Picture

Here's one valuable way to use kinesthetic memory to reinforce verbal and visual memory. Let's say that you must leave your car keys in a number of places because various members of the family use

You can have a visual and aural image of what happened, plus the kines- thetic memory of physically snapping a picture of it.

them, or you are lending some albums, or you are up on a ladder fixing something and decide to lay the screws on the top of the window frame. You suspect that you might not recall who, where, and what later on, so you "take a picture." Raise your hands to your eyes, miming a camera and click the button. As you do this, say outloud, "My keys are on the dining room table," or "Charles is borrowing my Aretha Franklin albums for his party on Thursday," or "The screws are on the window frame." You now have an aural and a visual image of what happened, plus the kinesthetic memory cue of physically snapping a picture of it.

Another way to use kinesthetic memory to jog other memories is to repeat a motion. (You may do this already.) Resume the position you were in when you originally had the experience you are trying to recall. Sit down at your desk or lie down in bed or backtrack and walk down the hall again. Recreating the sequence frequently lets you remember the verbal and visual parts.

Try This...

to Determine Your Kind of Memory

Some people are good at all three kinds of memory: verbal, visual, and kinesthetic. Others are best at one kind. Rate yourself with this test. If your answer to a question is "yes" or "true," check the box that follows it. If no, leave blank. Then add the vertical columns of checks to compare your verbal, visual, and kinesthetic memory.

Think about what you had for breakfast this morning.

	Verbal	Visual	Kines-thetic
1. Do you have a vivid visual picture of it?		☐	
2. Did you just re-experience the tastes and smells?			☐
3. Can you list everything you ate?	☐		
4. Can you recall the brand names of the eggs, cereal, coffee, bread, jam, juice, etc.?	☐		
5. Can you remember the color of the plate and cup? The tablecloth? The shape of the spoon? Whether it was sunny or cloudy?		☐	
6. Can you recall where you ate? How you sat? The position of the food on your plate?			☐

Now imagine you are standing in front of the first house you can remember living in as a child.

	Verbal	Visual	Kines-thetic
7. Do you see the color clearly? Do you have a strong image of how many windows there are? The kind of steps? How many steps?		☐	
8. Do you remember the address and phone number?	☐		
9. Go up to the door. Can you remember whether the doorknob is on the left or right? Do you step up after you have opened the door? Is there a closet on the left or right inside?			☐

If the answers to the questions below are "true," check the box at the right.

10. I am usually very aware of the furniture arrangement in a room.			☐
11. If friends painted their living room a new color, I would definitely notice.		☐	
12. I know whether the numbers on my watch are Arabic or Roman numerals.		☐	
13. I know my National Insurance number.	☐		
14. I'm good at sports and/ or dancing.			☐

107

	Verbal	Visual	Kines-thetic
15. I respond to the colors around me.		☐	
16. I always got good grades in English.	☐		
17. I didn't have much trouble learning to ride a bike.			☐
18. I love to do crossword puzzles.	☐		
Add up your scores.	_____	_____	_____

If you scored about the same in all three kinds of memory, you have three good ways to code and file each new memory. You can reinforce a primarily verbal, visual, or kinesthetic piece of information with two other backup memories (i.e., remember the three of clubs with a visual image of the card, the verbal memory of saying and writing the words, and the kinesthetic memory of sitting holding the cards and noticing that the three of clubs is the third card from the left).

If you are strongest in visual memory, you will remember better if you reinforce verbal and kinesthetic memories with a visual image. Write out names, addresses, and phone numbers and look at them. Make a visual image of the items on a list. See new people you meet with their names written on their chests or holding objects that suggest their names. When you learn a new physical skill, see yourself doing it, watch your body and hands as you experience the physical sensations in your muscles. Remember the colors and shapes of trees, signs, and buildings at the bus stop where you want to get off.

If you are strongest in verbal memory, you will help yourself remember better if you name things. Reinforce the memory of the faces of people you meet with private verbal descriptions—"Gladys Carpenter doesn't look like a glad carpenter, she looks like a sad carp." Make mental lists of the signs or the names of stores at the bus stop where you need to get off. You probably do much of this already without thinking, but expand it so you consciously reinforce visual and kinesthetic memories with a verbal backup.

If you are strongest in kinesthetic memory, you probably recall where you put things, but you may have trouble remembering written instructions or new people at parties or your shopping list. You will want to add strong kinesthetic memories to other information so you will have more ways to remember it. Shake hands with people you meet and repeat their name while you experience the texture of their hand, the feel of their muscles, your impression of their stature and movement. Feel the pattern when you dial a phone number.

When you learn something new, study it in a situation that is physically similar to where you will need to recall the information. Read the drivers' manual sitting in your car. Study the new postal regulations while you stand at the table where you will process mail. If you want to remember people's names at parties, practise them while standing or sitting in a rehearsal of the physical situation.

As you remind yourself to pick up your cleaning, feel the cold wire hangers and the slick polythene. Add the smell of the cleaning fluid in the store, the sight of the cheery assistant, the tinkle of the bell as you open the door, and the hiss of the pressing machines. See yourself turning off your regular route to stop at the cleaners and feel yourself doing it.

If you are good at two kinds of memory, use them both to reinforce information that is primarily of the third kind. If you are poor at kinesthetic memory, try visualizing your fingers on the typewriter keys and writing yourself instructions for operating simple appliances. If you are poor at verbal memory, make pictures and use your body to reinforce the words. If you lack visualization ability, write yourself a story about the thing and feel yourself handling it or responding to it.

11
Four Ways to Remember

Dividing memory in different ways often tells us more about our perceptions than about memory itself. The advantage of these divisions is that we can concentrate our attention on a small, manageable piece of a huge puzzle. The disadvantage is that labeling can limit our perceptions.

Episodic memories are personal, autobiographical reminiscences of experiences which occurred directly to you. Semantic memories are pieces of data about the external world, linguistic or mathematical for example, which you learn but which are not personal experiences.

Getting spanked by your mother for throwing bologna at your brother is episodic. Learning that bologna is spelled *b-o-l-o-g-n-a,* is pronounced "baloney," and when capitalized, is a city in Italy with a Communist administration, a reputation for efficiency, and a history of terrorist attacks by neo-Fascists, represents some subcategories of semantic memory—written and spoken language, history, and geography. Of course, this division is not absolute, since many tasks contain both episodic and semantic features.

Episodic Memory—
"Where Did I Put It?"

Episodic memory is primarily emotional. Much of this book explores how emotions can block memory and how they can be used to stimulate it. Here's one example of how experiences can be recorded episodically (emotionally) but not semantically.

A woman in one of my workshops wanted to remember the names of restaurants she had visited: "I love going to restaurants! Later I describe everything in minute detail to my friends—the menu, the tastes, the smells, the decor. I rave. But when they ask me the name of the restaurant or where it is, I can't remember."

Her mistake was in thinking she had recorded all this information at the same level. She was emotionally involved with the food, emotionally stimulated by the decor, but not by the name and address. I suggested that she pretend she was a newspaper reporter and keep a notebook or diary of where and what she ate. Not only would this *aide memoire* help her recall her dining experiences later, but waiters might assume she was a restaurant reviewer in disguise and give her better service.

Because episodic memory is, by definition, emotional, it is subject to emotional blocks and emotionally enhanced retrieval. Of course, even the dryest semantic facts can come with emotional overcoats— parental approval, society's messages, even the instinct for survival. William James, the early twentieth-century author and psychologist, said, "Memory requires more than mere dating of the fact in the past. It must be dated in *my* past." Fortunately we don't have to remember *where* or *how* we learned something to recall it later, although the emotional trappings may come along for the ride.

In the decade since a study on episodic and semantic memory by Canadian psychologist Endel Tulving, researchers have come up with literally hundreds of studies about semantic memory, but almost nothing about episodic memory. This may mean that such a division has not proved useful, or that our current explanations—emotional, mechanical, and physical blocks—are sufficient to explain why we lose our car keys and forget to post the phone bill.

Semantic Memory—Naming Things to Remember Them

Lots of invisible things have names—"memory," for example. When we give names to objects and concepts and moods and ideas and then use these names to remember them, we are using "semantic memory." It's unclear and usually unimportant whether we are remembering the letters *h-a-p-p-y* or the feeling of happiness.

Semantics has several dictionary definitions including the study of the meanings of words and symbols. "For the normal person,

111

every experience, real or potential, is saturated with verbalism," said linguist Edward Sapir. He believed that language not only recorded experience, but could substitute for it.

When we name something, put a label on it, then we have a powerful handle for remembering it. But don't forget that naming something also limits it. The minute something is labeled and cate-gorized, it is ready for convenient filing, but it is also unlikely to be re-evaluated. Information that we have filed away and not used every day, such as "world's tallest building" or "Ted's skinny kid-sister," needs periodic re-evaluation in the light of recent developments and discoveries.

Information we file away in our long-term memory needs periodic re-evaluation.

Political factions frequently use emotionally charged, easy-to-remember slogans to make their points. "The Army needs you!", I wish I could walk away from this poster too" and "Nuclear power, no thanks" are all slogans we remember. The presumption is that few will stop to analyse exactly *why* the Army should need *us*, what we can do to help the disabled walk or what question about nuclear power should elicit such a polite answer.

A Chicken and Egg Dilemma
Concerning Language and Perception
Here's the current debate:

- Does language shape our perceptions of the world around us by categorizing and labeling things?
- Or do perceptions shape our languages?
- Or both?
- Or neither?

Linguist Benjamin Lee Whorf argues that the language we speak determines our view of the world and how we sort, categorize, and evaluate the information around us so that we can remember it. He offers strong proofs . . . and so do researchers who hold the opposite view.

Language and Memory
If memory is categorizing and storing information and *if* each language divides the many natural variations of the world into different categories, then language and memory are totally dependent on each other.
Very roughly, the languages of the world can be divided (there we go again!) into:

Action languages
Languages (including all European tongues) that see the world as full of objects which then act or are acted upon. These could be called "physical" languages, conveying meaning by moving words around like blocks.

Condition languages
Languages that see the world as consisting of various states that are either transitory or permanent, i.e., Indian languages that assign shape to all things (round like ball, round and flat like pancake, round like spiral, etc.) or condition (wet, dry, hard, soft) or, most basic of all, animate or inanimate. These languages construct meaning by a process that is closer to a chemical action than a physical one.

An example of a chemical-type language in which the words *verb* and *noun* become meaningless is Nootka, the language of Vancouver Island, in which a sentence is one compound word. The idea—

> He invites people to a feast

is represented in Nootka as the root *boil* or *cook* (tl'imsh) and five suffixes:

> Boil -   ed eat - ers go-for he-does
>
> Tl'imsh - ya - 'is - ita - 'itl - ma

Similarly the Nootka sentence "He had been absent for four days" would be built around the root *four*, with *he, absent,* and *days* as suffixes. (If this sounds impossibly esoteric, consider our ancestral Latin which combines nouns and verbs into a single word—vini, vidi, vici. And some English words can act alternately as nouns, verbs, adjectives, adverbs, and prepositions, for instance the word *down*.)

Is it any wonder that Eastern and Western thought have taken such different routes when the road they traveled forked in such different ways?

Language and Thought

The next time you are at a party, mention casually that other languages can be very different from English. I will bet you that someone replies that Eskimos have many words for snow. One of the most obvious differences in languages is the number of ways they divide natural phenomena. But do these vocabulary differences demonstrate a sharper natural perception on the part of the speaker, or do the additional divisions of information require the speaker to develop those perceptions? Memory expert Alan Baddeley slyly suggests that one way to test whether perceptions of snow are limited genetically and culturally to northern denizens would be to see if the polar bear can discriminate between more kinds of snow than the honey bear. He acknowledges, of course, that conducting and interpreting such a test would be "a challenge."

It may be impossible to resolve this argument either way, since experiments support both sides. In one study that was somewhat easier than leading bears to snow, a linguist tested speakers of Dani, a stone-age language of New Guinea. The only words for color in Dani are roughly *light* and *dark*. Yet she found that Dani speakers could readily discriminate between colors, although not as efficiently as American test subjects. This suggests that perception is not limited by language, although language can enhance perception.

"Real Men" Don't See Colors

Color names present a good way to compare perception and memory. There are probably millions of colors and even more names for them. Yet it is popular in our western culture for "real men" not to discriminate between shades of red, blue, or green unless they are in professions that require that discrimination. Industrial designers, printers, house painters, and fabric manufacturers can and do describe colors as *spider web, cumulus,* and *moccasin* without their masculinity being in doubt, but fashion designers, art directors, and fine artists who use words like *scarlet* and *vermilion* are questionable — and if they can actually distinguish between *"cerise, fuchsia,* and *magenta*, they are definitely suspect! Yet it would be surprising if a western woman could not tell the difference between *buff, beige, camel,* and *tan.* Does this mean that women see more colors than men? (More men than women are color-blind but only a small percentage.) Or does it mean that culture has suppressed or enhanced a natural perception?

Language, declared Benjamin Lee Whorf, is "the best show that man puts on." Other creatures may communicate, but only man speaks. He added that, "thinking is most mysterious, and by far the greatest light upon it that we have is thrown by the study of language."

Can we have thought without language? Linguist Edward Sapir replies impishly that we *should* be able to, since he has observed that many people use language without thought. Theoretically it's possible, but close your eyes and try to imagine thinking and reasoning and remembering without language.

Skill Memory and Fact Memory

As you have seen, dividing memory in different ways to study it may tell as much about our own perceptions as about memory itself. There is one suggested division, however, that seems to have a definite physical basis. Before we tell more about it, let's look at some of the facts that the theorists had to work with in devising it.

HM had brain surgery 30 years ago in an attempt to cure his epilepsy. Now he cannot remember anything for more than a few minutes. Twenty-two-year-old NA was injured in 1960 when a fencing foil penetrated his brain. He, too, lost his ability to remember. In both cases, the hippocampus was severely damaged. Both men are now unable to remember any new material, that is, anything they have experienced since their brain trauma. In addition, NA cannot remember events that occurred just before his accident. Neither man can remember telephone numbers, words or shapes in a standard memory test, addresses, the current date, or even the identities of those who work with them every day.

Yet both men can work the tricky Tower of Hanoi puzzle in a minimum of moves, a feat that requires memory of previous moves. NA also drives a car and has no trouble getting around, but could not tell you the name of the street his home is on. What would you make of this? Let's look further.

Researchers noticed that other victims of severe organic amnesia (amnesia caused by injury to the brain and especially the hippocampus) also could not remember anything that has happened to them since they were injured. However, they *were* able to remember newly learned skills such as mirror writing or how to work a complex puzzle, although they frequently protested that they couldn't remember ever doing the task before. They also seemed to remember rules for games. Now, what theory can you come up with to explain this paradox?

Well, Richard Hirsh of McGill University considered all these conflicting facts and suggested that we have two kinds of memory: "fact" memory and "skill" memory.

Fact memory, he concluded, is remembering information — names, places, dates, words, historical and personal events. Fact memories are easily acquired and lost, and your distress at misplacing them is probably why you are reading this book.

Skill memory is less consciously summoned up, and perhaps because so much of it is unconscious, it is harder to lose. Riding a bicycle is the classic example. Other hard-to-forget skills are tying a shoe, hitting a tennis ball, playing the piano, or taking a spoonful of soup from a bowl and placing it in one's mouth. As you can see, these are primarily examples of kinesthetic memory.

Fact memory seems to be a later development in man, supporting the theory that our brains have retained their original primitive memory system (skills) which now interacts with the newer, more recent outer layer (facts). Experiments with baby monkeys (and our own observations of human babies) show that skills are acquired much earlier than "knowledge." The more primitive skill memory seems to mature earlier than the more sophisticated and recently acquired fact memory. This would explain why we have so few memories of our early childhood. Our neuron connections simply had not matured enough to store factual information.

Our Primitive Switchboard

The hippocampus is part of our brain's ancient limbic system. Along with the hypothalmus and pituitary gland, it forms our "second brain," the first step up and out from the simple reptilian brain that has served many species very nicely for millions of years. But man has added yet another layer on top of the limbic system—the neocortex.

Most theories about memory storage concentrate on our flashy new "third brains," but one group of researchers is concentrating on the more modest hippocampus. Neil Cohen and Larry Squire of the University of California at San Diego and Lynn Nadel of the University of California at Irvine theorize that the hippocampus is an invaluable switchboard. It assesses new facts and routes them to match up with and reinforce similar old ones in other parts of the brain. After enough similar memories accumulate, the neocortex learns to make direct connections, bypassing the hippocampus. The fact that NA could not remember events that happened just before his accident may mean that he had not processed them completely through his hippocampus and into his long-term memory.

We know that when a human hippocampus is damaged, the victim suffers from organic memory loss. However, researchers who tried to get the same results in rats were surprised that the rats without a hippocampus were still able to remember new things. Several theories were offered—that the hippocampus affects memory only in humans; that speech, exclusive to humans, plays some part in memory; or that injury to a neighboring part of the brain had actually caused the human memory loss.

The most recent theory was developed by John O'Keefe of University College, London, and Lynn Nadel of the University of California, Irvine. They found that rats that have had their hippocampi removed cannot learn mazes or perform tests that require spatial memory. They concluded that the hippocampus may be the storehouse for information about space, that the hippocampus makes maps.

Maps are essential for efficient memory storage. It *is* possible to store such information as lists in other parts of the brain, but maps do it much better. Imagine remembering the floor plan of your house as a list of directives: "Enter door, take two steps forward, turn right, enter living room, turn left, take four steps, turn, sit down." Map makers estimate that a map of the United States contains 100 million to 200 million bits of information. Much of that information is inferred by the viewer, for example, is Boise west or east of Chicago?

The Problem with Theories

Theories can (and should) offer an explanation for most of the known facts about a phenomenon, but there are usually a few niggling loose ends, colloquially if inaccurately known as "the exceptions that prove the rule." Have you noticed a basic conflict in these theories about the hippocampus?

Here it is. If the hippocampus allows us to draw mental maps so we can negotiate our surroundings, and if rats without a hippocampus cannot find their way about a maze, then how is poor, injured NA able to drive a car, a skill assuredly, but one that should require a sense of space? As you can see, each answer brings us just a little closer to understanding our complex memory systems, and each answer also creates new questions.

Memory research used to be almost incomprehensible to anybody but the researchers, discussing such things as the "empirical relations governing acquisition, transfer and extinction of habits." Fortunately for us, today's researchers are more interested in learning how the mind registers and stores and uses information—studies that may give us more direct and practical clues to using our own memory more efficiently.

Try This...

to See *How* You Remember

Episodic Memory

Notice *how* you try to remember these things, not *whether* you can remember them.

- What did you have for breakfast two days ago?

- Think of the bedroom you slept in when you were five years old. Were the windows on the north, south, east, or west side? Where was the doorway?

- Think about your first real job as an adult. Where did you hang up your coat? How often were you paid? By cheque or cash? What did you spend the money on?

- Where did you spend New Year's Eve ten years ago?

- What did you do the weekend before last?

Semantic Memory

An ancient Chinese encyclopedia divided animals as follows: belonging to the Emperor, embalmed, tame, sucking pigs, sirens, fabulous, stray dogs, included in the present classification, frenzied, innumerable, drawn with a very fine camel hair brush, etcetera, having just broken the water pitcher, those that, from a long way off, look like flies.

Semantic memory consists of comparing, pairing, opposing, and dividing information. One contemporary way to divide animals is mammals, birds, reptiles. Another is by the number of legs they have. A third is whether they are warm blooded or cold blooded. Let your mind float freely and come up with as many other ways as you can think of to divide animals _____

_____.

A few of the many other possibilities are nocturnal or diurnal; by size, larger or smaller than X; by diet, herbivorous, carnivorous, or omnivorous; egg layers or nonegg layers; flyers or nonflyers; etc. Yours may be much better.

119

12
Remembering – Young vs. Old

It's not true that we forget more as we get older. We may take longer to make the search of our mental filing cabinets, but we have much more structure and more retrievable information to compare new things to.

We've already discussed the myth of senility, and we have considered the illnesses of old age that can affect memory, but what about the healthy older person who decides that his memory is failing because he forgot to post a letter or stop at the cleaners? He's probably no more forgetful than he was at 18.

Edison, Goethe, Victor Hugo, Monet, and Titian did some of their best work in their 70s and 80s. George Bernard Shaw, Pablo Picasso, and pianist Arthur Rubinstein continued to work in their 90s. Composers particularly seem to have long productive careers, in which imagination and memory are essential tools. Handel wrote the *Messiah* when he was 56, and Haydn wrote the *Creation* when he was 67. Wagner wrote *Parsifal* at 69, and Verdi composed *Falstaff* when he was 80. Conductor Arthur Fiedler was active until weeks before his death at 88. Photographer Imogene Cunningham worked into her 90s. Grandma Moses didn't start painting until well after retirement age, when arthritis kept her from crocheting. Though remaining active in your chosen field doesn't necessarily prove that your memory is good, it certainly shows that you can remember what is necessary.

Of course, some older people do become forgetful. This can be caused by disease, by medication, by poor nutrition, by loneliness and isolation, by the attitude of those around them, or by their own expectation that they will become forgetful as they age. Older people also tend to use familiar, tried-and-true retrieval strategies and are less likely to try something else if the first approach fails.

Of course all of us get in problem-solving ruts. In *Whack on the Side of the Head* (Creative Think Publishers, 1982), Roger von Oech describes creative solutions reached by playing "what if?"

> *First idea:* What if paint contained gunpowder so that it could be exploded off buildings when it got old and cracked?
> *Problem:* The building would blow up, too.

Now many people would stop here, but von Oech shows how to use this first "what if?" as a stepping stone to further solutions.

> *Ultimate solution:* Put inert ingredients in paint that will react later when another solution is applied, causing the paint to drop off the surface.

Here's another example of creative thinking:

> *First idea:* What if we kept the streets clean by having public trash cans that pay people to put trash in them?
> *Problem:* No city could afford that.

Can you think of five new ways to get people to use trash cans?

> *Ultimate solution:* A city in the Netherlands rewarded people who deposited their trash in public cans with a tape-recorded joke, different for every can and changed every two weeks. Certain cans got reputations for having the best jokes, and people went out of their way to hear them.

Before you give up and decide that you're "getting old" when you forget something, try remembering in some of the new ways outlined in this book. Lots of older people see themselves as "forgetful," but tests have shown that people are poor judges of their own overall memory ability. (Ironically, most people are excellent judges of how well they will be able to remember.) But because more and more people are older than 65 – there are 27 million right now in the US and 35 million predicted by the year 2000 – scientists are now ignoring the myth that older people are naturally forgetful and exploring the memory process in older people.

How Older People Learn New Things

Most people are no more likely to forget at 80 than they were at 20. People in their 80s and even 90s can go back to school and learn new things as well as their grandchildren. They just need to use different techniques for remembering the new material. Here are some valuable tips from the National Institute for Aging in the US, plus some of my own.

- Give yourself plenty of uninterrupted time to learn new things. It may take longer than it used to, and you may have to concentrate more.

- Give yourself a good place to work. Be sure lighting is bright and your glasses appropriate.

- Ask questions. At your age you shouldn't let shyness keep you from understanding. Maybe the teacher isn't being clear, and the younger students in the class are afraid they'll look stupid if they ask questions.

- Don't try to do more than you can handle comfortably. Processing information at any age is difficult if you try to deal with too many elements at once.

- Don't expect to remember things as *quickly* as you used to. Develop tricks for giving yourself a little extra recall time. Smile, clear your throat, adjust your glasses, take a deep breath. These are all tricks used by accomplished actors to gain their composure and get the audience's attention. Use them.

How Children Remember

Children remember well because they use more of their senses simultaneously to store their impressions. They also haven't learned abstract thinking yet, so they store original information rather than concepts. Indeed, this absence of structure in the early years is probably why we have so few memories of our childhood. We can summon up vivid full-color images of particular moments, complete with smells, sounds, and tastes, but we lack an overall view of our first few years.

"Why, Mummy?"
Children are intensely curious about the world around them. Keep your childhood curiosity with you all your life to enhance your ability to remember.

To indulge our curiosity is to get closer, to become more intimate. If childhood "why, why, whys" go unanswered, curiosity soon withers. A child who is discouraged from asking will have to start asking later as an adult. We must begin noticing and prying if we are to absorb and savor the infinite variety of the world around us.

Perhaps the reason children learn things like second languages more easily than adults do is that they have an abundance of synaptic connections, the tiny wires between the brain's neurons that send information back and forth. The average child under six learns a new word every two waking hours.

Then why do we rarely remember our early childhood? One possibility is that, although children have an abundance of circuits, they haven't become sophisticated enough to provide storage structures for everything they see. They have no place to put much of the information, so they discard it until they have built storage systems to hold it.

Losing Synaptic Connections

By the time we reach adulthood, we have lost half of our synaptic connections. Most of these were never used and withered away. Yet, the peak years for storing memories appear to be the late 20s. At 30, our brains start to shrink. Fortunately, by then we have so many mental structures for organizing and storing information that the lessened circuitry doesn't affect us.

Why do our brains shrink? One reason may be that we lose our ability to make the proteins and enzymes that activate the receptors for long-term memory. When protein synthesis in animals is blocked, the animals can still learn things, but they can't remember what they learned. Unfortunately eating a high-protein diet doesn't produce the necessary enzymes directly, so we're going to have to find other ways to keep our memories in top form.

Another theory of age-related memory loss is that we experience diminished blood flow and send less oxygen to our simultaneously diminishing neurons. This would then slow down our response time. Some doctors also think that environmental pollution is attacking the nervous system with harmful elements, weakening both our bodies and brains as we grow older. For example, today quantities of lead found in the human brain are higher than before. Obviously we need to work on the world without while we work on the world within.

"Am I Getting Senile?"

How can you be certain you're not getting "senile"? Senility in the past has been a catchall term for any memory loss in later years. We now know that memory loss in older people can be caused by hundreds of temporary and permanent conditions. Older people can be profoundly affected by the loss of work and isolation of retirement, by the deaths of spouse, friends, and relatives, or by failing health. They can also be victims of several debilitating diseases that cause memory loss. The most common of these is Alzheimer's disease, also known as senile dementia of the Alzheimer's type or SDAT. It results in memory loss, disorientation, severe behavior changes, and ultimately death. Vigorous and active people of all ages can be struck down by it. Approximately 1 in 10 people over 65 are affected by senile dementia. This translates into 750,000 in the UK alone, excluding those in the pre-senile group.

If you've ever observed an elderly neighbor or relative with senile dementia, you may be concerned that you are next every time you misplace something or forget the name of an old friend. In some cases, the very fear of forgetting produces an emotional block that results in a self-fulfilling prophecy.

So, how can you tell if forgetfulness is caused by more than overloaded circuits or emotional blocks? Here are some clues that should send you to your doctor.

- You forget entire and important experiences, not just the details.

- Your forgetfulness limits your ability to function – your family, financial, social, and/or business responsibilities are suffering.

- You sometimes behave in uncomfortable, unfamiliar ways and are not sure why.

- Your forgetfulness is causing you distress.

Prompt medical testing can result in early treatment or, more likely, in assuring you that your memory lapses are not caused by disease and *don't* indicate the beginning of an inexorable mental decline.

About half of the older people who experience confusion and extreme forgetfulness have Alzheimer's disease. So far no one knows the cause or the cure, but it is being studied intently. Scientists know that the disease produces physical and chemical changes in the brain, and they are trying to find out if correcting or reversing these changes will reverse the disease. Possible causes may be heredity or a slow-acting virus. The fast-progressing SDAT that hits young adults tends to run in families, although the more common kind associated with advanced age does not.

The disease, first identified in 1906 by Alois Alzheimer in a 51-year-old patient, usually progresses slowly. The victim's early lapses can be attributed to normal causes. Those around him might begin to take over business and personal tasks on occasion. As the disease progresses, the victim may lose responsibilities at work or even lose his job. Friends may begin subconsciously withdrawing because of the behavior changes they see. When the victim succumbs, an autopsy will show a severely atrophied and distorted brain.

Although Alzheimer's Disease is a widespread illness that can leave the sufferer bewildered and anxious, there is as yet no cure. A lot of research is being done, however, to try to find the causes and a reliable cure. Meanwhile, there are drugs available that reduce the suffering and stress people experience who have this illness.

If memory loss is a constant problem, see your doctor as other causes of temporary memory loss, such as infections, cardiovascular and metabolic conditions or toxic reactions to drugs, need to be dealt with swiftly if they are not to result in permanent damage.

Competing Memories

Old and new memories are always jockeying for supremacy. The longer you live, the more you have to remember. Amazingly you are more likely to remember the names of childhood playmates than of people you worked with three years ago. This is because your brain was more efficient then, and you didn't have so many names to remember.

But collecting memories is essential for keeping the brain in order. Remember those synapses that withered because they were never used? This is a major clue to keeping your memory young. Stay active, stay interested, and keep your circuits open. In other words, use it or lose it.

Try This...

to Spot Abnormal Forgetfulness

Some of the following examples of forgetting should alert you to the possibility of disease rather than the normal reasons for forgetting that we have discussed: overload, fatigue, tension, emotional blocks, and the like.

1. You can't remember where you put your car keys.

2. You can't remember where you were married, no matter how hard you try.

3. You can't remember where you parked the car.

4. Your car is repossessed because you forgot to make the payments, even though you have the money.

5. You are demoted at work because you always forget where you put important papers, or you forget to return clients' phone calls.

6. You have almost started a fire two or more times because you turned on a burner on the stove and then forgot about it.

7. You often find your possessions in unusual places and don't know how they got there.

8. You fail to greet a neighbor or colleague on the street because you don't recognize him.

9. On several occasions, you have promised to meet a friend or relative and then forgotten all about it.

10. Your family has a joke about how you would lose your head if it weren't nailed on.

Score

If you answered yes to 2, 4, 5, 6, and 7, your forgetfulness may have a physical source. If you answered yes to 1, 3, or 8, remember that these things happen to all of us from time to time. They are only clues to a deeper problem if they happen consistently or disrupt your life in significant ways. The key word in example 9 is *several*. Everybody does double-think once in a while, planning to be in two places at the same time, but if this happens repeatedly, something may be wrong.

If you answered yes to 10, that your family jokes about your forgetfulness, you can regard their teasing in several ways: (a) They are using humor to relieve their genuine frustration or concern over your actions; (b) They are using an out-of-date label for you — like calling someone "Skinny" who has become fat, or "Red" who has become bald — and you have a choice. You can go along with their expectations (a comfortable position) or point out their error (an uncomfortable position); (c) They are embarrassed by their own mental slips and relieve their frustration by pointing out yours — unfair, but a human weakness.

There are other reasons than these, of course, but these may start you thinking about how your family role affects your remembering. Do you get positive "strokes" for remembering or for forgetting? Does forgetting reinforce or undermine your position with your family, your friends, your job?

13
Does Anyone Have a Perfect Memory?

In the 1920s, the famous Russian neuropsychologist A. R. Luria studied a man he called S who seemed to have a perfect memory. S was a journalist named Shereshevskii who could remember everything said to him, word for word, without taking notes. S had never thought this was unusual until his fellow reporters commented on it.

Luria found that S could remember 100-digit numbers, poetry in foreign languages he didn't know, and scientific formulas. S could

When S saw the number 32, it had a kind of sound, smell, and color to it.

remember a table of 400 numbers arranged randomly in a 20 by 20 grid pattern. Even after 30 years, he could recall all the numbers. His memory wasn't photographic. He had remarkably developed "synthesia," the ability to code information in several sensory ways.

We all have synthesia to some extent. It's what happens when we hear a favorite song and are flooded with poignant memories of a person, a perfume, a mood. When S saw the word *table* or the number 32, it had a kind of sound, smell, and color to it. This occurred automatically, and he had no control over it.

Ironically, S was not particularly successful in school. If someone said the same thing to him in two different tones of voice, he recorded it as two different messages. If someone coughed while S was reading, it was recorded as part of the story. The richness of his associations interfered with his solving mathematical problems. All sorts of sounds and shapes and smells would interfere with his functioning on an abstract level. To force himself to forget useless material, he taught himself to "write" it on a mental blackboard and then "erase" it. Eventually he went on the stage to support himself.

S shared one memory problem with the rest of us — he couldn't remember faces very well. To him the world was like a canvas by a primitive painter. All details were equally vibrant, equally detailed, and equally important whether they were near or far. He could not use the function of forgetting to separate important from unimportant details and therefore could not make value judgments.

VP and Professor Aitken

Before I leave you with the impression that people with super memories are generally misfits, I'd like to mention two "normal" people who practised to develop their memory skills and used them to enhance their lives. One was VP who was born in Latvia, not far from where S was born.

At the age of ten, VP memorized 150 poems for a contest. As an adult, he emigrated to the United States and found work as a shop assistant. He learned to speak all modern European languages except Greek and Hungarian, and loved chess, sometimes playing seven opponents simultaneously while blindfolded. Like S he could remember large grids of numbers; however, he did not appear to remember them as an overall visual image because he slowed down in recalling them when there were blank spaces in the grid. He appeared to rely mainly on semantic associations, aided by his knowledge of so many

129

languages. He denied having any superior gift and said that his skill was developed by his traditional Eastern European Jewish upbringing which valued and encouraged memorization.

Another memory whiz was Professor A. C. Aitken of Edinburgh University. Aitken could recite the first thousand decimal places of pi, which he regarded as an easy if useless skill. He compared it to learning a Bach fugue. He was given several memory tests in 1933. In 1960, he was able to recall lists of words and stories that he had memorized 27 years earlier. Apparently numbers were so lively and interesting to him that he was not conscious of making mechanical associations between them, but when someone mentioned the year 1961, he immediately responded that it was 37 times 53 and also 44 squared plus 5 squared and also 40 squared plus 19 squared.

Idiot Savants

Some people with very low I.Q.s have remarkable memories. A blind young Frenchman in an asylum for mental defectives could give the cube root of any six-figure number in 6 seconds and the sum of 64 progressive doublings of a number in 45 seconds. You may wonder if this young man actually had a high I.Q.; it is possible. However, there are contemporary cases of people who have difficulty functioning, who can barely speak, and who cannot read or write, yet who have remarkable talents. The academic term for such people is "idiot savant"—learned idiots.

Dr. Bernard Rimland, director of the Institute for Child Behavior Research in San Diego, is an expert on this condition. Among the theories advanced to explain this phenomenon are extraordinary development of certain nerve cells or the division of functions between left and right cerebral hemispheres. However, Dr. Rimland believes that these people have a unique power of concentration, that their impairment lets them shut out everything else and put all their effort into one task.

For instance, mentally retarded twin brothers who lived at the New York Psychiatric Institute in the 1960s were able to do lightening calendar calculations into the next century, even though they could not add or subtract. Another fascinating case is that of a retarded young man in Milwaukee. Blind and suffering from cerebral palsy, the 19-year-old astounded his adoptive parents one morning by sitting down at the piano and playing Tchaikovsky's First Piano Concerto from memory after hearing it on the radio. He could not walk or speak a complete sentence, but he was able to remember and reproduce a large repertoire of classical, jazz, and popular music, and he even performed on television. Another mentally disabled boy can compute square roots in his head, play the piano by ear, and write songs.

About 1 out of every 2,000 retarded people seems to have this unique power of concentration that produces an extraordinary talent—usually for mathematics, art, or music, and frequently involving memory. This occurs more commonly in men than women, about a three to one ratio. "As we learn more about the mind and machines that work like the mind," says Dr. Rimland, "the savants become more and more intriguing. In the past there was a tendency to view these people as freaks with bizarre abilities. We now tend to view them as special people, as human beings who have unique and individual talents."

Famous People with Good Memories

Extraordinary memories and powers of concentration are not the exclusive property of misfits and idiot savants, however. Many famous people have used their memories to great advantage in their careers. Toscanini conducted long, complex symphonies and operas without a score. Napoleon could greet thousands of soldiers by name. American politician James Farley claimed he was able to call 50,000 people by their first names, and Charles Schwab, manager of the Homestead Mill, knew all of his 8,000 employees by name. General George Marshall could recall almost every event of World War II, and English statesman and writer Thomas Macaulay could recite all of the epic *Paradise Lost* without error. Many of today's corporation heads have reputations for being able to call up thousands of names and figures at a moment's notice. And while we may find comfort in the tales of Albert Einstein's absentmindedness, he was certainly able to remember what he wanted to remember.

Napoleon and James Farley used the same strategies for remembering that you do. They just did it more efficiently, motivated by their ambition. Most of us go blank to some extent when we encounter a large group of strangers, but to a motivated person—a politician, a salesman, even a gregarious people-lover—remembering each new face and name can be a fascinating way to enhance himself. Toscanini was also motivated by a desire for power, but in a different way. He knew that if he had to keep looking at the score, he could not maintain eye contact with his musicians to control them.

Most people can remember all sorts of information about their hobbies, something that gives them great pleasure. It's hard to forget the details of our rich uncle's will or the winning score of our favorite team or the intricacies of a juicy scandal involving a long-time enemy. We remember what interests us, and people who remember "everything" are probably interested in everything.

We remember what interests us.

Try This...

to Pinpoint What You Remember Easily

What do you enjoy remembering? What enhances you? Put yourself in a relaxed, fantasy state.

You are on a platform before an adoring audience. You are filled with pleasure as you are introduced as the world's greatest expert on _____.

Or you pick up a newspaper, trade journal, or scholarly publication and see your photograph. The caption says that you are noted for your ability to remember all about _____.

Do you remember these things well in real life? If so, why? If not, why?

Part III

How To

14
How to Improve Your Memory

When people perform incredible memory feats, we assume that they have a unique and superior memory structure. "I could never remember that much!" Don't bet on it. The gulf between your memory and the kind of memory you envy is not so wide as you might think it is.

How do people with exceptional memories differ from "ordinary people"? The most obvious way is that they remember more. But are they just remembering more efficiently or do they use an entirely different method of remembering? Most of us make verbal "strings" to help us remember — words in a sentence, the days of the week, or the 1-2-3 sequence of numbers. People with a photographic memory, those who can remember huge charts of meaningless numbers after a few minutes of study, are assumed to remember visually; that is, they make a photograph-like mental image of the information. This is verified when they are able to repeat the numbers in any sequence — top to bottom, zig-zag, back and forth horizontally — as if they are reading it from the original chart.

The rest of us simply cannot remember that way, no matter how much we practise, but we *can* dramatically increase our ability to remember strings of information by using structures.

Rating Memory Capacity

Memory is too rich, complex, and elusive to be measured and weighed like a beef roast. This has never stopped scientists from trying. One early test, the "digit-span" measurement, was worked out by a London teacher in 1887. J. Jacobs wanted to find out how well his students could remember numbers, so he devised a system that has become a useful tool in psychology.

To test his students, Jacobs presented each with a sequence of digits and asked them to repeat it. He steadily increased the number until the student was able to repeat the list correctly only half of the time. This was the student's "digit span." A person's digit span seems to show the extent of his natural short-term memory ability.

Today, digit-span testing is a standard test. A series of numbers is read to the subject who immediately repeats them. An average ten-year-old can repeat three out of five sequences of six numbers. The average twelve-year-old can repeat backwards at least one of three series of five digits. The average adult can repeat two out of three series of seven numbers, and superior adults can do eight-digit sequences forward and seven-digit sequences backward. As with any testing, the results could be affected if the person taking the test feels rivalry with, or hostility towards, the test giver. While a few people might improve their performance under these conditions, most of us would decrease our scores because of tension.

Test Your Own Digit Span

To test your own digit span, have someone read you lists of four-digit numbers and repeat them. If you can say them back correctly more than 50 percent of the time, move on to five-digit numbers. Keep going through six- and seven-digit numbers, increasing the amount of digits, until you are correct only *half* the time. That is your digit span. Most people have digit spans of about 7 and just a few surpass 10 digits. Until a recent digit-span experiment with a "normal" volunteer, the highest digit span ever recorded was 18 digits, scored by the German mathematics professor, Rückle Müller, in 1911. (That means that half the time he was able to repeat a sequence of 36 numbers from memory.)

The World's Digit-Span Champion

In 1981, Anders Ericsson of the University of Colorado and William G. Chase of Carnegie-Mellon University set out to discover if the digit span of the average person could be increased. They found a hardy volunteer with normal memory capacity, and they tested his digit span. They kept retesting SF, as they called him, without giving him any instructions. He soon began to invent his own methods to increase his digit span. When SF was first tested, he had a digit span of seven. When he was through, his digit span was eighty! Was he really a genius in disguise, or did he discover a new way to use his memory? Here's what he did.

For 1 hour a day, 3 to 5 days a week, for 20 months — 230 hours of effort — SF was given a standard digit-span test. For the first four sessions, his digit span remained in the normal range, seven to nine. During this time, he either rehearsed the entire digit sequence or divided it into two groups and rehearsed each group. Sometimes he noticed patterns like 6-5-4 or 4-2-4, but mostly he just tried to remember random numbers.

But things were about to change. SF was a competitive runner and had lots of running times in his long-term memory. At the fifth session he began relating the random numbers read to him with the known running times in his memory. Naturally, only a few numbers would match up, but he went on to construct additional pegs. For instance, 3,492 would be 3 minutes, 49.2 seconds, an excellent speed for running a mile. Following this would be 893 which he would interpret as 89.3 years, a very old runner.

Eventually SF contrived super groups of numbers divided into three or four smaller groups. His organization for 80 digits consisted of sets of three-digit and four-digit groups in this pattern:

4-4-4   4-4-4   3-3-3   3-3-3   4-4-4   3-3-3   4-4-4   5

SF was actually putting these numbers in his long-term memory because he was able to recall more than 90 percent of the 200 to 300 digits presented to him at each hourly session. After 100 hours of practise, he reduced the time it took him to memorize a given number of digits by half.

You don't have to be a runner to use SF's system. Think of all the numbers you have in your head: birthdays, historical dates, phone numbers, the years that your favorite classic cars or films appeared. Remembering random lists of meaningless numbers isn't something we do very often, but we *do* run into number sequences that would be useful to know — serial numbers, Social Security numbers of family members, new car license numbers, and endless phone numbers. Maybe SF's system will work for you.

Shortening the Trip from Short-Term to Long-Term Memory

You control your short-term memory. You've noticed something, and you want to get it into your long-term memory, in other words to *remember* it. You have a choice. You can work hard to develop new strategies (groan, too much work), or you can go on working hard, trying to remember the way you do now.

Familiar solutions are "safe" and comfortable, so we tend to try them again and again, even if they don't always work. It's like the terrified horse that runs back into a burning barn to reach the safety of his stall. Here are some new strategies.

Strategy 1: Be Emotional

Why can we remember batting averages and scores or lengthy melodies and stories, but not recall a phone number or the correct spelling of a six-letter word like frieze? It's because we can remember when we take things like names, numbers, or musical notes and surround them with emotional trappings as well as structures.

Like computers, people need structures for storing information, but unlike computers, the human mind loves novelty. Fascinate it with tricks and toys while you give it some storage boxes, and it will do whatever you want. Emotionally charged events are easily remembered, probably because they are intensely personal. If you can impose emotion on something, you'll remember it. Love it. Hate it. Fear it. Be mad at it. You'll also remember it at the same time.

Strategy 2: Be Logical

Make structures for remembering. We'll talk more about that later on.

Strategy 3: Reward Yourself for Remembering

Any old reward doesn't work. You have to want it. Remember that "ought to remember" isn't the same as "will remember." Even

Use every means you have to help yourself remember.

"try to remember" is a cop-out because it implies that you might not succeed.

If you constantly forget certain things—car keys, names, birthdays, appointments—you can go into analysis to figure out what they really signify to you, *or* you can decide how remembering them will enrich you, enhance you, make you feel good about yourself. Not wanting to feel stupid isn't enough. You may trap yourself in a self-punishing cycle—"I'm so dumb that I deserve all this pain." Instead, you need to impose a real rush of pleasure around remembering the object or event. That holds true, also, for remembering to do something genuinely unpleasant that must be done. As a last resort, you could allow yourself a ridiculously puritanical sense of self-righteousness for having remembered to do such a grim task.

Strategy 4: Use All Your Senses

If you have "turn off copy machine before leaving office" in your short-term memory, you can form a multitude of sensory images around it that will help you get it into your long-term memory. Smell that copy fluid as you imagine holding your coat in one hand and flicking the switch with the other. See the machine and imagine it beckoning to you as you feel the sleek office doorknob in your hand. Listen to the hum of the copy machine as it purrs "turn me off, turn me off." If you routinely pop a breath mint, a cigarette, or a stick of gum in your mouth as you leave the office, you can even *taste* the copy machine's anxiety about being left on all night. Putting information in your long-term memory is an active process. Contrary to all laws of physics, you can speed up the trip by sending out more than one train.

The Uphill Struggle from Short to Long, or "How Scoop Flash Makes the Front Page"

Short-term memory is like a frame of photographic film intended for future use in a newspaper. Our fearless reporter, Scoop, has just gotten the news photo of a lifetime. He races back to the offices of the *Daily Blab,* clutching his precious roll of film, and hands it over to old Pop Slowpoke in the receiving room.

Pop sets it to one side while he answers the phone, then starts upstairs to the photo lab. His rheumatism is kicking up something terrible, so he is none too swift. Halfway up the stairs he is distracted as he stops to ogle Gloria Gorgeous, the *Blab's* ace reporter. He finally reaches the lab, but the technician is busy. "Just toss it over there, Pop. I'll get to it when I can."

The film may roll under a table and be lost before it is ever developed; or it may be spoiled when the darkroom door is opened; or, developed, it may not be printed; or printed, it may not be filed in the right place with the right caption. If it finally makes it through all these steps, then it is in "Long-Term Memory," ready to be yanked out and put on the front page when it is needed. Long-term storage of material is an active process that *must* go through stages and *must* take time. If the process is interrupted at any point, we don't get the final photograph.

The Mind As a Library

Long-term memory requires a structure or framework so that you can retrieve the information later. The mind is like a huge, jumbled library. Sometimes we have difficulty finding the exact book we want, but it is there. We increase our chances of finding a book if we put a thousand copies of it in our library instead of one. We do this in our mind's library by repetition, repeating something over and over until we are almost certain to recall it when we need it. However, each repetition may be slightly different from the others, like different editions of the same book.

Remembering can be like a detective story. Let's say you read *Tom Sawyer* and get interested in the books of Mark Twain. You then read *Huckleberry Finn* and are fascinated with the character Jim. This leads you to reading about Black people before and during the Civil War. You read *Uncle Tom's Cabin* and then Bruce Catton's *Peace at Appomatox*. To remember an event in the Catton book, you might have to run through the chain starting with *Tom Sawyer*. It might also help if you read *Peace at Appomatox* in your uncle's vacation cabin by the lake when you were recovering from a broken leg. This gives you even more paths to lead you back to Catton. The more images, the more context you can put around a piece of information, the more likely you are to find it again.

Using Retrieval Cues

A thread is sticking out of your sleeve and you pull it. It may come off in your hand, or you may have grabbed the end of the master thread that holds your whole jacket together. Memories are similar.

Sometimes we get a detached thread. "Pepys" leads to canaries and singing instead of Restoration London and diaries, or "Reuben" leads to sandwiches and dill pickles instead of Gen. 29:32, Jacob, and the tribes of Israel.

Word associations are a common way to retrieve information. For instance, fill in the missing words below:

_____ rampant	rant and _____
moot _____	diametrically _____
one _____ swoop	_____ dudgeon

Most people will reply — run rampant — moot point — one fell swoop — rant and rave — diametrically opposed — high dudgeon. In learning abstract lists of word combinations, subjects remember "hot-cold" much more easily than "cold curtains." Following familiar word clues to the wrong conclusion is a hazard to successful remembering. When a key retrieval word may lead you astray, you need to build a new, stronger image. To remember the phrase "cold curtains," you can create a dramatic mental scene of ice-covered draperies, crackling as an Arctic wind howls through the shattered windows of an abandoned mansion. Similar arresting images can help you set up new ways to retrieve information that might not respond to everyday retrieval cues.

"Depth of Processing"

Do we really store some information bits deeper than others? In a 1972 study, Craik and Lockhart suggested that the amount of information we retain depends on how deeply we process it. They decided that information processed in a simple way offers us vague memory traces, and that this shallow processing would decrease our ability to remember later. Information that is judged, categorized, and sorted in a number of ways, they felt, is processed "in depth" and will be remembered better. Their "depth" concept could also be seen as "horizontal," providing the information with many associations or handles for later retrieval. You may go through life never quite sure of the meaning of *dialectic* or *pragmatic,* no matter how many times you look the word up in the dictionary, but if you write an essay, poem, or series of puns about the meaning of the word, you will probably never forget it.

141

Pleasant vs. Unpleasant

If you have ever suspected that the really grating TV commercials are *intended* to irritate you, you're right. Studies show that, while we quickly respond to positive images, we remember the negative ones longer. This is the opposite of Freud's theory that we would forget anxiety and pain more quickly than pleasant memories.

As with much of memory study, tests on this point frequently contradict each other. For instance, a test designed to rate the effectiveness of different painkillers also found that, as time passed, the patients remembered their original pain as less and less severe.

"We've Got to Get Organized" — Using Structures

There is little order or pattern to the world except what we perceive or impose ourselves. Our lives are spent in rating, sorting, and coping with a tumult of ideas and objects.

Everyone loves "organizers." We buy them in walnut for our walls and desk tops, plastic for our drawers and closets. We fill every corner with gadgets to keep our life in order. These are the *structures* of modern life. The trick is to *use* them.

The ability to create structures for ourselves, to set priorities and separate the important from the less important, is one of the keys to a good memory. A good way to do this is to use your memory. "Memory is a great abstractor," says memory expert Alan Baddeley. His own career illustrates this point. Before beginning his first book on memory he reviewed all the available literature to ensure completeness. The result, five years later, was an all-inclusive specialist's text. For a second book, *Your Memory: A User's Guide* (Macmillan Publishing, New York, 1982), he let his memory abstract the material, racing over everything he knew to find highlights. He then wrote a delightful, readable book and checked the facts afterwards.

Anyone whose memory problems are caused by an inability to structure needs to learn mental organization. The optimum time to learn to structure things and ideas is between the ages 6 and 12. Given some encouragement and praise, children will involve themselves in how they want to arrange their rooms, their possessions, and even their time. However, if parents insist that children always conform to the parents' ideas of how things should be arranged, the children sometimes lose their incentive to experiment with structure. Parental help and recognition of the need for setting and keeping order encourages a child to learn to structure, if the help is judiciously given.

Fortunately, you can learn to structure at any age if you give yourself enough rewards for doing so. As you move about, notice what belongs to you and decide how you want to arrange it. Cook up convenient structures to retrieve your keys, wallet, glasses, and chequebook. Then applaud yourself as you stick to your system. It is this sense of order, supported eventually by habit, that will give you the security that comes from knowing where your things are. They are in a familiar and chosen place, impossible to forget.

People who are always losing glasses, car keys, and important papers are either overloaded and need to slow down, or else they can't see a sufficient reward for giving up the anxiety and even attention they experience as they frantically hunt for the misplaced objects.

Sometimes people blame themselves for having a faulty memory when the problem really lies in how they structure their time and their lives. If we accept that we are as responsible for our mental clutter as for the physical clutter that surrounds us, we can take the next steps.

> *Organize*
> Create a structure for your possessions.
>
> *Use it*
> Put things where you decide they belong. (No structure works if you don't use it.)

Does this sound like that boring adage from your childhood, "A place for everything and everything in its place?" Do you immediately imagine yourself surrounded by a cold, sterile environment of grim, tyrannical order that will crush every bit of joy from your already-overtaxed psyche? If so, perhaps your disorder is a delayed attempt to "show" your parents that you can structure your own environment, thank you.

Playing "Grown-up"

If the distant voice of a childhood critic is still ringing in your ears—"Hang up your coat," "Put away your bicycle," "How many times do I have to tell you to pick up your blocks,"—stop and decide if you still need to rebel or if you'd rather play "grown-up."

143

In this game, you have many more options than you did as a child. In addition to staying up late and eating as much candy as you want, you can choose between the deliciously naughty pleasure of tossing your things around or the comforting pleasure of finding them when you want them. Either way, when you play "grown-up," you're boss and *you* get to choose. You get to announce that "Setting things down anywhere I want makes me very powerful, but I think I'll skip the fun this time. It's more fun to find things the minute I want them. I'm even *more* powerful that way." (Logical considerations like wasted time, wasted energy, and emotional turmoil don't count when you're playing "grown-up." Go for the instant gratifications.)

Reinforcement— Writing Things Down or Rehearsing

We all know that writing things down helps us to remember. That's why we take notes and make lists. Writing is a form of rehearsing. You'll find an entire chapter on rehearsing later in this book, but let's look at everyday rehearsing right now.

You notice that you are out of mustard so you write *mustard* on your shopping list. You think "mustard," then you form the word with your pencil, then you look at the word after you've written it. You've just given yourself three copies of the thing to be remembered instead of one. You can also remember looking at the empty jar, smelling the fragrance, even licking a bit of mustard from your fingers after tossing the empty jar in the bin. The more copies you have, the more likely you are to remember.

In rehearsing, you generally read aloud what you want to remember or you listen to it over and over. Here's something that may make your work more efficient. In one experiment, people were asked to either read or listen to a long sequence of numbers, then say them back. Those who *heard* the numbers remembered them longer than people who only saw them, which seems to indicate that auditory memory lasts longer than visual. However, this is an individual thing. If you hear and see the material at the same time, you more than double your chances of remembering.

In the Mood to Remember

We've already mentioned that when divers learn something under water, even if it is entirely unrelated to diving, they can remember it better under water, and that if people memorize something while they are drunk, they will be better able to remember it later if they are drunk than if they are sober. This is called "state dependency" and also holds true when people are under the influence of marijuana, amphetamines, or barbiturates.

But what about moods? Are you ever "not in the mood" to remember something? Tests show that people also remember things according to the mood they were in when they acquired the information. Gordon H. Bower, chairman of the Psychology Department at Stanford University, has found that information acquired in a happy, sad, angry, or fearful state is most easily recalled in that state. He calls this "mood dependency/congruity."

Interestingly, while depression ordinarily blocks memory, Bower's "sad" subjects learned just as well as the "happy" ones. However, their sadness was hypnosis-induced, brought about by thinking of a sad experience while in a relaxed state. Bower compares mood dependency to having "Happy" and "Sad" bulletin boards that are most easily read when you are in these respective moods. Emotions act as filters for information.

This may be one reason why it is so hard to remember dreams. The dream state is unique and impossible to reproduce completely when we are awake.

Recall through Hypnotism

Does hypnosis really help people remember? Andre M. Weitzenhoffer found that people who had memorized prose or poetry and then were hypnotized remembered 50 percent more than they did in a normal state. He generalized that recall is improved by similar loose mental states: abstraction, free association, "twilight sleep," and simple relaxation.

Hypnosis may take away memory blocks, but it isn't foolproof. We can't retrieve what wasn't stored. Hypnosis simply removes distractions. Recently hypnotism has become a popular way to quiz witnesses of a crime. In a relaxed state they are sometimes able to visualize the scene clearly, recalling licence numbers and physical details that were glimpsed only briefly while under great stress. One of the dangers is that people usually feel very co-operative with their questioners during hypnosis and may imagine details just to please. In July, 1983, the New York State Court of Appeals barred testimony induced by hypnotism. It held that, even if safeguards are used, hypnosis tends to produce "a mixture of accurate recall, fantasy or pure fabrication in unknown quantities."

Seven out of ten people can be hypnotized, and 10 percent of those can achieve a deep trance. People with dominant right brains seem to be better subjects. Fifteen thousand doctors in the United States now use hypnotism. So far, there has been no proof that studying under hypnosis can improve learning, but this is an area that will certainly be explored in the future.

"I've Got Rhythm . . ."

Rhythm as an aid to memory has fallen into disrepute, probably neglected because some associate it with nineteenth-century memory drills, but rhythm is an instinctive way to remember. Watch the toddler rocking and chanting a two-note song again and again. Listen to the sing-song voice of a small child reciting a nursery rhyme. Or consider the cadences of most advertising slogans: "A hazelnut in every bite", "What's yours called" or "Plink, plink, fizz".

Rhythm is what makes poetry easy to remember. It can also help us to remember many other things. As we mentioned previously, Professor A. C. Aitken of Edinburgh University could remember pi to the first thousand decimals. It was easy, he said, because he simply grouped the digits in rows of 50 and divided the 50 into 10 groups of 5, "rather like learning a Bach fugue."

Misremembering

You've heard of Parkinson's Law and the Law of Gravity. In psychology there is a principle called Hodgson's Law: we often remember a thing in a way that we want to remember it. Once we have adjusted material to satisfy us emotionally, it remains in that form in our memory. This is one reason why witnesses rarely agree.

Sometimes people vividly remember things that didn't happen. The tabloids are always headlining stories like a housewife's journey to Mars or a bus driver's conversation with the spirit of Elvis Presley. Are these people crazy or just plain lying? Maybe neither.

Pioneer brain surgeon Wilder Penfield probed different parts of patients' brains during brain surgery and found that when he stimulated the cerebral cortex with an electrified needle the patient vividly recalled things that had happened as much as 50 years before. One woman remembered being at a parade when she was a child and hearing a band play. A girl thought that a phonograph had been turned on in the room, and a man heard his cousins talking and laughing. Penfield could also stimulate muscular movement with his probe. He concluded that he had caused a "ganglionic complex to re-create a steadily unfolding phenomenon, a psychical phenomenon . . ." Others quickly assumed that Penfield had proven that we never forget anything, and with proper stimuli, we should be able to summon up any information we have ever stored.

But Penfield's later experiments showed no consistency in the brain's reaction to electrical stimulation. There seems to be no direct relationship between the area of stimulation and the response. The brain is not a switchboard with neatly labeled plugs and circuits.

Contemporary brain experts know that stimulating the hypothalamus can produce bizarre images that seem totally real. This may have been what happened to a highly respected forest ranger who went to check out a strange light in the woods. His companions saw an explosion and fled. He later reappeared and described in great detail a trip in a space ship. Scientists speculate that his hypothalamus was stimulated by ground lightning, an electrical charge caused by rotting vegetation. This decomposition also produces a strong glow.

These may sound like exceptional cases, but what about ordinary people who misremember? The big advertising agency, J. Walter Thompson, quizzed viewers following a major 1983 TV miniseries. They learned that 32 percent of the sample audience remembered seeing commercials for Kodak, 32 percent recalled Prudential Insurance, 28 percent—Budweiser, 28 percent—American Express, 19 percent—Volkswagen, and 16 percent—Mobil. *None* of these sponsors advertised during the miniseries.

Making Structures for Remembering

Researcher George Mandler claims that all learning involves organization. Well . . . *most* of the time. Organization can be very helpful to remembering. Mandler divides organization into three types:

> *Sequencing*
> Putting things in a series such as A-B-C-D, 1-2-3, birth-life-death. We tend to remember events in a once-upon-a-time sequence, in the order of happening or presentation. We could not look up a phone number or find a book in a library without seriation.

Categorizing
Putting things in groups of similar things. Subjects were given 100 word cards to memorize. Some were told to divide them into categories. The more categories they created, the more words they were able to remember. (For instance, it would be harder to remember 25 animals than 4 birds, 3 farm animals, 6 reptiles, 5 fish, 3 house pets, and 4 zoo animals.)

SEQUENCING

RELATIONAL IMAGERY

CATEGORIZING

Try to structure information to remember it.

Relational imagery
Linking things that are visually similar — circular things, red things, sparkling things, things associated with Christmas, or sailing, or cooking.

Putting information in structures is essential to remembering it.

Structures Can Fool Us

Our love of order can also play tricks with our memories. We love dramatic structure so much that we fill in stories to make them complete. If several unrelated events happen at about the same time, we *want* to find a cause/effect sequence. That's why we remember later that we "left a dull job to take a more exciting one," when we actually were fired from the first and found the second one several months later. Or the old joke: they fell in love, got married, and had twins . . . but not in that order.

Material that doesn't mean anything to us is frequently discarded. In one experiment, a very complicated story was passed from one person to another, mimicking the game of "telephone" that we played as children. As the story was retold, it lost its conflicting elements, and by the fifth retelling, its meaning had been reversed altogether.

We also love to "improve" stories by adding detail. A simple statement gets embroidered in the retelling. Think of Pooh Bah in *The Mikado* who lent "verisimilitude" to his lies by adding colorful details.

So as you work to improve your memory, be aware that some of what you remember just isn't true. As Will Rogers said, "It's not what you know, it's what you know that ain't so."

Try This...

Exercise in Grouping-to-Remember

Here are some groups of objects. Try grouping them in different ways.

Group I
What categories could you make from these objects? Jot them down.

small child	teenager
hockey stick	cane
candy cane	old lady

Group II
What categories do these objects suggest?

coin	diamond
tyre	champagne bottle
slice of loaf cake	five pound note
licence plate	limousine
doughnut	

149

Answers

Group I—You could divide these things into child, teenager, old lady because they are all people; and candy cane, hockey stick, cane because they are all of a similar shape. You could also match the child to the candy, the teenager to the hockey stick, and the old lady to the cane.

Group II – You could group the coin, doughnut, tyre because they are all round; and the five pound note, cake, licence plate because they are all rectangular; and the diamond, champagne bottle, and limousine because they are all symbols of luxury. You could also cluster the coin, five pound note and diamond because they can all be used to buy something; the doughnut, cake, and champagne because they are all edible; the tyre, licence plate, and car because they are usually found together.

Now consider the 20 random objects below. If you try to "just remember" them, you will probably do fairly well. But try *grouping* them. There is no "right" answer. You have to make your own groups. Write them down on a sheet of paper if that helps, so you see the pattern you have made. Then start a fresh sheet and write down what you remember, using your clusters.

typewriter	cricket bat
gym shoe	top hat
stocking	riding hat
football	hot dog
dachshund	jar of mustard
book	cup and saucer
pencil	bicycle
cowboy hat	wheelbarrow
boxing gloves	automobile
tennis racket	horse

15
How to Use Memory Systems

Memory systems can seem overwhelming at first, but many people who approach them in a sufficiently playful manner discover that they can be invaluable tools for remembering.

"The advantage," says Dr. K. Anders Ericsson of Carnegie-Mellon University, "is that [mnemonics] relieves the burden on short-term memory because recall can be achieved through a single association with an already existing code in long-term memory."

What is mnemonics and how did it get such an odd name? Mnemosyne was the Greek goddess of memory and mother of the muses. Her namesake, mnemonics, simply means memory aids. A mnemonic can be simple or intricate, logical or silly. Sometimes the sillier or naughtier it is, the better we remember it. When I mentioned mnemonics to a room full of doctors, they spontaneously repeated a jovially vulgar memory aid:

> On old Olympus' towering top,
>
> A fat-assed German vaults and hops.

The first letter of each word is the first letter of the 12 cranial nerves. (A more genteel but less memorable version says, "A Finn and German viewed a hop.")

Many mnemonics are somewhat naughty and often not very specific. For instance, several of the cranial nerves obviously begin with the letter o, but which is which? Gordon H. Bower, chairman of the Psychology Department at Stanford University, suggests that a better mnemonic for the cranial nerves would contain more information.

At the *oil factory* (olfactory nerve) the *optician* (optic) looked for the *occupant* (oculomotor) of the *truck* (trochlear). He was searching because *three gems* (trigeminal) had been *abducted* (abducents) by a man who was hiding his *face* (facial) and *ears* (acoustic). A *glossy photograph* (glossopharyngeal) had been taken of him, but it was too *vague* (vagus) to use. He appeared to be *spineless* (spinal accessory) and *hypocritical* (hypoglossal).

Of course, a short, snappy, *and* exact mnemonic is best. The ones we remember are usually funny, naughty, or intriguing and have a rhyming structure. American children chant the names of the states as they jump rope:

How did Wiscon-Sin? Stole a New-Brass-Key.

What did Della-Wear? Wore a New-Jersey.

How did Flora-Die? Died in Misery.

You probably remember:

i before *e*, except after *c* or when sounded like *a*, as in *neighbor* or *weigh*.

A few of you may even have learned the sequel.

Exceptions: "Neither leisured foreigner seized the weird heights."

And there's the very useful first aid advice:

When the face is red, raise the head.

When the face is pale, raise the tail.

Mnemonic devices are useful when you can't record information in writing, for example for the very young or in societies where many are illiterate. Tribal lore and nursery rhymes, prayers, political slogans, magic incantations, "Thirty days hath September," "*i* before *e*, except after *c*," or even the sequential structure of numbers or the alphabet . . . all give us a map for remembering.

Numbering Things

Numbering or counting things can be an aid to learning. If you set out to name the 50 United States, you would probably do so in somewhat haphazard geographical or alphabetical order, checking yourself by counting how many you already had so you'd know how many were still missing. You probably don't associate numbers with states in a way that would let you "count" them. But if you wanted to name the elements or the amendments to the U.S. Constitution or the Ten Commandments, all of which are numbered, you'd most likely use their accompanying number as you went along, to make sure you got them all.

There are several counting systems that let you relate two visual images, one for the number and one for the object. If you tend to be verbal, try this one that uses rhyming words.

A Verbal Counting System

one	bun	six	sticks
two	shoe	seven	heaven
three	tree	eight	gate
four	door	nine	vine
five	hive	ten	hen

Or, if you tend to recall visually, here is a set of visual images described by popular memory writer Tony Buzan in his book *Make the Most of Your Mind* (New York; Simon and Schuster, 1984).

A Visual Counting System

one	pen	six	golf club
two	swan	seven	cliff
three	a pair of large breasts	eight	hourglass
four	sailboat	nine	pipe (hanging on a rack)
five	hook	ten	cricket ball and bat

A visual number system.

Having committed all those pens or hens to memory, you then match them to the new things you want to remember. For instance, you want to remember to do the following ten errands. You would list them mentally, matching them to either the rhyme number or the picture number.

1. *Buy stamps.*
   Rhyme: bun (A sticky cinnamon bun has stamps stuck all over it.)
   Picture: pen (Your pen pierces an assortment of stamps.)

2. *Buy tape at the hardware store.*
   Rhyme: shoe (Your shoe is wrapped tightly with tape so that it is hard to walk.)
   Picture: swan (A graceful swan is swathed in sticky tape. It is flapping about very inelegantly and squawking.)

3. *Buy washers at the hardware store.*
   Rhyme: tree (A Christmas tree is hung with rubber washers, like ornaments.)
   Picture: breasts (The doughnut-like washers are so big, they form the basis of a giant brassiere.)

4. *At the market you need bread . . .*
   Rhyme: door (A door won't shut because a big loaf of bread is in the way . . . it is getting crushed and scattering crumbs.)
   Picture: sailboat (A sailboat was unwisely baked out of bread. The foolish boatmaker is now sinking in his soggy craft as it sails in a sea of soup.)

5. *. . . and pickles . . .*
   Rhyme: hive (The bees have turned green as they tote pickle juice instead of nectar to their hive.)
   Picture: hook (Bait your hook with a pickle to catch a sourpuss catfish.)

6. *. . . and lightbulbs.*
   Rhyme: sticks (Smash burned-out light bulbs with a big stick as you anticipate your new ones.)
   Picture: golf club (Tee off with a lightbulb on your tee.)

7. *Go to the bank.*
   Rhyme: heaven (Imagine golden streets, angelic wings on the tellers as they run their hands through the coins in their drawers.)

Picture: cliff (You are pushing wheelbarrows of money off a cliff, watching the dollar bills swirl down to the rocks below.)

8. *Pick up your dry cleaning.*
Rhyme: gate (The plastic garment bags are draped over a gate . . . don't open it too fast or your best suit will fall in the mud.)
Picture: hourglass (Your dry cleaner is strapped into an old-fashioned hourglass corset. His or her eyes are bulging as he/she hands you your cleaning.)

9. *Buy a newspaper.*
Rhyme: vine (Your paper is sprouting tendrils.)
Picture: pipe (Dump the ashes out of your pipe into a newspaper, then fold the newspaper and put it in the bin.)

Nine/vine or nine/pipe—buy a newspaper.

10. *Get goldfish food at the pet store.*
Rhyme: hen (Your goldfish is so hungry it could eat a hen. See her chasing one around her bowl.)
Picture: cricket ball and bat (Your goldfish is playing cricket for England. Watch him lob that can of fish food for six.)

As you can see, all this is *work,* and it only works for you if you enjoy games. Otherwise, just make a list and look at it.

In chapter 21, "How to Remember Dates and Numbers," I will show you a comprehensive number system. If you decide to invest the energy in learning it, you will want to use the images of that system as mental "pegs" for fastening your lists.

A Foolproof Phone
Number System

Consider the Harvey Feinstein Foolproof Phone Number System. Harvey enjoys word puzzles, and one day, on the Illinois Central, he discovered that he could convert most phone numbers to words by selecting one of the three letters that share each number's hole or button. His own number became D-A-R-K-D-O-G (327-5364) while his girlfriend's number translated prophetically as Y-O-U-L-O-V-E (968-5683). Numbers with ones and zeros presented a problem since they have no accompanying letters, but he arbitrarily assigned *Q* or the word *one* to one and *Z* or the word *no!* to zero.

Here's how your phone dial divides the alphabet:

1 (Q or *one*)	6 M N O
2 A B C	7 P R S
3 D E F	8 T U V
4 G H I	9 W X Y
5 J K L	0 (Z or *No!*)

Write down a phone number you'd like to remember. Then write the three possible letters under each digit.

Phone number __ __ __ ‾ __ __ __ __

Possible
Letters __ __ __ ‾ __ __ __ __

Now use your crossword puzzle skills to contrive a word or words.

Phone word __ __ __ ‾ __ __ __ __

Try some more to get used to the idea.

Not every phone number can be made into words, but enough can to make it fun to try. At various times, various cities across America have recited the time or the weather to people who dialed P-O-P-C-O-R-N, N-E-R-V-O-U-S, or W-E-N-C-H-E-S, and the Yellow Pages reveal businesses that have worked their name, product, or service into their phone number—B-U-G-D-E-A-D for an exterminator or D-I-A-L-C-A-R for a limousine service. Maybe custom phone numbers will replace custom licence plates (and unlisted phone numbers) as a status system.

Abbreviations

Abbreviations are a quick way to say something complex, and they can also be a memory aid, furnishing the skeleton of the whole. You may not be sure what the initials stand for in TNT (trinitrotoluene) or UNICEF (United Nations International Children's Emergency Fund), but you probably know what they mean. See how many of the following you can identify.

U.S.A.	_____	IBM	_____
RSPCA	_____	JFK	_____
E.O.E.	_____	M.I.T.	_____
YHA	_____	E.T.	_____

Answers: United States of America, Royal Society for the Prevention of Cruelty to Animals, Equal Opportunity Employer, Youth Hostel Association, International Business Machines, John Fitzgerald Kennedy, Massachusetts Institute of Technology, Extra terrestrial.

Here are some other abbreviated or acrostic memory aids:

Every good boy does fine
The musical notes on the lines of the staff.

PEWSAGL
Pride, envy, wrath, sloth, anger, gluttony, and lust (the Seven Deadly Sins).

Kings play cards on fairly good soft velvet
Kingdom, phylum, class, order, family, genus, species, variety (biology classifications).

P. Cohn's Cafe
Phosphorus, carbon, oxygen, hydrogen, nitrogen, sulphur, calcium (Ca), and iron (Fe) (the chemical shorthand for the elements most common in the human body).

Use Location to Help Remember

Remembering things by where they are placed is useful. The socks without holes are at the front of the drawer; the freshest milk is on the left side of the refrigerator shelf; the new batteries are in the glove compartment, and the old ones that might still work in an emergency are on the bottom shelf of the workbench.

The Greek poet Simonides is credited with first demonstrating this system of remembering by location. He was called away from the table during a banquet, and while he was outside, the roof collapsed, crushing the other guests beneath the stones. The bodies were unrecognizable, but Simonides was able to identify them by remembering where each guest had been sitting. Later he realized that location could be a clue to memory, and that objects with no location, such as abstract ideas, could be attached to locations in the imagination and thus be remembered more easily.

Four hundred years later, the Roman orator Cicero used this system to remember his speeches. He would write his speech and place each section in different parts of his house and garden. Then he would walk from place to place, memorizing what he had written. Later, as he delivered his speech, he imagined strolling through his home, finding his next topic waiting. The Romans called this system "topology" from the Greek word *topos* meaning place. Our word *topic* comes from this. We use this placement principal in everyday speech: "In the first place" . . . "in the second place."

The Peg System

Are you yearning to learn some party tricks that will let you dazzle your friends and colleagues with your brilliant new memory? Try the system that the Greeks developed in the days before TelePrompTers and index cards. They used the structure of something they already knew, their homes, to arrange and remember lists of things such as the main points they wanted to make in a speech. They called this system *lochi* meaning rooms, and the Greek word has given us the English word, *locution*.

Lochi is a "peg system" that uses a structure you know to arrange what you want to remember. You can use the rooms of your home, your body, the streets between your home and office, any series of objects that is firmly fixed in your mind.

Now project the new items onto this structure. Exaggerate them. Make them ludicrous, bizarre, even naughty, so the picture will stand out. The crazier the image, the more likely you will be to remember it.

What Use Is It?

Most stage memory experts ask their audiences to shout out lists of objects—watch, roller coaster, rhubarb—which they then rattle back. You can have fun repeating this feat at parties (it's embarrassingly easy), but the really practical use for *lochi* is to fix in your mind the random thoughts that flit through it at precisely the times you couldn't possibly write them down or act on them: when you're driving, in the shower, drifting off to sleep, or "paying attention" to a boss, relative, or lover. Or a great idea for one project comes to you when you are totally involved in another project. If what you want to remember is an abstraction, try to make it into a solid image—a face, object, or symbol. Then, instead of reaching for a pencil, reach for a peg—a *lochi* peg that will record that thought until you can play it back.

Memory pegs also are useful when you need to read the information back in a setting where writing notes is difficult, for example, when you're making a speech or asking for a rise, or if you are the type who can never remember where you left your list.

How to Remember 20 Things in Less Than 2 Minutes

To remember 20 or 30 or even 50 things, it is essential to divide them into smaller units of 5 or 10. (I discussed grouping in the last chapter.) Having several structures lets you use them for different purposes—your body, say, for what you have to do on the way home from work and your kitchen for the calls you want to make after dinner. Having a number of different structures also lets us use some for short-term memory and some for long term—things you want to remember next week or next year. Also, several structures let you constantly insert new lists that won't get tangled. If you make five quick tours of the plant each morning, you may want five different structures to recall what you want to write down when you get back to your desk. That way, the information on location seven of the first structure—your belly button—won't collide with information stored minutes later in another location seven.

Let's start with ten always-available memory pegs on your body. Bodies are especially good for remembering objects—shopping lists—or things that have to be tended to—fix the *sink,* buy *stamps,* call *mother.*

1. *The top of your head*
   Make the first thing an incredible hat that perches or lurches there. Or the object you want to remember is running down over your face.

2. *Your forehead*
   It's a billboard or flashing neon sign advertising the second object.

3. *Your nose*
   It's a vending machine spurting out dozens of the third thing.

4. *Your mouth*
   It's a tunnel with the fourth item driving in or pouring out. Or your teeth or tongue become the object.

5. *Your throat*
   A transparent crystal cylinder that you think of as similar to Tiffany's window. The object it holds is very, very precious.

Your body has many always-available memory pegs for things that must be attended to (fix the sink, call Mum, buy petrol, do laundry, get the kids at school, get shoes repaired, a shopping list—stamps, light bulbs, roast, nail polish).

6. *Your chest*
   Here the object is stored in duplicate like a pair of lungs.

7. *Your belly button*
   The object is glued there or flashing there.

8. *Your hips*
   A belly dancer's hip belt is strung with dozens of the eighth object, and they move, clank, twinkle as you dance.

9. *Your knees*
   You are kneeling on the ninth object. Is it pleasant? Comfortable? Awful?

10. *Your feet*
    You stand on the tenth object. What does it feel like? What are your feet doing to the object?

Experience a silly burst of pleasure as you pass down your body, finding your speech or your shopping list or a sequence of battles, prime ministers, or rock formations as you go. You are able to digress endlessly when you want, yet always return to the preplanned sequence. Having a playful trick like this can make studying less arduous and more fun.

For the next five pegs, choose a room in your house. Imagine that you are standing at the door of your kitchen. (If it has more than one door, choose one.) Kitchens are marvelous because they are full of objects: an oven, a refrigerator, a toaster, a blender, a bin, cabinets, a food processor, a sink, In your mind's eye, move clockwise, from left to right around the room. Pick out the first dramatic part of your kitchen. We'll walk you through an imaginary sequence.

11. *The table*
    You want to post a letter so imagine sweeping everything off that table. Its surface becomes a giant letter, or letters are dancing on the top.

12. *The sink*
    You want to be sure to call someone, so put your telephone in the sink. Water is running all over it, and sparks are shooting all over the room.

13. *The refrigerator*
    You want to rewrite the letter to Mr. Jones and add three points. Three shelves of the refrigerator, or the freezer, butter drawer, and crisper hold each of those brilliant

new thoughts, and the refrigerator door becomes Mr. Jones's face or the logo of his company.

14. *The toaster*
You've got to get an important phone number you left at home and bring it to work tomorrow. See the slip of paper with the number on it popping up out of the toaster like a slice of toast; or see yourself burning with desire to get that number . . . or the numbers curling up like smoke from the slots.

15. *The stove*
You told your boss you'd pick up something on your way to work tomorrow. See your breakfast cooking while that object nestles, sizzling in your frying pan. It is so important that it shoves your usual eggs aside. If you don't eat eggs, imagine it staring out of your coffee cup or bobbing in your cereal.

Don't be tempted to use ten things in your kitchen even if you could. You need "white space" to group information.

Now go to your bathroom door. Bathrooms are usually full of things that rush and gush and flush. You can float things in the bathtub, unroll things like toilet paper, rain down on things with the shower. Tour the room from left to right, pegging things on prominent objects around the room. Here is an imaginary sequence:

16. *The bathroom basin*
It's probably different from your kitchen sink, maybe a different color and size. You want to remember to get petrol for the car. Imagine petrol pouring out of the taps as you try to shave or wash your hair. Ugh!

17. *The toilet*
Flush the thing. You want to remember to pay back the £1.51 you borrowed from Fred. Flush the money down the toilet as Fred hops up and down on the toilet cistern, clapping his hands with glee.

18. *Toilet paper*
The paper is printed all over with the next thing you want to remember. It unrolls and spills across the floor, till the room is full of colorful printed strips proclaiming your thought. You are engulfed with toilet paper.

19. *The shower*
   The object is pouring out over your bare body. Or it is under the shower, getting all wet. Your motor vehicle tax disc is getting waterlogged, floating pathetically in the swirling water, and you won't be able to drive unless you renew it. Or the flowers for your mother-in-law's birthday are pelting your back as you stand under the shower. They pile up at your feet, smiling up at you for your thoughtfulness.

20. *The towel rack*
   What you want to remember has replaced the towels and is hanging there. The steaks in the freezer that you have to leave out to thaw for dinner are right there on the rack. Or the cheque you promised to write and post immediately is folded neatly, giant-sized, over the bar. If you want to remember an abstract idea, you could imagine yourself naked at the board meeting, drying yourself with a giant towel while you deliver your brilliant plan.

Using *lochi* to remember points in a speech makes your talk look and sound spontaneous. The audience watches you search for the next idea and sees it come to you.

Once, when the *New York Times* went on strike, its movie critic, Richard Eder, was invited to do his reviews on television. He carefully read the first one and then saw it played back. He thought it was deadly dull. He decided that, instead of knowing exactly what he was going to say, he would jot down a few points and think through the material as he went. This approach proved much more lively and wonderfully effective.

Using Pegs as a Backup

Using pegs gives you two ways to remember things. One is rational—"Of course, I'll remember the five points of my speech or the eight things I have to do today." But if you block because of overload or nervousness, you have a second "list" to review. It's a marvelous backup, a way of putting ideas on hold.

Using Pegs to Learn New Things

You've just received a complicated new machine and have to do things in a certain sequence to make it work. For instance, imagine that you are learning to operate a new computer.

Step 1:
Turn on the green switch. (Imagine a green switch sticking out of the top of your head.)
Step 2:
Insert disc in slot. (Your forehead is a giant slot, opening to receive the disc.)
Step 3:
Hit the reset and shift buttons simultaneously. (Each nostril is a key with a huge sign sticking out of it. You must shove the signs back into the nostrils.)
Step 4:
Hit the "B" key. (Each of your teeth has a huge *B* on it.)
Step 5:
Hit the "return" key. (In the Tiffany's window of your throat is a golden key inscribed "Return to me.")
Step 6:
Type the name of the program you are about to do. (Make the alphabet soup of letters into a naughty brassiere. Remember, few people are mind readers and whatever connections you choose to make are strictly your property.)
Step 7:
. . . continue like this through all the steps.

You can use memory pegs to learn the steps to starting a car or opening a safe or any other sequence that must be done in order. It is simply another structure for storing information, temporarily or permanently.

It's OK
Not to Love Systems

If you've made a sporting try and you still feel frustrated and baffled by memory systems, that's OK. They work magnificently for some people and not at all for others. If you're one of the latter, you probably have many unconscious mental systems of your own that just don't mesh with outside ones. Try to keep a relaxed, open-minded, and playful attitude toward these external memory structures, and they may come in handy some day.

I prefer an approach to remembering that begins with what a person needs to recall. If you *need* to know it and *want* to know it, then you can usually find a way to remember it. The way may or may not include using a system, and the system may be a large, formal one (the alphabet, mathematics, the laws of physics), or it may be a ridiculous limerick. Both work.

Try This...

to Impress Friends with Your Ability to Remember

This is a great party trick. Get today's newspaper. You are going to memorize a key story or ad on each of the first 20 pages as your friends watch, or ask your friends to call the stories and ads out to you.

Your Peg	The Story or Ad	Your Silent Image (Make it funny.)
1. top of your head	_____	_____
2. forehead	_____	_____
3. nose	_____	_____
4. mouth	_____	_____
5. throat	_____	_____
6. chest	_____	_____
7. belly button	_____	_____
8. hips	_____	_____
9. knees	_____	_____
10. feet	_____	_____

Now enter your kitchen and, starting on the left, circle the room mentally and write down the five major things you see. Then choose a story or ad from pages 11 through 15 of your newspaper.

11. _____	_____	_____
12. _____	_____	_____
13. _____	_____	_____
14. _____	_____	_____
15. _____	_____	_____

165

Repeat the process with your bathroom.

16. _____   _____   _____

17. _____   _____   _____

18. _____   _____   _____

19. _____   _____   _____

20. _____   _____   _____

With a little practise, almost anyone can be a "memory whiz." If astounding your friends isn't your goal, use the above system to memorize a series of things you want to remember – the prime ministers of the 40s, the countries of Central and South America starting at the Mexican border, the operas of Verdi.

16
How to Study

"A student who changes the course of history," wrote humorist Franklin P. Adams, "is probably taking an exam." We are always students. One way or another, we never stop studying for exams. Even after surviving school physics tests, bar exams, and driving tests, there are always things to remember that affect our job, our family, and our society. That's why the way we remember as students is so important. Poor memory habits start in school.

Cramming has a bad reputation, yet cramming can be productive if you don't exhaust yourself and distort your perception. Just remember that cramming makes the material maximally available during the test but minimally available afterwards. If that's what you want, it's OK. The most efficient way to study, whether you cram or not, is to ask yourself questions about what you've already read, instead of rereading the material. Can you actively call the material back? Then you've increased your chances of recalling during the test.

Be Sure to Make Mistakes

Studying isn't easy because failure and errors have received a bad press. We are afraid not to be perfect, and therefore we unconsciously avoid the many small evidences of our "failure" during the learning process. As a result we end up with the one big failure of flunking the exam, or not learning a foreign language, or the new skill. We exchange freedom from small embarrassments for a major loss.

The Bad News

Here's some news you may not want to hear: studying requires concentration. If you work on seven things at once, you will get one-seventh of the total memory transfer for each that you would if you worked on one during the same time. It's like sharing time on a computer.

What is the benefit of flitting from one thing to another? If you stay with one thing until it is done, you may be judged by your product. The person who starts many new things and never finishes them delays this judgement.

To study successfully, you have to be inaccessible to external stimuli. The student, like the person who is beginning meditation, has to develop a spontaneous resistance to the enormous rush of distracting ideas, thoughts, and body sensations that greet him when he sits down to his task.

Why is it so hard? Well, reading and school work are very new ways to use a very old system, your mind. This system was designed millions of years ago to pay attention to what was happening at the moment. It was survival oriented.

The directed, focused way we use our minds today is a very specialized late addition. We always have a tendency to revert to the more spontaneous, less focused way of responding to new things. Like the caveman, we want to know, "Can I eat it or will it eat me?" This "mind wandering" is invaluable to us in terms of what we understand of the world, but mind wandering can make it hard to study.

Memorizing

Memorizing is done in two ways. We can learn mechanically by rote, or we can learn by understanding. Some things can only be learned one way or the other, but most memorizing benefits by a combination of both.

One example is the way people approach the computers that are flooding the world's business offices. One person, forced to deal with them, may say, "Don't bother me with details. Just show me which buttons to push." Another may want to know how they work, what they are capable of, and even how to take them apart for repairs and cleaning. The first person is trying to learn by rote, the second by understanding. Both may perform just as well in the short run, but the second probably has the long-term advantage.

Mechanical memorization may help you learn faster and perform better. This can be the best way to remember simple tasks. You don't need to know how a watch or a lock or an elevator works to use one effectively. Of course, you'd be helpless if one of them broke down in a crucial moment and you needed to fix it, but this happens so rarely that you really don't need to burden yourself with the intricacies of escapements, cylinders, or counterweights if you choose not to.

There are some drawbacks to mechanical rote learning. We may be mislearning the information. Children who learn so much by rote can be heard singing, "Land of the pills inside," instead of "Land of the pilgrim's pride;" or praying, "Lead us not into Penn Station." This can be charming and usually has no ill effects, but it may not aid later remembering unless the adult transposes pills and pilgrims.

Rote memorization, especially of something that has no meaning, rarely stays with us as long as information we truly understand. (An exception may be a particularly delightful bit of nonsense, such as "T'was brillig and the slithy toves did gyre and gimble in the wabe" from *Alice's Adventures in Wonderland* or the popular song of the 1940s, "Mairzy Doats and Dozy Doats.")

The role of meaning in memory was tested in a study that divided students into six groups. Each was shown the same set of paintings, accompanied by varying degrees of information about the artist and the art. Those who received the most information were able to remember the most paintings later.

Adding meaning to memorization helps lock the information in place. This is why we can summon up poems and quotes memorized decades earlier in school. Much of what we learn by rote as children forms the basis of our adult knowledge when we add understanding.

To Understand or to Memorize?

The simplest way to remember anything is to understand it, but with the vast amount of information in the world, that isn't always possible. Sometimes we need to memorize information solely for survival—the battles of the Civil War for a history class, the towns on a commuter train so we don't miss our stop, the wives of Henry VIII to do crossword puzzles. Dr. Albert Schweitzer had his illiterate patients repeat his instructions ten times so he was sure they would remember them even if they didn't understand the medical reasons behind them.

If you're absolutely sure that surface knowledge is enough, that you really don't want to *know* the information, just remember it, then you can use a trick. For instance, convert the information to a readily remembered sentence with the first letter of each word representing one of the parts you want to remember. The popular mnemonic for the stations on the Paoli Local, a train that services many colleges and prep schools outside Philadelphia, is "Old Maids Never Wed And Have Babies Rarely." Students use this sentence to keep from missing their closely spaced stops at Overbrook, Merion, Narberth, Wynnewood, Ardmore, Haverford, Bryn Mawr, or Rosemont.

Memorizing Techniques

The bookstores are full of good books on how to study, and those books are full of good study techniques. Here are two offbeat ones:

- Write the information on index cards (an active process), and tape the cards around the house in surprising places. When you run into a card, repeat the information out loud (another active process).

- Tape-record the information, and play it back as you bathe, wash dishes, drive.

Write what you want to remember on index cards and put them in unexpected places where you'll see them.

Conjuring Your Own Tricks

Let's say you want to remember the wives of Henry VIII. The easiest way would be to understand the rich and colorful drama of the time, the intense struggles between church and state, the heartache of a robust young king whose devoted, older wife bore him son after son, all stillborn, and of noble Sir Thomas More defying his king in the cause of his God. Understanding, in this case, would give you vivid, unforgetable pictures of the participants in this human historical drama. But you have neither the time nor the interest to do this. You just want to remember Henry's wives in sequence, with perhaps a few details on the side. How do you do it? Let's look at the list.

Catherine of Aragon (divorced)

Anne Boleyn (beheaded)

Jane Seymour (died)

Anne of Cleves (divorced)

Catherine Howard (beheaded)

Catherine Parr (survived)

Obviously you could make a quick rhythmic sequence of their fates:

Divorced, beheaded, died,

Divorced, beheaded, survived

But that's not much help if you don't know which was which. Let's look at the first letters of their names:

C A A B J S A C C H C P

Not very promising. The letters don't suggest a simple acronym (such as CREEP for Committee to Re-Elect the President or OPEC for Organization of Petroleum Exporting Countries). Maybe a verse could be contrived.

The Spanish Princess said her prayers
While pretty Anne leaped in bed.
Catherine of Aragon
Lost her paragon
But Anne Boleyn lost her head.

171

Lady Jane could see more (Seymour)
But died in childbirth's fever.
Then over the seas
Came Anne of Cleves,
Too smart for Henry's cleaver.

Little Catherine Howard
Thought she'd be his star.
But she was discovered
With more than one lover,
And — chop, chop — Catherine Parr.

This is admittedly dreadful doggerel, but the five minutes or so you spend contriving something like it are far more *active* than five minutes spent reciting the names again and again, and this active process has a better chance of fixing the ladies' names permanently in your mind, even if you ultimately (as is likely) forget your poetic attempt. If your talents tend to be visual, rather than verbal, you could try a series of cartoons, logos, or caricatures to help lock your subjects in your mind.

How Long Should You Study?

In studying, as in everything, we get what we "pay" for, but there are ways to get the most for our money. Do you learn twice as much if you study twice as long? Or does the "rate of diminishing returns" apply? Or do you become more efficient as you study longer? Results of experiments have been somewhat contradictory.

One nineteenth-century study by Ebbinghaus, the first modern memory researcher, indicated that dividing study time into equal periods was more efficient. Those who alternate between long and short study periods, will remember less than those who study in more equal periods.

A 1978 experiment tested the "Total Time Hypothesis" and found a direct ratio between learning and the amount of time spent. When British postmen had to learn to operate a complex number typewriter, it was the perfect opportunity for a study. The postmen were divided arbitrarily into four groups with four different study schedules. Here is how they did.

Those who studied one hour a day learned twice as fast as those who studied four hours a day in two two-hour sessions. The second group learned in half as many days but spent four times as many hours learning, a plus only if trying to meet a deadline. The other two groups studied either two hours once a day or one hour twice a day. They learned equally fast, and their speed fell between the first two groups.

This study indicates that if you don't have a deadline and want to spend the least number of hours studying, one hour a day is the most efficient way to study. Of course, if results are needed fast, like the famed 90-Day Wonders of World War II—officers trained and shipped to the battlefront in just 90 days—then the more hours spent each day, the fewer days or weeks needed to achieve the goal, even if many more hours are required.

Predicting Your Performance

People were shown a lengthy list of objects and asked to assign a number to each item, indicating how likely they were to remember it. It turned out that their estimates were very close to their actual performance on a test of recall. If you can do this kind of estimating, you can decide how much time you need to devote to studying something that you want to remember later.

Aural Repetition— an Inferior Study Aid

Recently the British Broadcasting Corporation had to change frequencies. In the weeks before the change, they broadcast the complex new channel information thousands of times. Surveys showed that almost no one could recall the information. When the change was made, most people referred to written instructions they had received and had few problems. The aural instructions failed because they were too complicated. Conclusion: complex information is better understood visually.

Forgetting and Restudying

We forget on a curve. It's rather like shooting down a steep slide that levels out at the bottom until we are scooting along on the level. At a specific moment we may have two memories at exactly the same spot on the downhill slide, but one started its trip long before the other. Jost's law, named after the nineteenth-century psychologist, says that if two memory traces are equally strong at the same moment, then the older of the two will be more durable and forgotten less rapidly. In other words, the older has already "leveled out" in its descent. Conclusion: spaced presentation enhances recall. Keep memories fresh by tracing over them periodically, and they will stay with you longer.

Theories about Forgetting—
Fading vs. Interference

There are two basic theories about how we forget and neither can be proven. The first says that memory fades. If this is so, then time should be a constant factor, but it rarely is. The second theory says that memories are obscured or disrupted. Rugby players were asked to describe games in which they had played. Most could remember the greatest number of details about the most recent game they had played, no matter how many weeks had elapsed since they had played it. The elapsed time affected memory less than the number of intervening games.

The less that happens between learning and recall, the better. Subjects who learned just before going to bed, remembered more 12 hours later than people who learned something first thing in the morning and had to recall it that night. (Of course, this is a generality . . . if you are bright and functioning first thing in the morning and a near-vegetable at night, this may not hold for you.)

Memories That Interfere
with Memory

Memories can get in each other's way, just like people in a crowded corridor. When you are trying to remember a specific fact, older memories and more recent ones can both get in the way.

Newer Memories
Newer memories interfere because we tend to forget in reverse. New material pushes out old, so we can remember where we set something down today more easily than where we set it last week.

Lots of studies of this "overwriting," have been done. In 1900, two German researchers had volunteers memorize a long list. Then the volunteers were divided into two groups. One group relaxed while the other memorized a new list. Then both were retested on the first list. The ones who had been idle were able to remember 56 percent of the first list, but the ones who had been busy with a new list recalled only 26 percent.

Older Memories

Older memories interfere when the older, more familiar material overcomes the new. The more similar two experiences are, the more likely we are to combine them. This may be helpful in strengthening a memory or it may not.

Husband: Remember that romantic weekend we spent in St. Louis?

Wife: (grimly) I've never *been* in St. Louis.

When more recent memories are blocked by earlier, stronger ones, we dilute the new information with lots of similar information. If we have only seen one football game or one opera or one airplane crash in our life, the details would probably remain fairly clear. But if we had seen dozens, even hundreds, the distinctions might begin to blur, unless we had a great interest in the information and formed structures to file it (as football fans, opera buffs, and crash investigators would do).

In another experiment in the 1930s, college students were asked to memorize lists of nonsense syllables. When their work periods were interrupted with such things as humorous readings, they remembered little of what they had been memorizing. The same experimenter did another study that indicated there is less interference between different kinds of information. In other words, if we have to study several different things in sequence, we can remember better when the subjects aren't similar. For instance, studying maths immediately after history wouldn't erase much of the earlier history information, but studying American history after English history might blur the distinctions.

And, despite the accepted idea that good study habits are consistent, another 1930s study found that consistently using similar study habits also resulted in retroactive inhibition. This may mean that varying your procedure or schedule or even the place you study could help you remember better. You could try studying chemistry in one place, languages in another.

Studying Formulas

Sometimes it is absolutely essential to understand something to remember it. Of course, some people are always trying to come up with an easier way. In an American book *How to Remember Anything* (Arco, 1976) by David Markoff and Andre Dubin, the authors say that remembering the classic formula $E = mc^2$ is easy if you translate it according to their memory table into "he, scale, ham, sea, and Noah." Then they suggest:

> See[ing] thousands of *he's* (men) weighing themselves on a *scale* . . . next we see a scale, or better a million scales being sucked into a steaming hot ham. Then we see the ham drowning in a sea . . . we now see thousands of hams dotting the sea and they're all drowning. Finally there is Noah sipping up the whole sea through a straw.

Now, it is just possible that some of you may find this easier to remember than $E = mc^2$, but I am not going to tell you to remember that way. There are lots of tricks to get us through life's memory chores, and you should use any of them that work for you, but images of Noah sipping a sea full of hams and scales should not replace the elegance, power, and poetry of $E = mc^2$!

Maybe chemistry is a dark, miserable sea to you, something you have to get through just to graduate. The formulas are relatively meaningless, but you have to show the teacher you "know" them. S, the man with the incredible memory, knew no chemistry, but he could remember lengthy formulas by converting them to visual images. For instance, he was given this meaningless formula to memorize:

$$N. \sqrt{d^2 . \times \frac{85.}{vx}} \quad \sqrt{\frac{276^2 . \quad 86 \times n^2b}{n^2v \quad . \quad 264}}$$

This is how he did it.

> Neiman (N) came out and jabbed at the ground with his cane (.). He looked up at a tall tree which reminded him of a root ($\sqrt{}$) and thought to himself: "No wonder the tree has withered and begun to expose its roots. After all, it was here when I built these two houses (d^2)." And again he poked with this stick (.). He said, "The houses are old, a cross ($\times$) should be placed on them." This gives a

great return on his original capital because he had invested 85,000 rubles to build them. The roof finishes off the building (−), and down below a man is standing and playing a harmonica (the ×). He is standing near the Post Office and at the corner is a large stone (.) to prevent carts from bashing the corner of the house . . .

This bizarre tale allowed him to remember it perfectly, both at the time and 15 years later.

To summarize, understanding a formula is best. Tricks are second best. And sometimes tricks get you through until real understanding comes.

Studying History

History has traditionally been structured chronologically by country—each culture standing apart from the others like separate columns. We may be able to rattle off lists of Chinese dynasties or English monarchs or American presidents, but we have to stop and think to relate them "sideways," to figure out who was King of England at the end of the Ming Dynasty (Charles I); who was President during the reign of William IV (Andrew Jackson); or who was the Russian Premier when President Kennedy was shot (Nikita Khruschev); unless there had been an important interaction, such as that between Marco Polo and Kublai Khan.

Sometimes these relationships can strengthen our concept of the world as a whole in exciting ways. For instance:

1. Catherine the Great of Russia was a contemporary of:

    a. Queen Elizabeth I of England

    b. George Washington

    c. Abraham Lincoln

2. Beethoven was still alive when which of these people were born?

    a. Renoir

    b. Pasteur

    c. Gershwin

3. Which of the following things happened during Rembrandt's lifetime?

    a. The pilgrims landed at Plymouth Rock.

    b. Mozart was born.

    c. Leonardo da Vinci died.

    d. Molière wrote plays.

    e. The French Revolution began.

4. Which of the following people, chronologically if not geographically, could have met?

    a. Jane Fonda and Freud

    b. Sarah Bernhardt and Ernest Borgnine

    c. Thomas Edison and John F. Kennedy

    d. Abraham Lincoln and Henry Ford

    e. Shakespeare and Pocahontas

5. When the atomic bomb dropped on Hiroshima, which of the following things were true?

    a. Women were wearing ankle-length skirts.

    b. The countries of Tanzania, Estonia, and Montenegro did not exist.

    c. Betty Grable was a pinup girl.

    d. Most Americans had never heard of pizza or seen a television.

    e. There was no immunization against smallpox, and epidemics caused many deaths.

Answers: 1—b   2—b   3—a,d   4—a,b,c,d,e   5—b,c,d

Did these exercises stretch your mind and help you imagine history as a gigantic structure, full of relationships and "pegs" to hang things on? When you need to memorize a date, try summoning up all the things that happened on that date. Knit a web of horizontal associations to hold your vertical date in place.

Even though we are frequently taught to study history in neat sequential columns, events are never this tidy. History is a tumult, and it is only we poor mortals who try to make a story of it, to have beginnings and ends, causes and effects. Forcing a structure, a viewpoint, and a purpose on sometimes-random happenings helps us to remember them, even though it distorts and occasionally falsifies them.

Studying Music

There was a vogue, some years ago, to teach music appreciation by having hapless students memorize the titles and composers of hundreds of pieces of music. The teacher reasoned that she could not test their true appreciation, but she could sure find out if they knew Schubert from Schumann. As a result, tens of thousands of Americans cannot hear the *Surprise* Symphony without muttering to themselves:

> Papa Haydn's dead and gone.
>
> But his memory lingers on.
>
> When his mood was one of bliss.
>
> He wrote jolly tunes like this.

(Haydn had the last laugh on that one, for this work is now attributed to another composer.)

About the only kind thing to say for a process that has left a generation of Americans putting doggerel lyrics to great music is that recognition *can* aid appreciation. A walk through the woods may be a pleasant experience, but if we can say, "Oh, that's a *Silene caroliniana* and that's a *Meleagrie gallopavo silvestris,* and over there is *Viola tricoleur,* also called Johnny-Jump-Up or Love-in-Idleness" and then launch into Oberon's speech from *Midsummer Night's Dream:*

> . . . a little western flower,
>
> Before milk-white, now purple with love's wound,
>
> And maidens call it Love-in-Idleness.

our pleasant walk can become a sublime and memorable experience.

So, if you were spared the lyrical "learning" process, treasure each unencumbered moment of Mozart, ripple of Rachmaninoff, bar of Beethoven, and thunder of Tchaikovsky. If not, seek out the wordless magnificence of Monteverdi, Scarlatti, Poulenc, and Stravinsky who probably escaped the degradations of this particular school of "memory training."

Auditory memory includes recognizing a friend's voice, the sound of glass breaking, or a piece of music. There has not been a great deal of auditory memory research, but two studies showed that people can remember a melody, even if the key and timing are different, as long as the "contour" is similar.

Both Eastern and Western music employ variations on a theme. The symphony form requires the composer to state his simple melodies and then elaborate and embellish them with great sophistication. Mozart once built an astounding tour de force of variations on the nursery melody we know as "Twinkle, Twinkle Little Star." Jazz and raga take a tune and then dissect, enlarge, twist, and exhort it to sublime heights of reinterpretation. Yet the melody in all cases must remain recognizable or the exercise loses its purpose.

What changes can we tolerate before we "lose" the melody? One researcher played well-known melodies like "Auld Lang Syne" for his subjects with various distortions. They recognized the melodies 94 percent of the time when they were played "straight." This dropped to 80 percent when the pitch was changed and to 54 percent when the time between notes was changed. (Some relevant trivia: The estate of the opera composer Giacomo Puccini successfully sued Al Jolson and Vincent Rose because the first 12 notes of their song "Avalon" were identical to the first 12 notes of the tenor's third act aria, "E lucevan le stelle" from *Tosca*. The notes are the same, but the timing is so different that almost nobody, probably including Jolson and Rose, recognized the similarities. Something similar happened to George Harrison of the Beatles. He was successfully sued by the author of the Ronette's hit "Be My Baby" which was judged to be too similar to Harrison's "My Sweet Lord.")

It seems that pitch and rhythm changes affect individual recognition of melodies to some extent and that music is a profoundly cultural experience. We learn to recognize patterns in our music, just as we recognize patterns in our language. Patterns that differ a little can sound fresh and exciting (I remember the fuss over Leonard Bernstein's dissonant score for *West Side Story* when it first came out, but now it sounds "normal" and even "traditional"), but patterns that differ too much can leave the listeners bored, confused, or angry (the riots that greeted Stravinsky's *Rite of Spring* or the ennui that engulfs most listeners of the works of Schönberg).

Studying to Music

Many of us put on a record or turn on the radio when we want to study. We're convinced that it soothes us, blocks extraneous noises, and helps us concentrate (especially if we did not have to memorize instructive lyrics to identify major composers). This may be wrong, according to a Bradley University study. Forty volunteers were divided into four groups of ten, with five men and five women each. All studied a passage from a law book and then were tested. Twenty of the students listened to their favorite "study" records while they studied, and the other twenty studied in silence. Afterwards, half of each group relaxed while the others did unrelated work.

Surprise! The silent group did slightly better than the group that listened to music, but even more surprising, the relaxation groups did about twice as well as the groups that did unrelated work between studying and taking the test. Here is a rundown on their scores, based on a maximum possible score of ten:

	Females	Males
music/relaxation	7.2	6.0
music/activity	2.8	3.2
silence/relaxation	8.8	8.0
silence/activity	3.6	4.0

Notice that women did slightly better than men in the same group if they relaxed before testing, and men did slightly better than women if they did an unrelated activity before testing. However, the relaxers are the big winners.

Some Laws for Learning

If you want a way to visualize the learning process, consider this equation:

$$readiness + frequency = learning$$

Edward E. Thorndike made groups of cats and chickens memorize things in order to eat. Later he repeated the experiment with college students. From their actions he decided there were key factors to learning including readiness, frequency, and effect. A hungry cat has readiness to learn. At first it tried many things to open the door of the cage to get to its food, but when it accidentally did so, it didn't connect the act and the door opening. But after the cause-effect repeated several times, the frequency impressed the cat. (Practise makes perfect.)

Frequency, however, isn't necessary if the thing being learned is so striking that it would be hard to ignore—your house is on fire; George makes more money than you do; Jupiter is about to crash into the earth. Anything that impresses you will go into your memory. An equation for this would be

$$\frac{\text{meaning}}{\text{reward}} = \text{learning}$$

Thorndike experimented with rewards for learning. People, he observed, will learn something that seems irrelevant at the time (like the alphabet, multiplication tables, or how to get along with a fussy boss) for an immediate reward. Occasionally the reward will be a personal sense of satisfaction. More often it is external—approval (including good grades, acceptance at college, degrees), power, fame, money, or personal possessions. The concept of reward can include avoiding punishment. Neurologist Richard M. Restak says that "novelty is a reward." I suggest tempting and charming yourself into remembering with the reward of novelty, rather than imagining all the terrible things that will happen if you forget (punishment).

Thorndike thought that people would remember pleasant things and forget unpleasant things, but other experiments and our own experiences show that this isn't always true. Thorndike amended his original theories to include the Law of Belongingness: meaningful associations are easier to remember than meaningless associations.

Experimenting with Rats, Cats, and College Students

Perhaps the ever-present rats, cats, and college students in memory experiments have you wondering, "What has all this got to do with *me*?" The answer is, not much and quite a lot.

When you read that a kangaroo learned to tap dance twice as fast when he was fed bananas while a red light flashed, you can easily dismiss it as nonsense. Much scientific study *does* seem like nonsense, but it's such delightful nonsense that makes up the building blocks of all human knowledge. To find out about the kangaroo, the experimenter had to design an experiment with strict controls.

For instance, was the kangaroo compared to a frog or only to other kangaroos? What were the variables? In other words, what was compared to what? Was it the task learned or the food ingested or the color of the light, or whether the light flashed or was steady? How was the speed of learning evaluated? Most important, can other experimenters duplicate the results?

If they can, then this bit of esoterica goes into the giant library of What-We-Know. Other researchers can try to apply its implications to other areas. If the implications prove to be broad enough, we could end up teaching every kangaroo in the country to tap dance, or we could increase the learning speed of school children by changing their diets, or we could change the lighting design of schools, or we could teach kinesthetic skills more quickly, or . . . Much of science is finding answers to questions that haven't been asked yet.

Discouraging Learning

Some of us constantly rise to meet challenges, and others fold up under disparagement. If you often find yourself in the latter group, you have plenty of company. In one experiment, volunteers were asked to memorize lists of numbers. One group was arbitrarily criticized for not being as good as the others. These subjects remembered less than the uncriticized group.

A controversial experimenter, A. F. Zeller, also repressed learning with criticism in an experiment that has drawn some criticism itself. A subject who had learned a list of syllables was then verbally abused in this manner:

> Great concern was expressed . . . over [his] mental ability. He was asked if he had not considered the possibility that he could not get through college and was informed that he probably would not. On the other hand, it was pointed out his mechanical ability was so poor he probably couldn't succeed in any of the trades. Nothing was omitted which would serve to make [him] feel insecure and inadequate.

Subjects who got this kind of feedback remembered significantly less than their control counterparts. Then these abused subjects were told that the criticism had been part of the experiment. Their performances improved dramatically, but it never equaled that of the control group. Similar results have been obtained by other experimenters.

The Ethics of Experimentation

This experiment has some strong inferences for educators. It may have contributed positively to teaching philosophy, but the danger of such tactics to the lives and psychic health of the participants can't be overlooked. It is possible that some of the subjects were permanently damaged by the process, just as people in similar real-life situations can be damaged.

Risky experimentation is a constant moral dilemma for researchers. (In the 1930s, a syphilis cure was tested on convicts by letting a control group go untreated!) These abuses are usually criticized — Baddeley comments on "the dubious ethical status" of the Zeller experiment — but enthusiasm can sometimes cloud ethics when we are consumed with curiousity — "How does this work? Let's tear it apart and see!"

Darwin's Law for Studying

While we are seeking guidelines for effective studying, let's check in with a top-notch observer, Charles Darwin. Darwin formulated what we have dubbed the Law of Contrariness. While collecting evidence for his theory of evolution, he forced himself to write down everything *contrary* to his theory because he knew he would forget the contradictions otherwise.

Try This...

to Determine Your Best Studying Technique

What type of fact—grammatical, historical, mathematical, general—is difficult for you to remember, no matter how often you study it? Or what concepts or what sequence, series, or group of things do you want to be able to recall? Go look up the information, if necessary, and write it down.

What studying technique might help you remember it? Look over the list below.

_____ repeating it over and over

_____ really understanding it

_____ studying it in a structured, regular way on a regular schedule

_____ studying it randomly, whenever time permits

_____ approaching it in an unusual, new way

_____ creating your own mnemonic about it

_____ drawing a picture of it

_____ being serious

_____ being silly

_____ being persistent

_____ being innovative

Check what you think will work. There are no right answers. Now test your predictions.

17
How to
Remember Facts

It is easier to think, plan, persuade, and make decisions if you have the facts to back you up. What the diplomatic community calls "intelligence" is simply facts, facts to use or ignore in dealing with people and events.

Schools say that they teach people how to think, but usually what they want to hear back from their students is a list of facts. To pass those exams, you will need to remember facts, arrange them in a logical way, and interpret the whole constructively. This can be true of life too.

Learning is knowing how to locate data and analyse it, not storing it in your memory. We are overloaded with data, but the more we know, the easier it is to learn. Each new piece of information has more places to go in our large, structured mental filing cabinet. As we get older, we may take longer to retrieve a crucial bit of information, but we have more file drawers in action.

Much that we see and hear each day would be meaningless if we didn't recognize it and categorize it. Imagine a bushman dropped down in the Louvre or, the opposite, a cultured Frenchman whisked to the great Australian desert. Each would have little understanding of what he saw and therefore would remember few details. In his own territory, the bushman might spot an impression in the sand, note the angle of the sun, sniff the air, and draw a valuable conclusion about impending danger. The Frenchman might view the works of Flemish painters and draw valuable conclusions about life in Europe in the seventeenth century. The reverse would be unlikely.

Intelligence and Memory

The ability to express things precisely depends upon the depth of one's vocabulary. Memory, then, is really one of the building blocks of intelligence. By intelligence, we mean novel ways of using information, of putting things together in ways they have never been before. This is a creative act, not a repeat of something, and therefore not memory.

Do smart people remember better? No one knows because there is little agreement on what intelligence is. Is it how fast a person can process information? How long it takes to react? (This is inherited.) Or is it thoroughness which can be taught? If intelligence is defined as the "ability to learn," then all intelligence is based in some way on memory. However, I.Q. tests like Stanford-Binet and Wechsler-Bellevue test only portions of a student's memory.

Some superior memories are obviously built in and probably genetic. Chess masters are able to remember the arrangement of pieces on a chessboard more quickly than average club players, indicating that some people have more memory ability than others, no matter how much desire is involved. Most tests indicate that effort and training can't improve a person's memory capacity. Don't despair, though, because effort and training *can* increase efficiency.

And if anyone tries to persuade you that memory really is intelligence, tell them about the monkey in Texas who proved that monkeys remember just about as well as we do. In a test at the University of Texas Health Science Center in Houston, a five-year-old rhesus monkey competed against human volunteers. Both the monkey and the humans were shown a series of slides. Then they were shown a second set that contained some of the slides in the first series plus new slides. Both man and monkey were taught to hit a lever when a familiar picture from the first group appeared. (The monkey, we assume, got a reward for his trouble.) In a ten-item test, both monkey and humans were right 86 percent of the time, and in a twenty-item test, both succeeded 81 percent of the time.

Do You Understand?

It is much harder to learn something if you have no framework to organize and store the information that's coming in. In other words, the better you understand what it is, the better you can remember it. Understanding is an active brain process, and memory ability is high when the information comes into the brain in a way that is easy to retrieve. For example, to remember the table of elements, you can divide the list into classifications like metal and nonmetal. This scheme gives you an organized way to search for and recall information.

One instructor of a class on statistics tried to help his students by giving them a framework of philosophy about the material. The students simply wanted answers, not background. As a result they had no way of structuring the information and failed to learn it.

There is more than one way to organize information. You can classify it: apple belongs to fruit which belongs to growing things. This is a vertical scheme, going from top to bottom or bottom to top. Then there is the horizontal order: an apple a day keeps the doctor away, Eve gave Adam an apple, Bramleys make good pies. Both vertical and horizontal schemes enrich the context, the surrounding material that inevitably leads us to what we want to remember.

In any information system there is noise. When you listen to a radio program, there is static. Whether you can hear the signal through the noise depends on how strong the signal is and on how redundant or repetitive the information is. If the information is repeated again and again, we can lose part of the signal and still reconstruct the material we want.

You can increase your chances of remembering a fact by:

- classifying the fact in several ways

- making multiple copies—if one is lost, you still have others

- giving the fact so much context that outside noise can't block it

More memory benefits come from spending an hour trying to recall what you've read than by spending the same time rereading the material. By recalling, you are actively involved in trying to retrieve the information.

Try This...

to Test and Enhance Your Powers of Recall

A few seconds ago you read about three ways to remember facts. Without looking, *actively* recall them by writing them down.

Compare what you wrote to the list on the previous page and make any corrections. Now, read over what you wrote. Then shut your eyes and repeat it out loud. You have just reinforced the information three ways: writing, seeing, hearing. Think you'll remember it?

Just the Facts

Remembering facts doesn't have to be a "grind." For a bit of fun, try this "Tribute to the Mystery."

"I can discover facts, Watson," said Sherlock Holmes, "but I cannot change them." In *The Problem of Thor Bridge,* Sir Arthur Conan Doyle put forth one of the most perfect of the great sleuth's cases. All the facts the reader needs to solve the case are clearly presented. Try to remember each fact as you read it. Then match your solution to Holmes's.

1. Neil Gibson, "the Gold King," was once an American senator of a western state. He now lives on a large country estate in England with his middle-aged wife and their two children who are tended by a pretty young governess.

2. The wife was once a great Brazilian beauty, but her charms have faded. Although she adores her husband, he no longer loves her. He is cruel to her, and there are rumors that he loves the governess.

3. At 11:00 one evening the body of the wife is found a half-mile from the house, in the middle of the roadway a few yards from Thor Bridge.

4. She has been shot at close range in the right temple.

5. No gun is found.

6. The road is hard, and there are no footprints.

7. Clutched tightly in the wife's left hand is a note. "I will be at Thor Bridge at 9:00." It is signed by the governess who admits writing it. She also admits that she met the wife at the bridge at 9:00, but that the woman was alive when she left her.

8. The next day a gun of the same caliber as the murder weapon is found on the floor of the governess's wardrobe under some dresses. One bullet has been fired from it.

9. Neil Gibson owns many guns. The gun found in the wardrobe is one of a pair, but the other gun cannot be found.

10. The estate manager says he suspects that Gibson, an attractive but ruthless man, has murdered his wife so he can marry the governess. The servants all love and pity their warm-hearted, passionate mistress, while distrusting their cold, arrogant master.

11. The governess says that she found a note on her school desk signed by the wife, asking to meet her that evening at Thor Bridge. It also asked her to leave a reply at the sundial so that Gibson would not know of their meeting. The governess says she left such a note at the sundial, and it is the one found in the murdered woman's hand.

12. The governess says that when she met the wife at the bridge, the woman began screaming jealous accusations at her. The governess put her hands over her ears and fled back to the house. She heard no shot.

13. The governess says that the gun could not have been in her wardrobe the previous day, because she would have seen it.

All this is known to the police. The governess is arrested for murder. She seems to have no chance of acquittal until Sherlock Holmes discovers an additional fact.

14. Sherlock Holmes finds a fresh chip in the underside of the bridge railing, about 15 feet from where the body was found. Although he strikes the rail repeatedly with his heavy cane, he cannot make a similar mark. The stone is too hard.

At this point, Holmes has solved the case. Watson, not so swift as his friend, requires more hints. Here is Watson's final clue.

15. Sherlock Holmes asks why the governess would carry out a carefully premeditated murder and then leave an incriminating note in the dead woman's hand? Why, too, would she carry the gun back to her room, rather than tossing it in the bullrushes below the bridge?

Now stop and decide what conclusions could be reached from the above facts. Have you solved the case? There is another fact that should make everything clear.

16. Sherlock Holmes asks that the area immediately below the white chip on the bridge be dragged. Searchers find the twin to the gun in the wardrobe. It is tied to one end of a 20-foot cord and a heavy rock is tied to the other end. One shot has been fired.

Do you have a final solution now?

Answer

The wife, in a jealous rage, committed suicide after planting evidence to make it look like a murder by her supposed rival. First she took a pair of identical pistols from her husband's collection. She fired one shot from the first gun, probably in the woods where it would not be noticed, and hid it in the governess's wardrobe. Then she met the governess as planned.

After the young woman had fled her jealous outburst, she tied a heavy rock to one end of a cord and tied the other end to the gun. She stretched the cord across the road with the rock hanging over the side of the bridge. She then held the note in her left hand and shot herself in the right temple. As she fell, the gun dropped from her hand and was pulled over the edge of the bridge and into the bullrushes. The metal gun hit the rail with a sharp blow, causing the chip.

The first step to deciding and solving is to remember the facts. The second step is to use them.

18
How to Remember What You Read

Do you ever find yourself reading and rereading a page without knowing what you've read?

If it's fiction and you're not remembering it, then you and the author are probably a bad match. Don't bother with each other. We read fiction either to experience something strange and new or to learn another perspective from someone with very similar experiences to our own in dealing with life.

It's non-fiction that most people want to remember. Whether you are reading for business or pleasure, it helps to recognize five basic patterns that authors use to organize their material.

Structures for Nonfiction Books and Articles

When you walk into a strange house, you can usually find the kitchen or bedroom because you recognize a familiar structure. When you buy a new TV set or a new car, you can usually figure out how to operate it, even if the controls are in a different place than on the one you owned before.

Non-fiction is similar. When you learn to recognize the structure of what you are reading, you can find what you are looking for quickly and easily, and recall the parts that make up the pattern of organization.

As you begin reading, look for the structure. Make a guess and then see if you are right. You can change your mind and try another structure if the first doesn't fit. When you find the structure and then arrange the information bits on that structure, you will have a much better chance of remembering than if you stack all the information up like old magazines in the garage for sorting later.

Speed Reading— Good or Bad?

Some people think that speed reading means skipping over the printed words without really absorbing them. You *can* skim through a book, sailing high over the landscape until you spot what you want and swoop down on it. But that's skimming, not speed reading.

We remember more if we concentrate. We concentrate more if we read at a speed closer to the speed at which we process information—in other words, very fast. When we take in more ideas instead of lingering over each sentence, it is actually easier to notice the information. The difference between casual reading and speed reading is the difference between driving on a flat highway in the desert and on a twisty mountain road. Our concentration rises on the twisty road, and we process much more information. Like mountain driving, speed reading is *work*, but it gives us back much more than it asks.

Misreading

You're sitting on the bus or subway and someone in front of you is holding the latest newspaper with part of the headline obscured. You may be able to fill in the missing part quickly, or you may remain tantalized, needing the missing letters to complete the message.

RAPE IS

NO SIN

becomes

GRAPE IS KING AT

VINO SINGFEST

when the paper is straightened and unfolded.

Much of our reading (indeed much of life) is filling in the blanks. They can be letters in words or words in sentences. We also fill in meaning, tying things together so they form patterns. Sir Frederick Bartlett used complicated stories to test memory. He found that several kinds of changes occurred when the subjects tried to recall the story later.

Omissions
Parts of the story that were hard to understand or which did not fit the reader's expectations were dropped.

Rationalization
New features were added to explain difficult or confusing parts of the story.

Dominant detail
The reader usually selected a key point to "anchor" the story.

Transformation of detail
Unfamiliar words and concepts were changed to more familiar words or concepts.

Transformation of order
The order was changed. This happened more often with material that was a series of random descriptions than with a tightly organized narrative.

Importance of the subject's attitude
Readers tend to recall their attitude towards a story before they recalled the story. The recall of the story then tended to be a justification of that attitude.

So what we read, like what we hear and see, is subject to misremembering. Let's explore some ways to remember more and remember it better.

The Patterns

Listed below are five main structures for non-fiction: problem, opinion, thesis, information, and instruction. A few pieces of non-fiction are combinations of two or more of these structures, but most of what you read falls into one of these structures.

The Problem Pattern
Problem: I need more money.
Effect: outgoings exceed income. Bankruptcy is imminent.
Causes: unemployment.
Solution: find a job, steal, join the army, shoot my rich uncle.

The Opinion Pattern
Opinion: the next president should be a woman.
Reasons: women are better business managers, less likely to start wars, and have more compassion for people.
Significance: you should support a woman candidate.

The Thesis Pattern
Thesis: alcoholism is caused by a metabolic difference.
Proofs: results of recent experiments.
Significance: testing blood samples from children might prevent alcoholism in adults.

The Information Pattern
Facet 1: location and description of Easter Island.
Facet 2: discovery by early explorers.
Facet 3: current inhabitants.
Facet 4: etc. . . .

The Instruction Pattern
Step 1: place egg in saucepan of cold water.
Step 2: place saucepan on stove.
Step 3: turn burner on to medium heat.
Step 4: etc. . . .

A Need to Know

When you want to remember what you read, but you haven't decided exactly what you'd like to get from your reading effort, try analysing the structure or organization of the piece. Unless you have a particular purpose or a "need to know," it's easy to fall into your old habit of just passing your eyes from left to right over each word or phrase. Then you end up with a random collection of miscellaneous ideas. This can be very pleasant if you are reading for pleasure only, but when you are reading to remember, you need to sort the information into structures.

Buckminster Fuller said that only 20 percent of a book can consist of new ideas, or the book won't be popular. We need that familiar 80 percent as our structure or framework for positioning the new 20 percent. The trick is to be aware of what you don't know and then use your natural predicting skills and your new knowledge of non-fiction structure to dive in for the new 20 percent.

Start reading with a purpose. It's OK to be tantalized into side-trips if you wish, and you can change your destination along the way, but at least you start out with an itinerary. Having a purpose increases your memory of what you are reading.

Distraction is the enemy of memory. When you look for the organization and the pattern parts, it's like taking an X ray or looking at a map. Have you ever found your mind wandering when you were lost and examining a road map? It's unlikely. You had a purpose (figuring out where you were) and a structure (a map full of streets, highways, and landmarks). Reading to remember requires the same two things. The structure has an added bonus: by organizing the material you read into the non-fiction pattern, you *pay attention* to it and probably remember it better.

Is all information arranged logically? Of course not! There are miserable writers, misguided editors, and inept publishers. If you run into any of these, you may have to rewrite the information in your own head in order to remember it.

Try This...

to Test Your Memory of What You Read

If remembering what you read is important to you, you might like to take the following quizzes on material in this book.

The Problem Pattern
Reread chapter 2, "Emotional Blocks," looking for the problem, effects, causes, and solutions. Then fill in these sentences.

The problem is _____ .

Some effects are _____ .

Some causes are _____ .

Some solutions are _____ .

The Opinion Pattern
    Reread chapter 5, "When It's OK to Forget," looking for the opinion, reasons, and significance. Then fill in these sentences.

The opinion is _____ .

The reasons are _____ .
(list supports for each reason if you wish.)

The significance is _____ .

The Thesis Pattern
    We don't have a classic thesis-pattern chapter in this book, but you can learn how to look for working hypotheses by spotting the theories in chapter 7, "How the Brain Remembers." Skim this chapter, looking for the four current theories on how the brain stores information. Now list the theories on how the brain remembers.

The Information Pattern
    Turn to chapter 11, "Four Ways to Remember." Get a pencil and read through the chapter fairly quickly, making a pencil slash wherever the facet (the subject being discussed) changes. Then go back and write a heading for each facet, describing the contents. Compare them to the answers.

The Instruction Pattern
    Turn ahead and read chapter 20, "How to Remember Names and Faces," stopping on page 213. Then list the five steps to remembering names.

Answers

The Problem Pattern – chapter 2, "Emotional Blocks."
Problem: Emotions can block memory. (Memory blocks can be a casual annoyance, a major inconvenience, or a life-threatening disaster.)

Effects:

    People "go blank."

    Negative feelings about self: frustration, embarrassment, disappointment, guilt.

    Blocks threaten job, personal relationships.

        Also:

- Gisela couldn't remember men's names at work.
- Mary couldn't remember lyrics of songs.
- Louise couldn't remember first names.
- Dan couldn't remember police station phone number.
- Barbara couldn't remember addresses and phone numbers.
- Rose could not remember how to read.
- Leslie misplaced things.

Causes: caring, conflict, self-protection.

Solutions:

    Discard blocks because you don't need them anymore.

    Develop new strategies for dealing with them.

    Accept block.

The Opinion Pattern – Chapter 5, "When It's OK to Forget."
Opinion: It's OK to forget some things.

Reasons:

    Forgetting can be safer (forgetting for self-preservation) – protecting ourselves from danger.

- Doctor forgot to return call to avoid disturbed patient.
- Student forgot to file crucial forms and avoided being accepted at law school.
- Woman forgot husband's death to concentrate on baby.

    Forgetting painful experiences – enables us to function despite pain.

- Toddlers forget bumps and learn to walk.
- Women forget pain of childbirth and have another child.

Forgetting sorrow—enables us to survive tragedy.

Forgetting for attention and support—gets us needed help.

> • Harry got attention at office by not shaving.

> • Eunice got help of children by forgetting insurance.

Forgetting because you are finished.

Significance:
Forgetting can be healthful.
• It's OK to forget – when you have to . . .
when you need to . . .
when you want to . . .
as long as it doesn't hurt you.

Also:
Negative memories can be used for humor, future income, and to reinforce positive future actions.

Healthy people can choose their memories.

Healthy people can "rehearse" positive mental images to replace negative ones.

The Thesis Pattern—chapter 7, "How the Brain Remembers."

Theories on how we remember

1. *Holographic theory*—memory occurs in all parts of the brain simultaneously.

2. *Mechanical theory*—information is stored physically on neurons.

3. *Electrical theory*—information is transmitted by electrical signals.

4. *Chemical theory*—information changes the chemical structure of the neurons.

The Information Pattern—chapter 11, "Four Ways to Remember."
Facet 1:   paragraph 1   Introduction

Facet 2:	paragraphs 2–3	Differences between epi-sodic and semantic memory
Facet 3:	paragraphs 4–8	Episodic memory
Facet 4:	paragraphs 9–22	Semantic memory
Facet 5:	paragraph 23	History of skill and fact memory
Facet 6:	paragraphs 24–26	Evidence of skill and fact division
Facet 7:	paragraphs 27–30	Current research on skill and fact division
Facet 8:	paragraphs 31–37	Role of hippocampus in skill and fact memory
Facet 9:	paragraph 38	Importance of research into memory

The Instruction Pattern — Chapter 20, "How to Remember Names and Faces."
How to remember names.

1. Decide to remember.

2. Be impressed before you hear the name.

3. Listen to the name, then match the name to your impression.

4. Repeat the name.

5. Lock the name to the face.

Also: Make a survival kit of things to say when you can't remember immediately.

19
How to Remember What You Hear

Remembering what you hear requires the same structuring tools you use to remember what you read, with one important exception — what is said is not always what is meant.

When we "listen," we interpret more than just the words we hear. We hear the tone of voice, see the body posture and facial expressions (unless we are on the telephone), get subtle or not-so-subtle inferences from the context and atmosphere.

For instance, here is what was *said*. What do you think was *meant*?

- "Oh, I couldn't possibly have any dessert. I'm on a diet."

- "I'm sure you have much better things to do than waste an evening playing draughts with your old grandpa."

- "Of course, if you want to have an affair with your secretary, go right ahead. We don't *own* each other . . ."

Did you "hear" anything in those statements that wasn't actually stated? Rightly or wrongly, we often hear things that aren't said. Criticism is an especially delicate area. A child who is criticized in moderate tones may respond, "Don't shout at me!" "My boss really yelled at me," is another commonly heard phrase, although the boss may have spoken softly.

As in reading, you often hear what you expect to hear or want to hear. A carefully phrased refusal may leave a lover or job applicant still hopeful if he chooses to overlook the negative whole for the positive tone.

Understanding what you hear is the first step in remembering it. This may be a skill you were born with. Just as some people most clearly understand and remember things they see, others need to hear it before it is locked in their memory. A good example of this was the experience of Stella, the head of the publications department of a major company. She found that much of her day was spent on the phone, *reading* portions of the company's *Manual of Procedures* to puzzled employees. It wasn't that the written description wasn't clear. These employees simply didn't understand the information until they *heard* it.

Fortunately, most of us absorb information both visually and aurally and can use one to reinforce the other. Students who take notes while listening to a lecturer are doing this and so are the people who read important instructions out loud to themselves. They are hearing and seeing the information at the same time.

Speed Listening

Processing the information we hear presents the same problems as processing the information we read, only more so. No one can talk as fast as we can listen, even those salesmen on television. The split second left over after we have absorbed one word and are waiting for the next gives us lots of time for mind wandering. Probably you have been at a lecture or at church or a meeting and found that your mind "took off" from something that was said. You miss several minutes of the speaker's comments while you mentally elaborate on or rebut an earlier remark.

Sometimes this can be very valuable—your conclusions outshine the speaker's and give you a new insight into the problem. But if you really need to hear what is *said*, you can set up a system to keep you anchored during the spaces between words.

- Predict what the speaker will say next.

- Confirm that prediction.

- Note your success or failure on a mental tote board. Fill in the listening gaps with this activity. *Don't* let your mind drift off into wondering why your prediction "failed," or you're back where you started.

Recently a process has been developed that will permit speed-recording for the blind. In the past, blind people have had access to magazines and newspapers through recordings. This is a slow, tedious method — imagine reading every word of your morning paper. But now it is possible to clip milliseconds out of a tape, speeding up the voice without raising it to a Minnie Mouse pitch. This is indeed speed listening and may find many uses among sighted listeners also.

Mishearing

I estimate that about 40 percent of spoken communication is either not heard or misheard. This may be a low guess. The wonder is that the other 60 percent gets through.

An incredible amount of talk is just friendly noise, a sort of social glue acknowledging that other people are present and letting them know you are there too. "How are you doing?" "Have a nice weekend." "Lovely weather." "Boy, are these buses slow." Much of what you hear is unimportant, uninteresting, or unrelated to you.

The chances of mishearing in English are great. We have homonyms: tide/tied, die/dye, plane/plain. We have poor pronunciation: use/youse, go on/gone, grandma/grammar. Simple words have multiple meanings: bill, check, let. Poor grammar can sabotage meaning. Here are three real examples:

- Our tuxedos are cut ridiculously.
- Police kill six coyotes after mauling girl.
- Shoes are required to eat in the dining room.

Analysing What You Hear

Remember the people who were shown a film of two cars running into each other (page 21)? Half were asked, "How fast were the cars going when they *contacted* each other?" The other half were asked, "How fast were the cars going when they *smashed* into each other?" Guess which group thought the cars were going the fastest?

What we hear can easily be colored by the emotions of the moment, by the skills of the speaker, by the power of the words themselves. Shakespeare was good at writing crowd-motivating speeches. Think of Mark Anthony in *Julius Caesar* who turns all Rome against the hero Brutus with a few sentences. Or the incredible St. Crispian speech in *Henry V* that changes Henry's dispirited rag-tag troops into invincible warriors. John F. Kennedy is said to have quoted this speech to his advisors during the Cuban missile crisis when the world seemed a hair's breadth away from nuclear destruction.

Listening to Silence

Neurologist Richard M. Restak tells of a professor leaving a faculty meeting. He remarked to several of his colleagues that the matter they had discussed was certain to be approved. "Why do you say that?" one of them asked. The professor listed the distinguished speakers who had spoken in favor of the proposal. "Yes," replied the other, "but the meeting arrived at the opposite conclusion, and the motion was defeated. You heard the words spoken, but you didn't understand the silences between them."

Giving Directions

Psychologist Douglas Kingsbury stopped people on the street and asked them how to get to a nearby place. He found that when he dressed and acted like a "local" the instructions were brief but adequate. When he assumed the air of an out-of-towner, people gave much longer, more detailed instructions. He concluded that we base our communication on how we perceive the knowledge and background of the listener. A cook who seems experienced will be told, "Sauté the chicken." An obvious novice will be told: "Get out a heavy iron frying pan and put it on the stove. Turn on the burner. When the pan is hot, put in some butter or lard . . ."

When Everyone Talks at Once

Everybody is excited and everybody starts talking at once. Since no one responds to what you have said (the others are too busy talking), you repeat yourself . . . only louder. The result is bedlam and wasted time.

Sound familiar? Try this trick. Create a diversion to provide a moment of silence—drop something or sprawl full-length on the floor—then say, "Let's take turns, starting with the youngest." While everyone tries to figure that out, order is restored, and a one-at-a-time approach allows each speaker to feel *heard*. Constant repetition in a conversation usually means that the speaker doesn't feel he has made his point, that he is not being listened to. You can save lots of precious time by *listening*.

Inadmissible Evidence

Ear-witness testimony may be more suspect than previously supposed, according to one study by University of Florida anthropologists. They found that most people can't remember with whom they talked the previous week. People were able to estimate correctly how many conversations they had had, but half the time they couldn't remember with whom they spoke. This indicates that courtroom reconstructions of conversations may be less than accurate.

Structuring What You Hear

Structuring what you hear is similar to structuring what you read, only harder because the most organized person rarely speaks in a straight line from A to B. Speech is a "hot" medium, easily deflected by the response of the listener and the rushing thoughts of the speaker. "I don't know what I'm going to say, until I hear myself say it," said American semanticist Wendell Johnson in his book *People in Quandries: The Semantics of Personal Adjustment* (Harper & Row, 1946). And sometimes, even then, neither the speaker nor the listener knows what was said.

Try This...

to Sharpen Your Listening Memory

Let's do some exercises to structure what is being said. Have someone read the following passages aloud to you and try to arrange the information logically, just as you did in reading.

Your wife says:

We have a lot to do before the party tonight. I don't know if we have enough glasses. Could you call your brother, George, and ask him to bring ice when he comes if he's coming before 7:00. If he won't get here until later, ask Harriet to pick it up on her way home from work. The tablecloths are still in the dryer, and the folding chairs have to be brought up from the basement. I suppose George can do that if he comes early. I don't know if we have enough glasses. I better go get those tablecloths out of the dryer before they get wrinkled. Do you think your brother and Harriet will hit it off?

You just got a lot of extraneous information. Your goals here are to decide what you were being asked to do and arrange them in proper sequence.

Here's what you should have "heard."

Call George and see if he is coming before 7:00 P.M.

If yes: (a) ask him to bring ice; (b) tell your wife he will be early, so he will bring the ice and can help carry the chairs up from the basement.

If no: (a) call Harriet and ask her to buy ice on her way home from work; (b) tell your wife that Harriet is bringing the ice, and you will have to carry the chairs up from the basement.

Optional: count the glasses.

That was a typical family situation. Now try one that you may have run into in your business life. Your boss, Mr. Fickle, also likes to "think out loud."

Mr. Fickle says:

I need some cigarettes from the newsagents downstairs. Get me a pack of Camel Lights and charge it to my wife's account. Try to get Steve to take care of you because the older guy may give you a hard time. Before you go down, take this report to Mr. Samson on the 13th floor in the annex and give it to his secretary. If she's not there, get somebody to sign for it. Last month some jerk lost the report and I got my ear bent. Make two Xeroxes of it just to be safe. One of those copies has to go to headquarters today, so drop it off at shipping, but tell them to send it second class. Mr. Samson says we're spending too much on postage, so if it takes longer to get there, that's his sweet problem. Do you think something's wrong in his department? He's been crabby as the devil lately.

This was a hard one, but typical of many busy offices. Most of what was said was instructions, spoken and implied, but it certainly wasn't in order. You might even have had to grab a pencil and write down what was wanted to be sure you got it all.

Here's what you were being asked to do.

1. Address an envelope to headquarters (implied).

2. Make two photocopies of the report. Place one copy in the envelope you just addressed.

3. Deliver the original report to Mr. Samson's secretary on the 13th floor in the annex. If she is not there, leave the report with someone else and get a signed receipt.

4. Deliver the "headquarters" envelope containing the photocopied report to shipping and ask them to send it second class.

5. Buy a pack of Camel Lights at the drugstore and charge them to Mrs. Fickle's account. Try to be waited on by the younger assistant.

6. File the second photocopy of the report as a backup, in case one of the other copies is lost (implied).

Remember that the skills acquired in the mail room will serve you equally well in the board room. Getting instructions from a teacher, colleague or sales assistant can be tricky. See how much of the following you actually need to remember, and try to organize it into a sequence.

The paint store sales assistant says:

Put the stain on with a soft brush and really rub it in. If you try to put it on too thickly, the surface will dry while the underneath part is still wet. Then you'll get a rippled surface because the hard top skates over the wet bottom. Did I tell you that you have to mix it well before you start? Don't use your best screwdriver. The lighter colors really look good in this finish, but I think the dark color you've chosen will be OK. You have to seal it afterwards with two or three coats of polyurethane varnish, otherwise the rain will soak in and warp the wood. Oh, but you're using it inside, so that's not a problem, but be sure you clean the wood first to free it of dust and dirt.

You had to discard some of the information you got here. If you put the remainder in a working sequence, it should come out like this:

1. Clean the wood first.

2. Stir the stain if necessary.

3. Rub the stain into the wood thoroughly with a soft brush.

4. The sales assistant doesn't like dark stains.

20
How to Remember Names and Faces

What's the worst thing that can happen when you forget a name or a face? In a Hollywood thriller it might mean getting shot at sunrise or losing the million dollar inheritance. In real life it is rarely so devastating.

What *is* the worst thing?

- "I might get fired."

- "I lose important business contacts."

- "My employees think I don't care about them."

- "I feel like a nerd."

If someone walked up to you and said, "I'll give you £1,000 if you can remember that my name is Fred Jones," you would probably be able to remember "Fred Jones." First of all, he has made himself memorable. Secondly he has given you a way to enhance yourself personally by remembering him. This what's-in-it-for-me is important, though the reward doesn't have to be monetary or even a social advantage. It can also be the joy of curiosity rewarded.

People who don't remember people may be protecting themselves.

- Some people are trying to avoid overload and may be acting sensibly — "Why remember the 50 people at that party or all my child's classmates when I probably will never encounter them again?"

- Some people may be enjoying a bit of egomania — "I am much too important to bother remembering people."

- Some people may see themselves as helpless to control the comings and goings of those around them. They avoid bereavement by deciding, "I won't miss you if I don't give you a name or a face."

- And for some people all of life is threatening—"The world is full of dark and terrible creatures ready to zap me, so I won't give them any more power over me by allowing them names and faces." (This is a popular device of little kids that can extend into adulthood if we're not careful.)

People who don't remember people should consider whether they still need to protect themselves or whether the method has outlived its usefulness.

People who *remember* people are usually those who retain their sense of wonder. Once my friend's three-year-old daughter opened the door and stared in astonishment at the visitor on the porch. "Oh, mummy," she cried, "come see how much makeup the lady's wearing!" When the child in us is struck with the novelty of those we meet, we can approach each new person with the same enthusiasm and perceptiveness.

Sharing a Common Weakness

People rarely disclose their true shortcomings to other people. Instead they expose their subtle vices, assuming that the perceptive listener will see them as the virtues they are.

- "I have such a weakness for emeralds."

- "I guess I'm hard to work for—I'm such a perfectionist."

- "I have a terrible memory for names."

In fact, when someone says, "I can't remember names (or faces)," he is usually doing something very close to bragging. He may think he is establishing a sense of camaraderie by showing he shares a common weakness. He is also warning you in advance that he is not responsible for remembering you or anyone else he meets.

Do we have a choice about forgetting or remembering people? Yes. Here are two sets of "How To's" for you to choose from.

How to Forget People
When You're Introduced

Be preoccupied — worry about what they think of you.
Be distracted — think about what you will say.

How to Remember People
When You're Introduced

Decide to remember. How many names and faces have you forgotten when you really made an effort?

Be impressed . . . before you hear the name. Use the first three seconds to notice a person's characteristics. Pick something positive or negative. Look with the eyes of a child. You can change your mind later if you want.

What if the person has no outstanding characteristics, is mousy and almost invisible? Then play "knock, knock, who's there." Make up a story to dramatize the person in your mind. "She works for the CIA" or "He's really a male stripper" or "Where's the last place in the world I'd expect to meet this person?"

Exercise: talk to someone you plan *not* to remember and, as you remain passive, be aware of what is passing through your mind when you *don't* focus on the name. This awareness will help you to be in charge of forgetting or remembering, two very different behaviors.

Listen to the name. Then ask yourself if this name matches your initial impression. It doesn't matter if your answer is yes or no. The point is you've made a decision that will affect your memory. Have you met a beautiful girl named Euphemia? A straightforward young man named Marmaduke? A man named Carol or a girl named Sydney?

"CYNTHIA"   "BERTHA"   "MARMADUKE"   "SPIKE"

Ask yourself if the name matches your initial impression.

We tend to define the aptness of names by people we know. Sheilas should look a certain way. Unless you decide *why* this Sheila is different, you may forget her because she doesn't match your template.

Memory lecturer Hermine Hilton suggests that we categorize names as we meet new people. The energy spent mentally filing a name under one or more of various headings helps us retrieve it later. She recommends the following categories:

- The same as someone I know?
- The same as a celebrity?
- An occupation (Singer, Shoemaker, Smith)?
- A thing (Cane, Woods, Car)?
- A brand name (Campbell, Kellogg, Ford)?
- Can you rhyme it?
- Can you convert it to a familiar word or words (Askew to ask-you)?
- Can you make a euphonious description (Jovial Jones, Smiling Smith)?
- Can you translate it (Morgenstern is morning star)?

Perhaps you can devise your own system for categorizing names that will make them memorable to you.

Repeat the name. Is it Dan or Don? Joan or Joann? When meeting a lot of people at once, slow down and try to lock on each one. Ask a question. "John? How do you spell your last name? Are you from New York, too?" Say your name so they can get an auditory image of you. Shake hands. Maybe that's one reason why shaking hands has stayed in fashion. It's an excellent slowing-down process and can work as a kinesthetic reinforcement.

It's also very flattering to turn to someone you've been chatting with for a few minutes at a party and say, "Tell me your name again." This helps you and lets them know you are interested in them.

Lock the name to the face. As the song from the musical *Gypsy* says, "Ya gotta have a gimmick." Her name is Joan. Imagine her on a horse as Joan of Arc. Does the name translate into another language? Boulanger—the baker? Verdi—green? Schwartz—black? Can you use that to remember them? Mr. Boulanger has French bread for ears. Miss Verdi is eating great strings of green Italian pasta. Mr. Schwartz has blond hair, so he belies his name—imagine black dye pouring over his handsome hair as he looks distressed. Pick an image — silly, bizarre, even obscene. Here's a typical workshop group.

Peggy Lindsay
Linseed oil? Imagine oil poured over her peg-like head. One student imagines Lindsay Water Softener — she's soft and cuddly. Or you might summon up images of former New York mayor John Lindsay or the bionic woman, actress Lindsay Wagner. Peggy's freckles might remind you of a pegboard. How about "Piggy?" Do her mannerisms suggest the bravura style of Miss Piggy, or is she shy and modest?

Nancy Smith
"Antsy?" Are ants crawling all over her face? Smith — imagine two horseshoes around her eyes. Or she has muscles like Longfellow's Village Smithy who stood under the spreading chestnut tree.

Al Fredericks
A free derrick? Alley for "Al?" Make a mental bowling alley out of his nose. Alexander the Great and Frederick the Great? A great guy, Al!

Giles Langlois
Foreign names can be hard because we have no preconceived notions. Here's where reading *The Three Musketeers* proves helpful. If you aren't a Dumas buff, try rhyming Giles with heel and Langlois with Bang-Wah. Imagine him hopping about in pain after banging his heel.

The more far-fetched the images, the more likely you are to remember them, but try to be specific. There may come a day when you call Mr. Lambreth "Mr. Ramsbottom."

Ask if you don't remember. Sometimes we forget names when we run into someone because we are so anxious to remember them that we panic. Try saying, "Where did we meet last time?" or, "How long has it been?" which gives you a few extra seconds and may furnish the clue you need. Or say, "I know we've met and I am not remembering your name . . ." Or, "We've had such good conversations, but your name has slipped right out of my head."

Memorable Names

A lovely red-haired woman waited on me in a New York store. I overheard her name as "Bridgit O'Keary" and complimented her on her "fine Irish name." "Actually my last name is 'Okuri,'" she replied. "My husband is Japanese." That's a name I've never forgotten.

Names that mix nationalities can be memorable. The Nanette Kennedy Laundry used to be a source of amusement to my friends ... until Jacqueline Kennedy graced the White House. Ming Toy Epstein, Boris Lopez, or Sean Giacometti would be hard to forget. As the global village becomes smaller, such international mixings will be more common, but right now such names are pure gold for name-remembers.

"Naughty" Names

Some people have memorable names through no fault of their own. People named "Gay," "Pratt," "Knocker," or "Tush" face unfair snickers because their very proper names have at one time or another been appropriated as slang words.

A friend of mine grew up in the state of Washington where few people knew Yiddish. When he went away to college in New York, he was astonished that his name was greeted with laughter when a professor called the roster. He didn't know that *Putz,* literally "clean" in German, had quite a different slang meaning in Yiddish. In fact, a Yiddish dictionary warned that, "*putz* is worse than *schmuck,* and should not be used by anyone unfamiliar with the martial arts."

Sometimes it's pronunciation, not translation, that gets giggles. Fine names like Lipschitz, Pissi, and Foq have unfortunate connotations in English.

During World War II, I went to school with a boy named Adolph. It was a fine family name, but the poor boy was teased mercilessly by his classmates who constantly gave him the Nazi salute. He was wild and unruly and did poorly in school until his parents changed his name to Franklin. Obviously names are very powerful stuff, one of the most intimate things we possess, and we can use that power to remember other people's names.

How to Remember Faces

Have you ever murmured, "Nice to have met you" to someone you encounter with a friend and found out later you had met him many times before? He had just never made an impression on you, or you didn't recognize him when you ran into him away from his usual setting. If you plead that you lack a strong visual memory, then the trick is to convert what you see at the moment into verbal information. Try pinpointing physical characteristics, not necessarily flattering ones, and locking them to the names. Warning: weight, beards, and hairstyles (even hair color) are all subject to sudden changes. Use them, but back them up with the shape of the eyes, nose, mouth, ears, and hairline.

Overall impression seems to be more important in recognizing faces than any particular feature. Notice—

- physical characteristics

- posture and attitude

- mannerisms

Most portraits show a three-quarter view of the face, giving the best impression of the relationship of the different features. Front and profile views are dramatic, but less informative. (This may be one reason that those Police mug shots rarely look like anyone we know.)

Most people would have trouble identifying a friend or a well-known person from just their eyes, ears, or nose unless that feature were outstanding and unique—Barbra Streisand's nose or Joan Crawford's eyes, for instance. But used as part of a bigger framework, they can be valuable clues to recall.

Start with the eyes. Are they round like an owl's? Perhaps they are triangular or oval. Do the brows slant, arch, march straight across? Now that you've noticed (half the work), try making up silly shorthand names for the characteristics, names that will stick in your memory. Repeat this with other features. Then lock them to the name. Let's try it with our original workshop group.

Peggy Lindsay

Linseed oil pouring over a peg-like head. The peg is a round one in a square hole because her eyes are round, and her jaw is square. The oil is golden like her eyes. It will pour off quickly because her eyebrows slant down at the sides.

Nancy Smith

Ants are crawling on her face which has two horseshoes around her eyes. The ants will be especially attracted to her mouth which is tiny and sweet like a gumdrop. The horses will want to drink from her lake-blue eyes and graze in the thick lashes surrounding them.

215

Al Fredericks
His nose is a bowling alley owned by an Italian because it is a Roman nose. His chin is a free derrick, his square jaw the shovel. Bulging tendons run up his neck to manipulate the derrick. The alley continues over his high forehead to his receding hairline, where— strike!—he sports a toupee.

Giles Langlois
He is hopping about from pain in his heel (heel bang-wah!), and his eyes are squinty with pain. His nose is a bulging one like a sore heel, and his ears have shrunk to a small size, so they won't hear his shouting.

All of the above is utter nonsense, of course, and much of it may be totally useless to you. The point is that you will make your own images, meaningful to you, and the effort you put into it will probably lock that person in your mind for good. You may even decide that all the tricks are too cumbersome, and it is easier just to remember.

How Well Do You Remember?

Some people say, "Oh, I never forget a face," or "I can never remember names." While most people are relatively good at predicting how successfully they will remember different items on a list, few people are accurate judges of their overall memory ability. In England, 100 housewives were asked to rate their memory for faces. Then they were tested with a series of slides. There proved to be no relationship between how well they did and how well they thought they would do.

Memory for faces may depend on a particular system located in the brain. Patients who suffer from prosopagnosia, a rare neurological condition, can't recognize faces, but can recognize other objects. Memory for faces is still being studied. Doctors have found that babies recognize their mothers from a small portion of their total face. Large portions of the mother's face could be masked and the baby would still recognize her, but when the crucial area—containing an eye and cheek area—was covered, the baby would respond as if she were a stranger.

Even newborns can recognize face-shaped designs. Dr. R. Fanz projected two designs on the ceiling over the cribs of infants only hours old. One design resembled a human face. The other contained the same features, rearranged into an abstract pattern. The infants preferred gazing at the face-like design.

Most people have trouble recognizing faces when the face is upside-down. However, patients with right brain damage were tested on ability to recognize faces and buildings, both right side up or upside-down. These patients did poorly on upright faces, compared to the control group, but they could recognize upside-down faces more readily. Both groups did almost equally well with famous buildings.

Divide and Conquer?

One theory is that dividing faces into parts helps us recognize them. In a treatise on painting, Leonardo da Vinci described dividing the face into four parts horizontally for classification. Recently Jacques Penry developed the "Photo-fit System," a set of pictures of noses, chins, ears, etc. He said that study of these parts would improve ability to recognize and remember faces. Students learned how to "read" faces by abstracting and categorizing types of features. But when students who had taken intensive Photo-fit training were tested against a control group by impartial observers, both groups did just as well, except in one photo-recognition test. In that test, the untutored group did *better.* One interpretation of this experiment is that the principle of dividing the face to recognize it is faulty. It's the relationship of the whole that we recognize, not separate parts.

Misnaming

"When I'm in the same house with my wife and sister," said a man in one of my workshops, "I start calling each by the other's name. My sister doesn't mind, but my wife gets mad as hell. Why do I do this?"

"What sort of things are you saying when you mix up their names?" I asked.

"Oh, stuff like, 'When do we eat?' or, 'Have you seen the paper?' Nothing heavy."

"Do you like your sister?"

"Sure."

"And do you like your wife?"

"Yeah!"

Now, it's possible to make a great deal of misnaming people. Pure Freudians might suggest everything from repressed incest to open hostility. But in this case, the answer seemed simpler.

I suggested that he really didn't care which of them he asked, that these were neutral exchanges, and it really didn't matter whether he was talking to his wife or sister. "You chose your wife partially because she had qualities you liked in your sister, mother, and other women you knew as a child. She may even have unpleasant qualities you associated with the other women in your life, but they were faults that you felt 'comfortable' dealing with. It doesn't matter that you mix them up in these neutral social situations. What *does* matter is that it upsets your wife. Your goal is probably to make a 'present' to your wife of never calling her by your sister's name."

I recommended that when he found himself in the company of both women, he pause before addressing either and concentrate on the name. Or if that concentration took too much enjoyment out of the situation, he could always fall back on the Hollywood trick:

Get into the habit of calling them 'dear'

For it not only sounds very sweet,

It helps to avoid the continual fear

Of calling 'Louise' 'Marguerite.'

Children sometimes call mummy "daddy" and vice versa. This is not because the child can't tell the difference, but because both are providers of things wanted. A mother may be crushed when her little darling calls her "Teacher" after returning from school or "Grandma" after a vacation with grandparents, but this is perfectly natural. If, in a moment of passion, a husband calls his second wife by his first wife's name, this *may* be significant and is *definitely* dangerous.

Why Fictional Names
Are Unforgettable

The names of fictional characters can stick in our memories better than the names of real people. This is because we may have few associations with the real people—we don't really "know" them well—while the fictional characters have rich personalities and, frequently, deliberately memorable names. Most people would recognize the names of Romeo and Juliet, Simple Simon, Camille, Captain Pugwash, Dr. Frankenstein, Heidi, King Kong, Mary Poppins, and Dougal.

Consider the colorful characters of Dickens: Ebenezer Scrooge, Uriah Heep, Mr. Bumble, Mr. Pickwick and Mr. Fezziwig, Tiny Tim and Little Nell. Or Tennessee Williams's way with names: Mrs. Wire, Stanley Kowalski, Amanda Wingfield, Alexandra Del Lago, Chance Wayne, and Heavenly Finley. The names stand out before we learn anything about the characters, and when we have added something about their physical appearance and character, they are locked in our brains.

Stage Names

Actors need memorable names. (Rosemary Clooney said she knew she had become famous when people began accusing her of changing her name—"*Who* would change [her] name to 'Rosemary Clooney'?") In the old days, many proudly used their own unusual names and endowed them with the magic of their personalities—Humphrey Bogart, Francis X. Bushman, Una Merkel, and Ida Lupino, for example. Others, rightly or wrongly, opted for name changes. Several used their middle names. Just plain Bill Gable became Clark; Eldred Peck became Gregory. Their new names were probably easier to remember. Then there were the manufactured names: Rock Hudson (Roy Scherer), Tab Hunter (Arthur Gelien), and Troy Donahue (Merle Johnson.)

We can regret the loss of the highly memorable and colorful names of Eunice Quedens, Archie Leach, Joe Yule, and Tula Ellice Finklea. These sprightly monikers were tamed to the bland (Eve Arden, Cary Grant), the cute (Mickey Rooney), and the exotic (Cyd Charisse). Today there is a simultaneous resurgence of "real names" (Meryl Streep, Tovah Feldshuh, Dustin Hoffman) and conjured ones (Engelbert Humperdink, Sid Vicious, Alice Cooper). The purpose of a performer's name, whenever it was acquired, is to make him unforgettable and to reinforce his public image. Maybe if we could choose our own names upon reaching our majority (as is done in some cultures) so that they reflected our adult selves, names would be much harder to forget.

Strategies for Coping
with Memory Lapses

The mayor of a large university town was well known to most of the residents, but there was almost no way he could have remembered the 40,000 or so people who "knew" *him.* However, he developed a useful technique for the times he appeared in public. When someone approached him with a smile of recognition, he would peer at them over his glasses and then extend his hand—"Well, *hello* there, I didn't recognize you for a moment. How have you been?" This got him over the first moments of the encounter and probably got him some votes besides.

One doctor has practiced for 30 years, training thousands of students. When they come up to him to say hello, he usually says jovially, "Well, who the hell are you anyway?" His wife is less flamboyant. She says, "I remember you very well, but your name has slipped my mind."

Give yourself permission to say one of the above. (I recommend the latter.) Otherwise, you're playing "let's pretend"—"let's pretend I can remember the name of everyone I've ever met."

Make up a survival kit of things to tell yourself and to tell other people. Suffering is optional when it comes to remembering names. Taking good care of yourself and keeping a sense of humor are the important things.

The people who are going to think that you're a creep for not remembering their names are probably not the kind of people you want in your life anyway. Who do you have fun with? Usually people with high nurturing and low critical attitudes.

Some of us are in the habit of harassing ourselves. We may have been brought up by very critical parents who wanted us to be perfect. Perfection comes in handy when you are flying a plane or building a nuclear reactor, but it is a nuisance most of the time. People who had a "do your best" upbringing seem to remember better than those who were told they had to be perfect.

New Strategies for Remembering People

You're so shy that you want to drop through the floor when someone says "hello." Or you're so involved in your own thoughts that you're rarely aware of the people around you. If you're not interested in people or if you're basically shy and feel you need to protect yourself from confrontation, involvement, or unwelcome requests, you won't remember the people you see. This can be valuable when striding down a crowded city street. Not noticing leaves your mind free to think of other things. But not noticing can become a bad habit that haunts you when it would be better to notice.

Here's a way to start noticing again. Begin a writer's notebook, real or imaginary, to write down characteristics of strangers for a novel you will write some day. Note quirks—bitten fingernails on a beautiful woman; dangling earlobes on a jogger; chipped front teeth, indicating perhaps a seamstress who bites her thread; an elegantly dressed man with raw, red, workman's hands or a laborer with soft, white hands unaccustomed to work; an old woman who walks like a ballet dancer; a teenager who alternately swaggers and scurries like a scared rabbit. Make up stories about total strangers on the street, across the aisle on the bus, or ahead of you in line at the bank. Once you can do this with strangers, try it with someone you want to remember.

Your Last Option

You have one last option: choose *not* to be embarrassed when you forget. Feeling mortified or guilty or stupid is a choice. If you choose to be comfortable despite your lapse, you will have a much greater chance of recalling the name or the face.

Survival Kit

What to say if the name won't come to you:

"It's been so long. When was the last time we met?"

"I remember you so well . . . your name has slipped my mind."

"I loved your speech at the meeting last month. Tell me your name again."

Introduce an old, but temporarily nameless, friend to a new acquaintance with, "This is Mary Jones," and hope he replies by saying, "Hi, I'm Harvey Smith."

And behaviorist B. F. Skinner proposes a conspiratorial strategy in his book *Enjoy Old Age* (with Margaret Vaughn, Hutchinson, 1984). For this you need a congenial partner (mate, friend, business associate, etc.). When a familiar stranger approaches you at a gathering, shake his or her hand and turn to your partner saying, "Of course you remember . . ." Your partner immediately extends a hand and replies, "Of course! How *are* you?" (If you are the conspiratorial partner, you may be able to fill in by adding the persons's name. If you've never seen the person before, you are free to approach him later alone and say, "Tell me your name again. I didn't want Sam to know it had slipped my mind.")

Try This...

Exercise for Remembering Names and Faces

The Name Game

Here's a game that may tell you something about how and why you remember names. Read over the list below.

Bob Baker	Molly Quinn
Rosanna Calcese	Sue Wong
Lazarus Hennenberg	Mary Foster
Marie DuBois	Horst Egensperger
Juan Lopez	Vincent Yoshihiro
Rose Cohen	Clyde Wyndham
Riordan McIlhenny	Eva Weber
LaTonya Robison	Jackson Davis
Cynthia Petherbridge	Etienne Giradoux
Gino Romano	Imelda Hermosilla

After you've looked them over, close the book and write down as many of the 20 names as you can remember, in any order you wish.

Check your answers, and note the number you got correct.

That was probably very hard. I'll make it a little easier for you. Try the quiz that follows.

Below are the original 20 names combined with 20 new ones. Take your pencil and check off the ones that look familiar.

_____ Lisa Dupree	_____ Joella Vincent
_____ Molly Quinn	_____ Bob Baker
_____ Sid Goldstein	_____ Jim Jordon
_____ Edward Temby	_____ Rosanna Calcese

_____	Sue Wong	_____	Benito Bustamente
_____	Mary Foster	_____	Lazarus Hennenberg
_____	Leticia Long	_____	Fifi d'Orsay
_____	Horst Egensperger	_____	Marie DuBois
_____	Fleyda Vetch	_____	Max Glotzbach
_____	Rhonda Weber	_____	Juan Lopez
_____	Vincent Yoshihiro	_____	Rose Cohen
_____	Clyde Wyndham	_____	Riordan McIlhenny
_____	Maryalice Mayberry	_____	LaTonya Robison
_____	Eva Weber	_____	Pedro Hernandez
_____	Jackson Davis	_____	Jeff Marshall
_____	Gordon Clark	_____	Cynthia Petherbridge
_____	Benjamin Bridges	_____	Gino Romano
_____	Humphrey Doxstater	_____	Jacob Jasinski
_____	Etienne Giradoux	_____	Crystal Clark
_____	Imelda Hermosilla	_____	Edward Taft

Check your answers with the original list, and note the number you got correct.

Was recognition easier than recall? Did you find yourself better able to recognize names of one sex or one ethnic group? Did simpler names seem simpler to remember, or did the unusual ones fix themselves in your mind? These can be valuable clues to your perceptions of others.

So far, you've been trying to remember names in a vacuum. Without the flesh and blood people attached to them, or at least a literary facsimile, it's pretty difficult to form images around the names. Now we're going to give you more information about our cast of characters.

- Bob Baker was your best friend in college. He has red hair and laughs a lot. He lent you £100 when you were broke and refused to let you pay it back. This bothers you, but you can't complain, so you get back at him by addressing your letters to him, Bob "Big Money" Baker.

- Your sister's roommate, Cynthia Petherbridge, has been telling vicious lies about you, and you are not sure why.

- The car that sideswiped you was driven by Gino Romano, a short, fat teenager with no insurance.

- Since Rosanna Calcese's big dinner party, everyone has been trying to get her recipe for chopped liver, but you are the only one she will give it to.

- The famous writer, Lazarus Hennenberg, is lecturing on Thursday.

- Rose Cohen has brown hair.

- When you got home, you found that you had accidentally taken Riordan McIlhenny's briefcase, and he was on a plane for Calcutta with yours at that very moment.

- Molly Quinn has got to be the hottest new TV star of the season. With her baby doll face, red curls, sea-green eyes, and sultry singing voice, she has 70 percent of the nation's viewers glued to their sets on Sunday night. Golly-Molly clubs are springing up all over the country.

- You weren't going to get the big promotion, but Sue Wong, the regional manager, put in a special plug for you. After she talked to several regional managers, the top man changed his mind, and you got the job. You call her true blue Sue.

- Your parking space by the main entrance is always grabbed by Vincent Yoshihiro, the lazy slob, so he can sleep late and still get to the coffee machine before your boss gets in.

- You can't stand that Clyde Wyndham. His jokes are terrible, and he laughs like a hyena whenever he tells one. Oh, oh . . . here he comes now. You duck out.

- Did you hear that Mary Foster is expecting triplets? She and her husband tried to have a baby for years, and then she went on fertility drugs. Now they're going to have a houseful!

- Our company's financial future hangs on a phone call that will come this morning. Horst Egensperger is calling from Switzerland, and if we can persuade him that the deal is sound, he will approve the contract worth millions of pounds.

- That snooty bank cashier who always wears lavender nail polish, what's her name . . . Eva Weber . . . ever since you took in the change from your piggy bank and asked her to count it, she shuts her window when she sees you coming.

- Jackson Davis is the elevator operator's brother.

- When you go to Paris, Etienne Giradoux and his wife would love to put you up and show you around. They share your interest in art and theatre and speak perfect English.

- Our neighbor, Imelda Hermosilla, accepted delivery of your package of live lobsters, but she's so dizzy, she forgot to give it to us before she left for the weekend. The box sat on her porch for three days and boy, did *she* have a surprise when she got back. The neighborhood kids were chanting "Imelda smelda!" She was so embarrased.

- Marie DuBois is trying to get you fired.

- One of the scholarship candidates is LaTonya Robison, a law student. LaTonya is an orphan with 11 brothers and sisters. Without the scholarship, LaTonya will have to go to work at a menial job.

- Juan Lopez has offered to buy out our foundering restaurants. We'll make a nice profit, and he'll merge it with his successful Juan's Weenies chain.

Now fill in the blanks.

1. The lady with smelly lobsters on her sunporch is _____ _____ .

2. In Paris, you are invited to stay with _____ .

3. The elevator man's brother is named _____ .

4. Your best friend in college was red-headed _____ .

5. The coveted chopped liver recipe came from _____ .

6. The wimp who nabs your parking place is _____ .

7. The snooty teller with lavender nails who hates pennies is _____ .

8. The woman with brown hair is _____ .

225

9. Your briefcase is on its way to Calcutta with _____ .

10. The regional manager who got you the promotion was _____ .

11. Your sister's lying room-mate is _____ .

12. The famous writer who is lecturing Thursday is _____ .

13. The lady expecting triplets is _____ .

14. The scholarship candidate is _____ .

15. Our restaurants are being bought by _____ .

16. Your car was sideswiped by _____ .

17. The beautiful new TV star is _____ .

18. The man who tells terrible jokes is _____ .

19. The important caller from Switzerland is _____ .

20. The woman who is trying to get you fired is _____ .

Check your answers on the chart below, and circle the letters that follow each correct answer. Then add each vertical column.

	Positive	Negative	Male	Female	Common	Uncommon
1. Imelda Hermosilla		N		F		U
2. Etienne Giradoux	P		M			U
3. Jackson Davis	—	—	M		C	
4. Bob Baker	P		M		C	
5. Rosanna Calcese	P			F		U
6. Vincent Yoshihiro		N	M			U
7. Eva Weber		N		F	C	
8. Rose Cohen	—	—		F	C	
9. Riordan McIlhenny		N	M			U

	Positive	Negative	Male	Female	Common	Uncommon
10. Sue Wong	P			F	C	
11. Cynthia Petherbridge		N		F		U
12. Lazarus Hennenberg	–	–	M			U
13. Mary Foster	P			F	C	
14. LaTonya Robison	–	–		F		U
15. Juan Lopez	P		M		C	
16. Gino Romano		N	M		C	
17. Molly Quinn	P			F	C	
18. Clyde Wyndham		N	M			U
19. Horst Egensperger	P		M			U
20. Marie DuBois		N		F	C	
	of 8 positive	of 8 negative	of 10 male	of 10 female	of 10 common	of 10 uncommon

Did you remember more names with positive or negative associations? More men or women? More common or uncommon names? Notice that four of the names had neutral associations. Did that affect your ability to remember them?

Several of the descriptions repeated the person's name and connected it to something else like a nickname or a business. Did you remember them better? If you did, notice that adding information to a name makes it more memorable.

Of course, these questions are highly subjective. You may regard having triplets as negative rather than positive, or think the name Gino Romano very unusual and hard to remember, rather than common. This small sampling can't give you a true picture of your memory patterns, but it may offer clues that you can follow up on your own.

Chaining Names

Here's a name-chaining game that may make you stretch the way you associate names for recall. The idea comes from a *New York Magazine* competition of several years ago, designed by Mary Ann Madden.

Start by writing down a name—a movie star, politician, historical character, your aunt, anyone—on the top line. Then make an association with another name. Continue making associations until you have chained ten names. Ready for the trick? Your assignment is to make the last name the same as the first, that is, to come full circle.

Here's a sample list:

1. Richard Nixon
2. John Mitchell
3. Margaret Mitchell
4. Scarlett O'Hara
5. Red Buttons

6. Santa Claus
7. Monty Woolley
8. Cybil Shepard
9. Richard Crooks
10. Richard Nixon

Do you see the connections between each descending pair of names? If they are too obscure, here is a rundown. Richard Nixon was President and his Attorney General was John Mitchell. John Mitchell and Margaret Mitchell share the same last name. Margaret Mitchell created the literary heroine, Scarlett O'Hara. Scarlet is a shade of red, so Red Buttons. Red Buttons would be found on the clothing of Santa Claus. Santa Claus has a white beard and so did Monty Woolley. Woolly sheep might be guarded by a Shepard. Shepherds carry hooked sticks called Crooks. Richard Crooks, the tenor, shares the same first name with Richard Nixon who, to avoid confusion, proclaimed, "I am not a crook."

Want to try? Make up some ten-line game sheets. While you have fun, notice the association tricks you use. How could these tricks help you remember the people you meet?

21
How to Remember Dates and Numbers

You may think that you simply can't remember numbers, that they have no emotional trappings to help you recall them, but that's not true. Read the story below and see how much you understand.

> 007, dressed to the 9s, sauntered off the 747. He yearned to spend the evening at 90 with a 36-26-36, but recalled the 86 he had experienced on his last visit. Instead, he hopped in his 5 and drove to a 8 til late where he bought a 19 and some 1001. Dropping them in his flight bag next to his .44, he drove off to see 2001 for the 10th time.

For those who need a translation: special agent James Bond, superbly dressed, sauntered of the airplane. He yearned to spend the evening at an expensive Park Lane restaurant with a shapely woman, but recalled that he had been thrown out on his last visit. Instead he hopped in his car and drove to a convenience store where he purchased a teen fashion magazine and some carpet cleaner, put them in his bag alongside his gun, and went to see a movie.

Now James Bond would *never* have done some of the things described above. Also some trademarked numbers are spelled out in their regular form (i.e., Ninety Park Lane), but I wanted you to see how much personality plain numbers can have.

Using Your Life as a Calendar

Many people date recent happenings by where they were living or working at the time. Women with several children frequently date an event by recalling which child they were pregnant with. It is a rare individual who can't tell you where he or she was when Pearl Harbor was bombed or when President Kennedy or John Lennon were shot.

These dates are signposts in our lives. Like the numbers on a clock, they give us markers so we can figure out the time in between. In the larger context of history, most people can identify key dates: A.D. 33, 1066, 1492, 1776, 1929, the Fourth of July, *Cinco de Mayo,* the Ides of March.

The Easiest Way to Remember

How do you remember a specific date? Your mother-in-law's birthday or an important meeting? The simplest way is to write it down and then acquire the habit of checking your calendar weekly or daily or hourly.

But what if you need to remember dates or numbers for business purposes or an exam? Students have to process and play back an incredible array of numbers to satisfy their teachers. Lawyers need to recall case numbers, and salesmen want to know model numbers. Librarians must memorize the Dewey decimal system, and a musician may want to memorize the Koechel listings for all of Mozart's works.

Since most people remember words better than numbers (that's why telephone exchanges used to have letters instead of numbers), you may want to try a memory system that turns numbers into words. We'll tell you about one in a moment.

Reciting and Grouping

Saying numbers aloud seems to give better results than reading them silently to yourself, and grouping digits in clusters greatly improves your ability to remember them. If you think of a number as 386-54-36 or 38-65-436, rather than 3865436 or even 386-5436, you'll remember it better. Indeed, that's how most European phone numbers are written. Our high rate of errors in reproducing phone numbers might be reduced if we divided them that way.

Of course, there *was* a time when phone numbers had *names* instead of prefixes. But British Telecom decided that numbers were better, and now we have to remember anemic 0604 or bland 091 instead.

When Should You Try a Number System?

S, the man with the incredible memory, said that numbers possessed colors, shapes, sounds, and personalities for him. Two, for instance, was a high-spirited woman, rectangular, whitish in color. He could remember long strings of numbers because each was as memorable as an interesting person he had met.

If you also feel that numbers have personalities, work to develop this perception. Forget number conversion systems and give each number a color, shape, size, texture, a musical theme, or a mood. Then strings of apparently arbitrary numbers will become parades of old friends, constantly rearranged into fascinating patterns.

Learning a letter/number conversion system is *hard work*. You should only do it if:

- You see numbers as just so many dreary squiggles — perhaps even slightly threatening in their incomprehensibility — and absolutely can't remember them.

- You have a strong verbal memory and enjoy word games and puzzles.

Otherwise, learning charts of words to replace numbers will just be another baffling, frustrating task that will leave you worse off than when you started.

Most numbers that you use every day — the combination of the office safe, the code that opens your garage door or lets you take cash out of a machine — get locked into your memory pretty quickly. You don't need a system to remember them.

But there are numbers that you only use once in a while that can be invaluable. For instance, being able to come up with the Social Security numbers or insurance policy numbers of every member of your family or the registration number of your car or the numbers of all your bank accounts and credit cards can save you lots of time and aggravation in an emergency. You may have this information written down in a safe place, but having it at the tip of your tongue can be mighty handy in our red-tape society.

This works just like the peg systems described in chapter 15. Let's say that either ketchup or milk is on your shopping list among other items. Depending on numerical position, here are images that would "peg" them for you.

1 = Tea (A Tea cup is poured full of ketchup to everyone's astonishment; a cow is giving milk into an elegant silver pitcher at a formal Tea party.)

2 = N.Y. (Even if you have never been to New York, you probably know something about it. Here, the Empire State Building becomes a giant red ketchup bottle; the Hudson River runs with white milk. You could also use Broadway, the Statue of Liberty, the United Nations, Madison Square Garden, Central Park, etc.)

3 = Ma (Ma is a grey-haired little old lady. She is pouring ketchup into bottles with a funnel and slopping it all over; for milk, a grey-haired lady is shampooing her hair in milk to make it white.)

4 = aiR (Ketchup bottles are floating everywhere in the aiR—you can't *catch up* with them; the aiR is white with milky rain pouring down—try to catch it in milk buckets.)

5 = eeL (A wiggly, squiggly eeL wraps itself around a ketchup bottle—you take off the cap, and more eeLs pop out and slither onto your hotdog; a group of eeLs are laying eggs in a stream—each little egg looks like a milk carton, and you try to scoop them up.)

6 = Bee (The Bees live in a hive shaped like a giant ketchup bottle—they are red and black and red ketchup oozes out of their hive; the milk case at the supermarket is surrounded by circling, buzzing Bees—everyone else is afraid, but you walk through and pick up your milk because the Bees are your friends and have been protecting the last carton until you got there.)

7 = Key   (A ketchup bottle forms the handle of a large Key that you must use to unlock your front door—try not to get the drippy red stuff on your clothes; you turn the Key in your front door, and a wall of white milk gushes out, carrying you along—the Key inflates and helps you keep afloat in the sea of milk.)

8 = Doe   (A Doe is suckling her fawn—her underside is covered with teats that look like ketchup bottles, and Bambi is covered with dripping red ketchup; the milk carton on your breakfast table suddenly sprouts antlers and hooves and begins running around the room.)

9 = Pie   (Ketchup Pie—yuck!—imagine the faces on your guests when you serve it; people are throwing Pies at an old-fashioned milkman— the street and all his bottles are covered with whipped cream Pies.)

10 = ToeS (Your ten little ToeS are covered with ketchup; you try to make shoes out of milk cartons, but your ToeS stick out—you need another milk carton to cover your ToeS.)

Try This...

if You Want to Learn a Number System

Most number systems turn numbers into words by giving each digit, 0 through 9, a consonant equivalent. Then you write down the number you want to remember, using consonants, and fill in with vowels—*a, e, i, o, u, y*—to make words, or you contrive a short sentence using the consonants at the beginning of each word. Words beginning with vowels can be used freely in the sentence method without affecting the number. To show you how this works, let's try an arbitrary list of consonants and see if you can make words or phrases out of them.

Consonants	Write Your Word(s) Here	Possible Answers
L D N S	_____	LouD NoiSe
		LeaDeN Sea
		Lazy Dogs Never Sit
B R M L	_____	BaRe MaLe
		beau BRuMeL
		Banks Rarely Make Love

Some Don't-Panic Number Charts

We are about to turn numbers into words on a systematic scale. Don't be intimidated. You're going to learn a *tool* for memory, not create another massive thing to memorize.

Some number systems use the *sounds* of letters to replace numbers. I think this just adds to the confusion. For instance, in one system, 6 can be represented by *shoe, chair, judge,* or *George,* while the letters *s* and *c* can be used for 0 if they are pronounced as in *soap* and *cipher,* and *c* can also be used for 7 if it is in *cow.* Are you following all this? Probably not.

In this system, a consonant is always exchanged for the same number, no matter how it is pronounced. The purpose of this exchange is to let you make words, sentences, rhymes, or riddles out of numbers that you would otherwise have a hard time remembering. The system assumes that you remember words more easily than you remember numbers.

You don't have to stop in the middle of your conversion to ponder whether *c* is 6 or 7 or 0. In this system, you always exchange the same letter for the same number.

How to Use the System

Here's how you do it. Each number is represented by a consonant.

1. Write down the number you want to remember.

2. Write the letter equivalent underneath.

3. Fill in vowels to make words. Or construct sentences in which each word starts with the number-equivalent letter.

   Use this system or plot your own. (Hint: avoid using extra consonants—ToSs and DoLl, for instance—because later you won't be sure which letters represent numbers and which are "silent.") If you decide to create your own exchange system, notice how the active, physical process of writing out the chart locks your code in your memory.

   In the number/letter conversion system below you *don't* have to memorize a word substitute for every number up to a hundred. (If you could do that, you probably wouldn't need a system!) Instead, you memorize just ten digit/consonant combinations, then form words and sentences as memory hooks.

Examples

Phone number:	381-1470	MaD aT TuRKeyS
Social Security number:	947-25-0028	PaRK iN LooSe SaND
Safe combination:	73-21-1	Key Me iNTo iT

Learn the system as you practise making words out of the key letters.

Numbers	Letters (Fill in a word.)	Possible Words
0	S	Sea, Say, So, iS
1	T	Tea, Tie, aTe, eaT
2	N	N.Y., No, Nee, Nay
3	M	Ma, Moo, May, aM
4	R	aiR, Ray, Rue, Rye
5	L	eeL, aLe, Loo, Lie, Lay
6	B	Bee, Be, aBe, oBoe
7	K	Key, oaK, a.K.a.
8	D	Doe, Do, Day, iD
9	P	Pie, Pea, aPe, Poo

10	T	S	ToeS, iTS, oaTS
11	T	T	ToT, TaT, TooT, iTTy
12	T	N	TaN, TiN, ToN
13	T	M	TaM, TaMe, TiMe
			(etc.)

You are probably asking what you can do with all these clue words. One thing would be to rehearse with a partner so you can amaze your friends at parties with your "mind reading" ability. But you can also use your hard work for more practical applications.

You want to remember the full citation for

Abrahamson v. Fleschner, 648 F.2d 862 (1977).

6	4	8	F.2d	8	6	2	1	9	7	7
B	R	D	FND	D	B	N	T	P	K	K
BiRD			FouND	DuBiN			ToP	Cook		

Fortunately I have a friend named Dubin who is a good cook. (Personalizing your memories helps rivet them.) For this one, I might relate the "flesh" of Fleschner to a succulent roast chicken cooked by my friend. You might prefer an "idea ban" or a "doe bone." Silly? Of course. That's why it takes energy to create and why that energy lets you recall it later.

Try these famous cases on your own.

Plessy v. Ferguson 163 U.S. 537 (1896)

| 1 | 6 | 3 | U | S | 5 | 3 | 7 | 1 | 8 | 9 | 6 |
| T | B | M | U | S | L | M | K | T | D | P | B |

Make some words or sentences here.

_____ ____ _____ _____

_____ ____ _____ _____

Plessy v. *Ferguson* established the "separate but equal" rule for schools and public accommodations in the United States. It took 58 years to reverse this with the *Brown* v. *Board of Education* decision.

Brown v. Board of Education 347 U.S. 483 (1954)

3	4	7		U	S		4	8	3		1	9	5	4
M	R	K		U	S		R	D	M		T	P	L	R

Make some words or sentences here.

———————   ——————   ————————

———————   ——————   ————————

     Let's say you are very anxious to remember pi to the 20th decimal point. Write your letter equivalent under each number below.

3 . 1 4 1 5 8 2 6 5 3 5 8 9 7 9 3 2 3 8 4 6

—.—————————————————————

Now convert your consonants into words by adding vowels. Divide the words anywhere you want.

     Here's how it would work with the standard conversion system, customized to my needs with a 6-b and 8-d combination.

3		1	4	1	5	8	2	6	5	3	5	8	9	7	9	3	2	3	8	4	6
M	.	T	R	T	L	D	N	B	L	M	L	D	P	K	P	M	N	M	D	R	B

This is a toughy, but perhaps you could use the first letter of each word in a verse:

May Tempestuous Roamed The Land
Delighting Naughty British Lords.
May Lured Dukes,
Princes and Kooks.
Presently a Majesty
Noticed May's Diversity:
Royal Board.

Another classic mnemonic for pi is the following:

Pie
I wish I could determine pi.
Eureka cried the great inventor.

Christmas pudding, Christmas pie
Is the problem's very centre.

This gives you pi to the 20th decimal if you count the
number of letters in each word. (As you can see, these
"systems" are a lot of work and only help people who are
great with words and terrible with numbers.)

Coding Dates

Say a student must remember the birthdates of Franklin
Delano Roosevelt, Harry S. Truman, and Dwight D.
Eisenhower. Here's how he does it.

Roosevelt	30 - 1 - 82	M S T D N
		MaST DoNe

Roosevelt – the one,
who got the MaST DoNe

Truman	8 - 5 - 84	D L D R
		DuLl DaRe

Harry was DuLl
but brave enough to DaRe to care.

Eisenhower	14 - 10 - 90	T R T S P S
		TaRT SiPS

Maybe Eisenhower eats his TaRT
between SiPS.

You are about to say that these are pretty bad, and you
are right. The reason they work is that *you* figure them out,
you write them down and *you* read back what you wrote,
actively locking them in your memory three ways.

Write down some dates you want to remember here,
family birthdays or anniversaries.

Event	Date	Letter Code	Word or Sentence
_____	_____	_____	_____
_____	_____	_____	_____

Use What Works

If some of these techniques for remembering numbers seem harder to remember than the numbers themselves, you may find that your poetical ear prefers the repetition of a number sequence until its cadences sing automatically in your memory. If that works for you, that's great. You're a natural number person. The point of these varied suggestions is that you select what works for *you* and forget the rest.

22
How to Rehearse

Rehearsal comes from the Middle English word *rehersen* which means to reharrow or redig the earth. Rehearsing something over and over until you have memorized it is a lot like hoeing a row. It's boring, exhausting, demeaning work, and it frequently results in very welcome fruit.

Memorizing a Script

Professional actors aren't the only people who must memorize scripts. You may also need to know something word for word so you can make proper introductions, do an effective business presentation, act in an amateur stage production, make a TV commercial about your company, or even stage an elaborate effort to persuade your boss to give you a rise. The many things that need memorization – words, stance, tone, gestures, emphasis–can be harder to master than just one component, but once you've meshed them, they reinforce each other.

> Step forwards, pick up the wrench, scratch ear, and say, "The problem with cantaloupes is . . ."

It would be difficult to take a step forwards or encounter a wrench or scratch your ear without going right on to cantaloupes.

Actors use two basic methods to memorize scripts–to "learn their lines." Some memorize all the lines and then explore their meaning in rehearsal. Others prefer to get a sense of the whole script and then memorize the specific words as they work on individual sections.

Actress Julie Harris says she likes to begin with the part fully memorized. "I prefer not to worry about the mechanics of the part when rehearsal starts. This allows me the freedom to concentrate fully on the meaning." She starts by reading the script over two or three times and underlining her part. Then she divides the amount of material she must learn by the number of days she has to do it. Each day she tackles the predetermined chunk, reading five lines and then repeating them and repeating them until they are memorized. She constantly backtracks and reviews material already studied, adding it on to the new chunk.

Christopher Plummer uses the second technique, beginning with the meaning and adding an exact reading of the text later. The great film actor, Paul Muni, used a tape recorder, listening to the lines over and over and hearing his own voice in different "readings" — emotional approaches — to the material. Sir John Gielgud writes his parts out in longhand two or three times, like a schoolboy writing, "I will not chew gum in class," on the blackboard. This is a valuable technique, as we have noted before, because it combines an *active* process (writing), a *visual* process (reading), and an *aural* process (saying it back).

Cues

All recall is based on "cues." Scripts consist of a series of responses, each triggered by what went before it. When you learn a script, you learn to respond to these cues. A cue can be something another person says or a sound or an action.

As you memorize your script, trigger your response with appropriate cues. If they are actions, act them out. If they are sounds — bells, clapping, music — simulate them. If they are words, mumble the preceding line to yourself or, better yet, have someone read it to you so that you respond automatically with what comes next. Once you're feeling cocky about knowing your "part," have your friend mix up the cues and see if you can respond correctly. (When you do this, you will come to appreciate the angst of professional actors when one of their stage fellows gives them the wrong cue.) Notice where repeated phrases or similar cues may lead you astray. If necessary, make up a mnemonic or numerical framework to keep them in order.

Some soap opera actors have to memorize more dialogue each day than most stage and film actors do in a week. They can be forgiven if they go for the sense of the scene, memorizing only key transitional lines that cue another actor's entrance or a change of scene. Probably few lines of deathless prose are lost to the world. However, an actor who tried to be similarly cavalier with the words of Shakespeare or Molière or Calderon would quickly be hooted off stage. Imagine a Hamlet who intones, "The question is whether to be or not," or a Rhett Butler who sneers, "Frankly, Scarlett, I couldn't care less." The "real" lines sing in our souls, and while we may accept unusual readings of them, we want each and every word as we remember it.

Should We Practise Memorizing?

Is memorization a skill that you can improve with practise? Some experts say no. For instance, in 1890, William James recorded how long it took him to memorize 158 lines of Hugo's *Satyr.* Then he memorized *Paradise Lost.* Then he memorized the next 158 lines of the *Satyr.* It took him longer than to learn the first 158 lines. He decided that the ability to memorize could not be improved by practising.

But most actors advocate memorizing for the fun of it as an everyday exercise, just as a pianist would practise scales. Julie Harris suggests learning one Shakespearean sonnet a day and then going on to famous speeches.

Children used to memorize long poems in school to train their minds, just as they now do calisthenics to train their bodies. Then the idea that memory capacity was genetic and unchangeable made such practise unpopular. Today, even the most curmudgeonly expert will usually concede that training improves the efficiency with which we use our inherited capacity. Memorizing just for the sake of memorizing has not yet made a comeback in our educational system, but many people get great pleasure from knowing long, complicated sequences of material—poems, songs, quotations, laws, chemical formulas, or equations – by heart. They savour both the usefulness of the information and the pleasure that mastering it gives them. It becomes a form of play.

Like the rest of us, some actors are "easy studies," committing lengthy parts to memory with little effort, while others agonize over every sentence, repeating it hundreds of times before they can remember it. Stage and film actor John Barrymore was famous for forgetting lines. He solved his problem by writing them down and placing them all about the set. Speeches were pasted on the back of chairs, pencilled in the pattern of the wallpaper, even inked on his cuffs. Then he practised his own mnemonic technique by literally walking to where his next lines appeared, reciting them and moving on. His delivery was so impressive that his audiences neither knew nor cared.

Memorizing a Speech

A mnemonic technique for remembering speeches is described in chapter 15, "How to Use Memory Systems," but here is a way to polish your presentation. First of all, I highly recommend memorizing *what* you are going to say, not the words that say it. You want to remember your ideas, your key phrases, your main points, but unless you are delivering someone else's speech in his absence or making a critical press statement after a disaster where your every word will be weighed by the press and the victims' lawyers, you don't *want* to read a speech or even say it word for word so that you sound like you're reciting *The Face on the Barroom Floor.* What you want to remember is the thought process.

Here is a technique that may help you do that. The following steps are adapted from the Lessac system devised by Professor Arthur Lessac of the State University of New York, Binghamton. He has applied his techniques of kinesthetic feedback not only to vocal presentations, but to body movement and relaxation.

Your written speech is a gem, beautifully phrased and polished, with each idea following the last like a string of pearls.

1. Write an outline of your speech, listing main points.

2. Divide the written speech into logical sections, not too long or short. Then stand in the middle of the room and read the first section to an imaginary audience. They are bright-faced students who will be tested on what you are saying as soon as you stop.

3. Done? OK, now put down your script and look at all those eager faces. You see questions in their eyes, so you repeat what you have just said naturally, in your own words, emphasizing and elaborating on points that they may not have understood. How do your gestures, facial expressions, pauses, emphases make your message clearer? What new ways do you find to strengthen what you want to get across? (Don't be afraid to ad lib. It may give you some of your best material.)

4. Look at your written speech again and see if you've left anything out. If you did, write it down on your outline.

5. Pick up your written speech and deliver it again, but look at the page *only* when you have to.

6. Now set down the written speech and deliver the section again, using only your outline. Don't be afraid that your imaginary audience will get bored. They're still there, hanging on your every word.

7. Repeat these steps with each section of the speech, until you are completely comfortable with the material.

8. Deliver the entire speech without notes. If you get stuck or realize that you left something out, stop and note it on the outline sheet. If you have trouble keeping the segments in order, try the techniques described in chapter 15, "How to Use Memory Systems."

9. Keep the outline sheet as a backup during your speech. (I'll bet that you won't need to look at it.)

Memorizing Movement

Did you ever watch a stage full of ballet dancers doing complex movements to the crash of metal bins, the cries of whales, or total silence? Do they really know what they are doing, or are they just making it up as they go along? Yes, they *do* know what they are doing because in silent accompaniment to "Concerto for Chevrolet Engines" or "Fugue for Tin Cans and Roller Skates" they are *counting:* a-one-and-a-two-and-a-three, dip, twist, six, kick, kick, slide, ten. You probably did the same thing when (or if) you learned the waltz—*one* two three, *one* two three, *one* two three.

Dancing is a fugitive art. Choreographers can write out a dance in any of several systems of dance notation or even in their own shorthand, but dancers can't move about the stage holding a script, and so they count.

Counting is a useful way to lock any movement into memory. Dancers count in variable units, depending on the music. The most common counts are four, eight, sixteen, or thirty-two, corresponding to common musical segments. Each set of counts is called a "combination." The counts within a combination can be thought of as words in a sentence. Each "sentence" follows the last until a "paragraph" is formed. Unless the dance is an incredibly complicated contemporary piece, the counts are soon locked into their muscles and become kinesthetic memory. No more conscious counting is necessary. The *music* becomes the *cue*.

How can dancers' counts help in nondance pursuits? Well, music or other sounds can serve as cues for motion. An assembly-line-type process could be "choreographed" to music so that you know exactly where you should be in relation to the music. You could time getting out of the house in the morning to songs from the musical *Annie*. ("Oh, oh, I'm late, I should be brushing my teeth by 'You're Never Fully Dressed without a Smile' and I'm only putting on my shoes." "Hard-Knock Life" reminds you to take your wallet and keys off the dresser and put them in your pocket.) You could wash the car to a Michael Jackson album ("The Girl Is Mine" means don't forget to scour the white walls). Clean the house to *The Marriage of Figaro* (scrub the refrigerator and set out the meat to defrost for dinner when "Se a casa Madama" comes on). Music keys action.

You may want to use counts to divide a complicated activity into simpler units. Five steps for a tummy-firming exercise before breakfast or changing the blades on a food processor, seven steps to threading a projector or setting up a computer.

Even Professionals Can Goof

The late pianist Artur Schnabel once got utterly lost in the midst of the *Brahms Piano Concerto in B Flat*. With great dignity he rose from the piano, walked to the podium, and studied the conductor's score, then returned to finish the piece.

Another master pianist, Andre Watts, played *Chopin's F Minor Fantasy* at 12 different concerts and 12 times forgot his place. He finally "conquered" the piece by scheduling it for the second half of a concert. During the intermission he rehearsed it over and over, and finally succeeded in playing it through correctly. "I said afterwards, 'Right, I'm never playing this piece again'," Watts recalls. "I refused to play it for a long, long time."

Rehearsing for Life

The methods professionals use to memorize their very special material can be applied in many ways in our day-to-day memory projects. Professionals have the advantage over the rest of us—they *want* to remember, *need* to remember, and *enjoy* remembering. When you add those three conditions to any memorization project you have a winning combination.

As you struggle with memorizing a few pages or paragraphs, think of this: Under the Chinese emperors, no one could become a civil servant until he could prove in a national examination that he had memorized several books of classical literature and poetry. The reasoning was that in order to serve wisely, you had to be wise in the history, morality, and beauty of the world. We can only imagine what it would be like today if all postal workers were also Shakespearean scholars and if every meter maid could recite T. S. Eliot and E. E. Cummings as she wrote out our tickets. What a lovely thought!

Try This...

to Celebrate Memory

Pick out something you would enjoy remembering— a poem, saying, song, or speech—and memorize it for sheer pleasure.

23
A Bag of
Miscellaneous
Memory Tricks

Now you know how to dazzle your friends and how to solve most of life's major memory problems. How about some simple tricks for coping with the pesky nuts and bolts of everyday remembering? Here is a collection.

The Old Watch-on-the-Wrong-Wrist Trick—You need to do something before you leave your home or office, or you need to remember to take something with you or to stop on the way and do an errand. Switch your wristwatch to the other wrist. Most people automatically check their watches whenever they make a transition. Your bare wrist will trigger the memory of what you want to do.

The Rubber Band/Safety Pin Trick—This is a variation of the string around the finger, much easier in these days of package tape.

The old tie-a-string-to-your-finger trick for remembering.

(When was the last time you owned a ball of string?) If you lack a watch or want to remember *two* things, try slipping a rubber band around your wrist or pinning a safety pin in the little metal loop that holds the handle on your handbag or briefcase. If you're incredibly forgetful or have lots of things to remember, make your left hand "home" and your right hand "office" (or any other suitable division) and assign fingers to different areas, then slip rubber bands around the appropriate fingers. You may look silly, but it beats burning the house down or arriving at work without the day's post that you were supposed to pick up at the post office.

The Tipped Lamp Shade Trick — An important thought floats into your mind as you drift off to sleep. If you leap up and get a pencil and paper, you will spend an hour getting back to sleep. If you don't, you'll have forgotten it in the morning. Try tipping the shade on your bedside lamp to a sharp angle. Or set the alarm clock on the floor. Or pull open the drawer of your bedside table, or toss a pillow across the room where you will have to step on it when you get up. In the morning you'll see what you've done and rebuild the memory connections.

The Billboard Trick — This only works occasionally. Like all good things, if you do it too much, it loses its effect. Simply write yourself a big note and stick it on the bathroom mirror or the front door, or your typewriter, someplace where you will have to physically remove it to go about your business.

The Phone Call at 10:35 Trick — Hardest of all is when you absolutely must call Mr. Bludgett at 10:35, not 10:30 or 10:40. Otherwise, Worldwide Widgetts will be bankrupt and you will be out in the street. Actually, if it were that important, you would probably sit staring at your watch from 8:30 on, so let's pretend that failing to reach Bludgett would only cause massive inconvenience and loss of money. You could count on the arrival of the tea lady to prompt you, but this may be the one morning it's late. You could trust your secretary, but she might get tied up on the phone and forget. Or you could set an alarm clock or timer to ring. My recommendation is to try all of them. Give yourself three ways to remember, then forget it and get on with your work.

The Step-On-It Trick — easiest of all. If you have to take something with you when you leave the house, set it in front of the door. If someone else might step on it first, have a special (and it *must* be special) place where everything that goes with you is laid out. If everything gets dumped there, forget it. A really organized person might even have a set of shelves labeled Monday, Tuesday, Wednesday, Thursday, Friday to lay out things for the whole week.

The Siamese Twins Trick – Behaviourist B. F. Skinner suggests remembering something you should do regularly by relating it to a similarly regular activity that has become habit. For instance, if you have to take pills twice a day, attach the pill bottle to your toothbrush with a big rubber band. When you reach automatically for the toothbrush, you will be reminded to take your pills. If you promise to wake up a friend each morning until he can find a new answering service, set the phone (or a note) on the toilet seat. Attach objects or notes to coffee pots, refrigerator door handles, shower heads, typewriters, mirrors, dog leashes—anything you use at regular intervals. Try to attach them in a way that will hinder the use of the regularly used object. For instance, if you put a note on the bathroom mirror, make it a big one. Cover the mirror. Otherwise you might shave, comb your hair, and stumble off to work without seeing it.

The Make-Life-Simpler Trick—an unattainable goal, but still worth the effort. Keep your brain cells free to ponder life's mysteries by doing most of your more boring remembering outside your head. Make lists and use them. Have a place for everything and everything in its place. Have a schedule for paying bills, ordering supplies, going to the dentist. If all this sounds impossibly idealistic, think of the energy you spend on chaos. We can't control how we spend every penny and every minute, but we do have a lot of choices in our expenditures.

24
How to Be Happy Though Forgetful

John went out on his lunch hour to pick up his shoes at the repair shop. On the way he stopped to fill a prescription, buy the new issue of his favorite magazine, deposit his pay cheque, and pick up the key for his new locker at the health club. When he got back to the office, flushed but on time, he realized he had forgotten to pick up his shoes.

Now if they were his only pair of black shoes and he was due to be best man at his brother-in-law's wedding that evening, a good case could be made for deliberate forgetting. But he probably just overloaded himself.

Clara went down to the basement for a jar of pickles. On the way, she stopped to toss a load of laundry in the washer and rinse out the plastic laundry basket that had become coated with detergent. As she hung up the basket, the hook came off the wall, so she got out the screwdriver and fixed it. While she was at it, she tightened some loose screws on the door hinges and got out the oil to lubricate them. Just then the phone rang and she raced upstairs to answer it. Twenty minutes later she realized she had not fetched the pickles.

Pretty stupid, eh? If the pickles had been *that* important, if she craved a pickle so intensely that she would have cheerfully knocked over ten rugby players in her rush to get one, then she wouldn't have stopped. And if the pickles were for her husband's lunch and they had just had a fight . . . but maybe the pickles were just as important as the other things.

Now Clara and John could spend a great deal of time berating themselves and their terrible memories. They could form strong images of themselves as useless, feebleminded failures, incapable of a simple task. If Clara's husband or John's brother-in-law subscribed to the theory that there are no accidents, John and Clara could have resonated with guilt for months or years to come. But let's look at the other side.

Both accomplished several useful tasks, worked off some extra calories, and enjoyed what they were doing. The fact that they had started the action that would result in the desired effect probably caused them to check it off their mental list. How often have you gone to the store for one particular thing and come home with everything else but?

You probably could train yourself to focus totally on the task at hand, denying any extraneous thought, and repeating your mission in mantra-like fashion. You *could* . . . but so far this is not your nature.

You may find it easier and more rewarding to tolerate occasional lapses of memory in order to be available to some of the pleasant notions that flit through your unconscious mind. The price for being unusually disciplined is less spontaneity. By making friends with the way you already use your memory, you will actually remember more of what you want to remember. Self-harassment rarely improves memory because it sets up a system of negative stimuli that is, at best, distracting and, at worst, destructive.

Buy a Memory Insurance Policy

Most people buy contents insurance and accident insurance. Treat yourself to some memory insurance. When forgetting turns out to be expensive—when you forget to make a payment and are charged a penalty or when you forget to buy petrol and have to be towed – you can either make yourself sick with regret and self-abuse or you can draw on your memory insurance policy.

A memory insurance policy is simple. At the beginning of each year, budget a certain amount of money for memory lapses. Forgetting that costs money is painful. If you plan for it, then expensive slips of the mind can be tolerated without self-recrimination.

Try the same technique with cost-free forgetting. When enough good things are happening in our lives, one or two low moments don't usually get us down. If you forget an umbrella, birthday, or appointment, remind yourself of all the essential things you *did* remember. Remedy the situation as best you can and then . . . forget it.

Three Things
You Should Never Forget

1. We remember what enhances us and gives us pleasure.

2. We forget what doesn't enrich our immediate lives.

3. Anyone with a belly button is allowed at least a 20 percent margin for error.

Bibliography

Anderson, John N., and Hubbard, Barbara M. "Sex Differences in Age-Related Brain Atrophy." *Lancet,* 25 June 1983, pp. 1447-48.

Baddeley, Alan D. *The Psychology of Memory.* Harper and Row, 1976.

——. *Your Memory: A User's Guide.* Penguin, 1983.

Baddeley, Alan D., and Hitch, G. J. "Recency Re-examined." In *Attention and Performance VI,* edited by S. Domic. Hillsdale, N.J.: Lawrence Erlbaum Associates, 1977.

Baddeley, Alan D., and Longman, D. J. A. "The Influence of Length and Frequency of Training Sessions on Rate of Learning to Type." *Ergonomics* 21 (1978):627-35.

Bartlett, F. C. *Remembering.* Cambridge University Press, 1932 (out of print but you may be able to find it in your library).

Bower, Gordon H. "How to . . . uh . . . Remember!" *Psychology Today,* October 1973, pp. 62-70.

——. "Mood and Memory." *Psychology Today,* June 1981, pp. 60-69.

"Brain's Record of Past: A Continuous Movie Film." *Science News Letter,* 27 April 1957, p. 265.

Brody, Jane E. "Head Injuries and the 'Silent Epidemic'." *New York Times,* 23 March 1983.

Burtt, H. E. "An Experimental Study of Early Childhood Memory." *Journal of Genetic Psychology* 40 (1932):287-95.

Butler, Robert N. "Alzheimer's Disease: An Examination." *Ambassador Magazine,* November 1982, pp. 69-83.

Buzan, Tony. *Make the Most of Your Mind.* Pan Books, 1981.

Clark, Ronald W. *Einstein: The Life and Times.* Hodder and Stoughton, 1979.

Craik, Fergus I. M., and Lockhart, Robert S. "Levels of Processing: A Framework for Memory Research." *Journal of Verbal Learning and Verbal Behavior* 11 (1972):671-84.

Del Rey, Patricia. "Effects of Contextual Interference on the Memory of

Older Females Differing in Levels of Physical Activity." *Perceptual and Motor Skills,* August 1982, pp. 171-80.

Dembart, Lee. "Mathematician [Paul] Erdos: In the World of Numbers, He's No. 1." *Los Angeles Times,* 26 March 1983.

The Diagram Group. *The Brain: A User's Manual.* New England Library, 1984.

Dowling, W. J., and Fujitani, D. S. "Contour, Interval and Pitch Recognition in Memory for Melodies." *Journal of the Acoustical Society of America* 49 (1971):524-31.

Drachman, David A. et al. "Memory Decline in the Aged: Treatment with Lecithin and Physostigmine." *Neurology* 32 (1982):944-50.

Eisenson, Marc. "Parents: Get Smart about Drugs ... and Drug Abuse!" *Family Circle Magazine,* 16 November 1982, pp. 195-99.

Ericsson, K. Anders, and Chase, William G. "Exceptional Memory." *American Scientist,* November-December 1982, pp. 607-15.

Etaugh, Claire, and Ptasnik, Patricia. "Effects of Studying to Music and Post-study Relaxation on Reading Comprehension." *Perceptual and Motor Skills,* August 1982, pp. 141-42.

Fanz, Dr. R. "The Origin of Form Perception." *Scientific American* 24 (1961):66.

Fernstrom, John D., and Wurtman, Richard J. "Nutrition and the Brain." *Scientific American,* February 1974, pp. 84-91.

Finn, Robert. "Amnesia: Case of a Fragmented Past." *Science Digest,* November 1983, pp. 72-74.

Foucault, Michel. *Order of Things: Archaeology of the Human Sciences.* Tavistock Publications, 1974.

Goodwin, D. W.; Othmer, E.; Halikas, J. A.; and Fremon, F. "Loss of Short-Term Memory as a Predictor of Alcoholic 'Blackout'." *Nature,* 11 July 1970, pp 201-2.

Green, Blake. "What Their Eyes Tell Us." *San Francisco Chronicle,* 3 November 1980.

Greene, E. B. "The Retention of Information Learned in College Courses." *Journal of Educational Research* 21 (1931):262-73.

Grinspoon, Lester. "Marijuana." *Scientific American,* December 1969, pp. 17-25.

Heider, Eleanor Rosch. "Universals in Color Naming and Memory."

Journal of Experimental Psychology, April 1972, pp. 10-20.

Houston, John R.; Schneider, Nina G.; and Jarvick, Murray E. "Effects of Smoking on Free Recall and Organization." *American Journal of Psychiatry,* February 1978, pp. 220-22.

Hunter, I. M. L. "An Exceptional Talent for Calculative Thinking." *British Journal of Psychology* 53 (1962):243-58.

Jacobs, J. "Experiments in 'Prehension'." *Mind* 12 (1887):75-82.

James, William. *Principles of Psychology.* volumes 1 and 2 in one volume, Harvard University Press, 1983; volume 3, Harvard University Press, 1981.

Jones, Marilyn K., and Jones, Ben Morgan. "The Relationship of Age and Drinking Habits to the Effects of Alcohol on Memory in Women." *Journal of Studies on Alcohol,* January 1980, pp. 179-86.

Killworth, Peter D., and Bernard, H. Russell. "Informant Accuracy in Social Network Data." *Human Organization,* 35 (1976):269-86.

Layton, E. T. "The Persistence of Learning in Elementary Algebra." *Journal of Educational Psychology* 23 (1932):46-55.

Lessac, Arthur. *The Use and Training of the Human Voice: A Practical Approach to Speech and Voice Dynamics.* 1960. Reprint. New York: Drama Book Publishers, 1967.

Lieber, Charles S. "The Metabolism of Alcohol." *Scientific American,* March 1976, pp. 25-33.

Loftus, E. F., and Palmer, J. C. "Reconstruction of Automobile Destruction: An Example of the Interaction Between Language and Memory." *Journal of Verbal Learning and Verbal Behavior* 13 (1974):585-89.

McGaugh, James L. "Role of Hormones and Adrenalin in Memory." Paper delivered at the Western Psychological Association, San Francisco, April 27, 1983.

McKean, Kevin. "Memory." *Discover,* November 1983, pp. 19-27.

MacLean, Paul. "The Brain's Generation Gap. Some Human Implications." *Zygon/Journal of Religion and Science,* June 1973, pp. 113-27.

McWhirter, Norris, ed. *Guinness Book of Records, 1983.* Guinness, 1983.

Mandler, George. "Organization and Memory." In *The Psychology of*

Learning and Motivation, edited by K. W. Spence and J. T. Spence, vol. 1. Academic Press, 1967.

Mandler, George; Pearlstone, Zena; and Koopman, Henry S. "Effects of Organization and Semantic Similarity on Recall and Recognition." *Journal of Verbal Learning and Verbal Behavior* 8 (1969):410-23.

Martinez, Joe L., Jr.; Jensen, Robert A.; Messing, Rita B.; Rigte, Hank; McGaugh, James L. "Endogenous Peptides and Learning and Memory Processes." *Contemporary Psychology,* September 1982, p. 727.

Mazer, Eileen. "Five Proven Ways to Sharpen Your Memory." *Prevention,* February 1982, pp. 58-62.

Miller, L. L. et al. "Marijuana: Effects on Free Recall and Subjective Organization of Pictures and Words." *Psychopharmacology,* 29 December 1977, pp. 257-62.

Penry, J. *Looking at Faces and Remembering Them: A Guide to Facial Identification.* Elek Books, 1971 (out of print but you may find a copy in the library).

Sagan, Carl. *Cosmos.* Macdonald, 1984.

Sands, S. F., and Wright, A. A. "Primate Memory: Retention of Serial List Items by a Rhesus Monkey." *Science,* 22 August 1980, pp. 938-40.

Sapir, Edward. *Selected Writings of Edward Sapir in Language, Culture and Personality.* Edited by David G. Mandlebaum. University of California Press, 1949.

Schmeck, Harold M., J. "The Biology of Fear and Anxiety: Evidence Points to Chemical Triggers." *New York Times,* 7 September 1982.

——. "How Does Memory Work?" *New York Times,* 26 October 1982.

Schmidt, William E. "Gifted Retardates: The Search for Clues to Mysterious Talent." *New York Times,* 12 July 1983.

Simpson, Christopher. "World Brain." *Science Digest,* May 1982, pp. 52-54, 95.

Skinner, B. F., and Vaughan, Margaret. *Enjoy Old Age.* Hutchinson, 1984.

"Social Drinking Tied to Cognitive Impairment While Sober." *Internal Medicine News,* 16 April 1983.

Sorabji, Richard. *Aristotle on Memory.* Duckworth, 1972.

"Tips to Making Learning Easier." *Modern Maturity,* June-July 1983, pp. 4-6.

Tulving, Endel. "Episodic and Semantic Memory." In *Organization of Memory,* edited by Endel Tulving and Wayne Donaldson. Academic Press, 1972.

Underwood, Benton J. "Forgetting." *Scientific American,* March 1964, pp. 91-99.

von Oech, Roger. *Whack on the Side of the Head: How to Unlock Your Mind for Innovation.* Creative Think Publishers, 1983.

Watson, Robert I. "An Experimental Study of the Permanence of Course Material in Introductory Psychology." *Archives of Psychology* 32 (1938):3-64.

Weeks, David J. "Do Chronic Cigarette Smokers Forget People's Names?" *British Medical Journal,* December 22-29, 1979, p. 1627.

Weingartner, Herbert et al. "Effects of Vasopressin on Human Memory Factors." *Science,* 6 February 1981, pp. 601-3.

Weitzenhoffer, Andre M. *General Techniques of Hypnotism.* Grune and Stratton, Inc., 1957 (distributed by Academic Press).

Wells, Gary L., and Murray, Donna M. "What Can Psychology Say about *Neil v. Biggers* Criteria for Judging Eyewitness Testimony?" *Journal of Applied Psychology,* April 1983, pp. 347-62.

White, B. "Recognition of Distorted Melodies." *American Journal of Psychology* 73 (1960):100-107.

Wilson, Jeanie. "The Amazing Brain." *Town & Country,* August 1982, pp. 73-84.

Zailian, Marian. "A Genius Who Eschews the Title of Prodigy." *San Francisco Examiner,* 4 September 1983.

Zeisel, Steven H. "The Effects of Dietary Components on Brain Function." In *Advances in Human Clinical Nutrition.* Littleton, Mass.: John Wright/PSG, 1982.

Zeller, Anchard F. "An Experimental Analogue of Repression: III the Effect of Induced Failure and Success on Memory Measured by Recall." *Journal of Experimental Psychology* 42 (1951):32-38.

Index

A

Abbreviations, as memory aid, 157
Absentmindedness. *See* Forgetting, abnormal
Actors and actresses
  memory problems of, 54, 55
  rehearsal techniques of, 242–45
  stage names of, 219
Additives in food, sensitivity of children to, 29
Adrenalin, and memory, 76–77
Adrenocorticotropic hormone/melanocyte-stimulating hormone combination, enhancing memory, 78
Advertisements
  duration of memory of, 142
  word associations in, 21
Ageing, memory in, 38, 120–27
  adrenalin affecting, 76–77
  brain changes affecting, 75, 123, 125
  calcium affecting, 76
  of competing memories, 125
  diet affecting, 28
  exercise affecting, 44
  and learning, 121–22
  and senility, 124–25
Aids to memory, 134–254
  abbreviations in, 157
  auditory, 201–8
  for facts, 186–91
  for history, 171–72, 177–79
  hypnosis in, 145–46
  location in, 158, 175
  miscellaneous tricks in, 249–51

for names and faces, 209–28
numbering systems in, 151–56, 246–47
for numbers, 137, 229–41
  in mathematical formulas, 176–77
  in phone numbers, 156–57
peg system in, 158–66, 178, 233–35
in reading, 192–200
rehearsal in, 242–48
reinforcement in, 144
in retrieval of information, 140–41
rewards in, 138–39
rhythm in, 146
in speech presentation, 245–46
structure and organization in, 142–44, 147–50, 251
in studying, 167–85
in transfer of short-term memory to long-term, 137–40
word associations in, 141, 213, 214, 215–16, 227
Alcohol use, affecting memory, 28, 42–43
Allergies, physical memory blocks in, 39
Alzheimer's disease, memory in, 28, 37–38, 124–25
  choline enhancing, 79
Amnesia, 36
  emotional, 36
  after head injuries, 36, 116
Animal models in memory research
  adrenalin in, 76–77
  brain size and intelligence comparisons in, 77

diet in, 27–28
hippocampus in, 117, 118
implications of, 182–83
learning process in, 181, 182–83
long-term memory in, 76
swallowing of memories in, 77–78
Appointments, memory of
Freud on, 68
trick improving, 250
Aristotle, on memory, 61–63
Arteriosclerosis, memory loss in, 37
Ascorbic acid, affecting memory, 31
Assessment procedures, quizzes and exercises in. See Quizzes and exercises
Associations stimulating memory, 62–63
and information retrieval, 141
for names and faces, 211–13, 214, 215–16, 227
Attention and support, forgetting for, 14–16, 50–51, 199
Attitudes toward forgetting, 4, 17, 252–54
Auditory memory, 101–2, 201–8
accuracy of, in courtroom reconstructions, 205
emotions affecting, 203–4
exercise on, 205–8
of faces and names, 211
in listening to multiple speakers, 204–5
in listening to silence, 204
and mishearing, 203
of music, 179–80
reinforcement of, 144
visual memory in, 202
in speed listening, 202–3
structuring in, 205–8
in studying, 173, 179–80
Automobile accidents, benefits of forgetting, 49

B

Bartlett, Frederick, on memory, 65–66
Bicycle riding, kinesthetic memory of, 102, 104

Billboard trick, as memory aid, 250
Birthday dates, memory of, 240
Blindness
kinesthetic memory in, 102
speed listening in, 202–3
Blocking processes, 3
emotional, 4–17
Freud on, 66–69
mechanical, 18–25
physical, 26–47
Body parts, as memory pegs, 159–61, 165
Books and articles, memory of information read in, 192–200
Brain, in memory, 1, 70–81, 197, 199
adrenalin in, 76–77
age-related changes of, 123, 125
alcohol use affecting, 42–43
in arteriosclerosis, 37
cigarette smoking affecting, 43
compared to computers, 64, 66
diet affecting, 27–29
electrical stimulation affecting, 146–47, 199
exercise affecting, 44
future research on, 79
holographic theory of, 64, 74–75, 199
limbic system in, 72, 117
locations of areas used in, 73, 75
mechanisms in, 74–77
models of, 63–64
of names and faces, 216, 217
neocortex in, 72, 117
neurotransmitters in, 75–76
percentage used in, 70–71
receptors in, 75
in reptilian brain, 71–72, 117
size of compared to intelligence measurements, 77
visual and verbal, 103

C

Calcium intake, affecting memory, 31, 76
Calpain, and memory, 75, 76

Capacity for remembering, 73, 79–81, 83
    aids improving, 134–254. *See also* Aids to memory
    digit-span measurement of, 135–37
    extraordinary, 128–33
    immediate memories in, 83
    inborn factors affecting, 73, 79
    long-term memories in, 85
    practise affecting, 244–45
    quiz for evaluation of, 79–81
    rating of, 135–36
    short-term memories in, 84, 85
Caring about others, and emotional memory blocks, 7–10
Categorization, as memory aid, 148
    exercise on, 149–50
Chemical theory of memory, 75–76, 199
Children, memory in, 122–23
    diet affecting, 29, 34
    for faces, 216
    for facts and skills, 116–17
    and learning about structure and organization, 142–43
    photographic, 102-3
    visual and verbal, 100
Choline intake, affecting memory, 27–29, 30, 78–79
Cigarette smoking, affecting memory, 43
Cold remedies, affecting memory, 40
Color names in language, 114–15
Commercials
    duration of memory of, 142
    word associations in, 21
Competing memories, 174–75
    in ageing, 125
Computers, compared to human brain, 56, 64, 66
Conflicts, internal, and emotional memory blocks, 5–10
Conscious mind, Freud on, 66–67
Constructive forgetting, 48–59
    quiz on, 57–59
Copper, affecting memory, 32
Counting system, as memory aid, 152–56
    kinesthetic, 246–47

verbal, 153–55
visual, 153–55
Cranial nerves, mnemonic for, 151–52
Creativity, in ageing, 120-21
Cues for remembering
    in movement memorization, 246–47
    picture-taking technique in, 104–5
    in retrieval of information, 140–41
    in script memorization, 243–44
Curiosity, and memory, 122–23
Cyanocobalamin, affecting memory, 30

D

Dance movements, memorization of, 246–47
Darwin's law for studying, 184
Dates, memory of, 229–41
    exercise on, 240
Deamino-D-Arginine Vasopressin (DDAVP), and memory, 75, 76
Déjà vu, kinesthetic memories in, 104
Dementia, senile, of Alzheimer's type, 124–25
Depressant drugs, affecting memory, 40
Depression, memory in, 37
Depth of information processing, affecting memory, 141
Diet, affecting memory, 27–35
    animal research on, 27–28
    in children, 29, 34
    in weight loss diets, 34
Digit-span measurements of memory, 135–37
    improving score on, 137
Discarding of information, 3, 20
Diseases, memory blocks in, 35–38, 124–27
Distractions, memory blocks from, 18–25
    in fatigue, 45
    in filing of information, 22
    in marijuana use, 42

in reading, 196
in registration of information,
91
in retrieval of information, 23
in studying, 168
Dreams, memory of, 145
Drugs
blocking memory, 40
enhancing memory, 40–41,
78–79
and memory aid for pill
taking, 251
Duration of memories, 83
and fading, 65, 174
immediate, 83
interferences affecting, 174–75
long-term, 85, 93
pleasant and unpleasant, 142
and restudying forgotten information, 93, 94, 173–74
short-term, 84, 85

E

Ebbinghaus, Hermann, on
memory, 65
Echoic memory, 101–2
Education and learning
in ageing, 121-22
capacity for memories in, 73,
79
of children, 123
diet affecting, 29, 34
duration of memories in,
93–94, 173–74
mechanical memory blocks in,
19
negative feedback affecting,
183
peg system in, 163–64
readiness for, 181
and re-learning of information,
93, 94, 173–74
rewards in, 182
study techniques in, 167–85
and variations in giving directions, 204
visual and verbal memory in,
101
Electrical theory of memory,
146–47, 199

Emotions
and auditory memory, 203–4
blocking memory, 4–17, 81,
110, 111, 196–97, 198
amnesia in, 36
causes of, 10
in fatigue, 45
Freud on, 66–69
and keeping of blocks,
11–13
of music, 5–6
of names, 5, 6, 8–9,
209–10, 217–18
as protective mechanism,
5–13
resolution of, 10, 13–16
of travel experiences,
9–10
enhancing memory, 111, 138
and episodic memory, 110–11
and mood dependency of
memories, 144–45
and number memory, 6–7,
229–30
Employment, memory affecting
success in, 53–55, 206-7, 209
Encoding of information distractions and interferences in,
18–25
Energy to accomplish goals, and
effects of absentmindedness, 54
Enthusiasm, and amount remembered, 73, 80
Environmental pollution, and age-
related memory loss, 123
Episodic memory, 110–11
exercise on, 119
long-term, 86, 87–88
Errands, memory aids in remembering, 154–55, 159–63
Ethical considerations in experimentation, 183–84
Evaluation
of information, 2
expectations affecting, 20
individual variations in,
19–20
of self, quizzes and exercises
for. See Quizzes and
exercises
Exercise, affecting memory, 44

Exercises and quizzes. *See* Quizzes and exercises
Expectations
    and evaluation of information, 20-21
    language affecting, 21
    sounds affecting, 21
Extraordinary memory, 128-33
    of famous people, 131-32
    of idiot savants, 130-31

F

Faces and names, memory of, 129, 197, 200, 209-28. *See also* Names and faces, memory of
Facts, memory of, 116-17, 186-91
    on dates, 229-41
    exercise on, 189-91
    and studying techniques, 167-85
    understanding affecting, 168-69, 176, 177, 187-88
Fading of memories, 65, 174
Famous people with good memories, 131-32
Fatigue, affecting memory, 45
Feingold diet, 29
Feinstein Foolproof Phone Number System, 156-57
Filing of information, 90, 91
    distractions and interferences in, 18-23
    and misfiling, 18-22
Financial cost of forgetting, 253
Focus on desired goals, and effects of absentmindedness, 54
Folic acid, affecting memory, 31
Food additives, sensitivity of children to, 29
Foreign language learning, mechanical memory blocks in, 19
Forgetting, 1-59
    abnormal
        in Alzheimer's disease, 124-25
        exercise on, 126-27
        and success in work, 53-55
    for attention and support, 14-16, 50-51, 199
    attitudes toward, 4, 17, 252-54
    on completion of tasks, 53
    in emotional blocks, 4-17
    Freud on, 67-68
    in mechanical blocks, 18-25
    of pain and sorrow, 49-50, 198-99
    in physical memory blocks, 26-47
    positive uses of, 11-13, 48-59, 197, 198-99
        quiz on, 57-59
    and restudying forgotten information, 93, 94, 173-74
    selective, 56
    for self-preservation, 11-13, 48-49, 198
    Zeigarnick effect in, 53
Formulas, mathematical, memory aids for remembering, 176-77
Freud, Sigmund, on memory, 66-69
Fugue states, 36

G

Grouping-to-remember, 147-50
    exercise on, 149-50
    in peg system, 158-66
Guilt, and emotional memory blocks, 5

H

Happiness
    memory of, 52
    in memory lapses, 252-54
Head injuries, memory after, 36, 39, 73, 116
Hearing, memory in, 201-8. *See also* Auditory memory
Hippocampus, and memory, 72, 75, 116, 117, 118
Historical theories on memory, 61-69
History, memory aids for remembering, 171-72, 177-79
Holographic model of brain, 64, 74-75, 199
Homonyms, and mechanical memory blocks, 19

Hormones, affecting memory, 77, 78

Hospital intensive care units, psychosis in, 37

House rooms, as memory pegs, 161–63, 165–66

How to techniques, for memory improvement, 134–254. *See also* Aids to memory

Hypnotism, recall in, 145–46

Hypothalamus, 72, 117, 147

I

Idiot savants, 130–31

Illnesses
    physical memory blocks in, 35–38, 124–25, 126–27
    psychosomatic and somatopsychic, 34–35

Imagery, as memory aid, 139, 148
    for faces and names, 212–13, 215–16
    for numbers, 234–35
    in peg system, 158–66

Immediate memory, 83

Improvement of memory, aids in, 134–254. *See also* Aids to memory

Inborn capacity for remembering, 73, 79

Information pattern in nonfiction, 195, 197, 199–200

Information processing
    depth of, 141
    distractions and interferences in, 18–25
    filing and retention in, 90, 91
    and misremembering, 146–47
    registration in, 90, 91, 123
    retrieval in, 90, 91–93. *See also* Retrieval of information
    in speed listening, 202–3
    in speed reading, 193

Injuries of head, memory after, 36, 39, 73, 116

Instinct, in immediate memory, 83

Instruction pattern in nonfiction, 195, 197, 200

Instructions, speaker variations in giving of, 204

Intelligence
    and brain size, 77
    of idiot savants, 130–31
    and memory, 187

Intensive care unit psychosis, 37

Interferences affecting memory, 18–25, 65, 73, 80–81
    in marijuana use, 42
    other memories in, 125, 174–75
    in registration of information, 91
    in studying, 168, 174–75
        music as, 180–81

Iodine, affecting memory, 32

Iron, affecting memory, 29, 32

K

Kinesthetic memory, 99–109
    counting cues in, 246–47
    and déjà vu, 104
    exercise on, 106–9
    of faces and names, 212
    rehearsals in, 246–47
    reinforcing verbal and visual memories, 104–5, 108–9

L

Labeling of items, and semantic memory, 111–15

Lamp shade trick, as memory aid, 250

Language
    action type of, 113
    condition type of, 113–14
    and perceptions, 21, 113, 114, 115
    and semantic memory, 111–15

Learning. *See* Education and learning

Lecithin intake, and memory, 27–29, 78

Letters and words, as memory aid for numbers, 230–41

Limbic system, 72, 117

Listening memory, 201–8. *See also* Auditory memory

List writing, as memory aid, 23, 144

Location, as memory aid, 158
    in peg system, 161–63, 165–66
    in studying, 175
Long-term memory, 66, 83, 85–86
    diet affecting, 28
    duration of, 85, 93
    episodic, 86, 87–88
    exercise on, 87–88
    norepinephrine in, 76
    semantic, 86, 87–88
    transfer of short-term memo-
      ries to, 85, 86
        aids in, 137–40
Lost articles
    and emotional memory blocks,
      14–16
    Freud on, 67–68
    improving memory about,
      143–44

M

Magnesium, affecting memory, 32
Manganese, affecting memory, 33
Maps, mental, in memory, 117, 118
Marijuana, affecting memory, 41–42
Mathematical formulas, memory
   aids for, 176–77
    on pi, 239–40
Mechanical memory blocks, 18–25,
   81
    in acquisition of information,
      22–23
    in alcohol use, 28
    in filing of information, 22
    in misfiled information, 18–22
    in overload of information, 23
    in retrieval of information, 22,
      23
    of travel experiences, 22–23
Mechanical theory of memory,
   74–75, 199
Medications. See Drugs
Melanocyte-stimulating hormone/
   adrenocorticotropic hormone
   combination, enhancing
   memory, 78
Memory. See also specific types of
   memory
    in ageing, 38, 120-27
    aids for improvement of,
      134–254

    auditory, 101–2, 201–8
    echoic, 101–2
    episodic, 86, 87–88, 110–11,
      119
    of idiot savants, 130–31
    immediate, 83
    kinesthetic, 99–109
    lapse of, 1–59
    long-term, 66, 83, 85–86
    perfect, 128–33
    photographic, 102–3, 135
    semantic, 110, 111–15
    short-term, 66, 83, 84–85
    verbal, 99, 100–102, 135
    visual, 99, 100–102, 144
Memory systems, use of, 151–66,
   246–47
Mercury in medications, affecting
   memory, 40
Misfiled information
    mechanical memory blocks in,
      18–22
    retrieval of, 22
Mishearing, 203
Misnaming, 217–18
Misreading, 193–94
Misremembering, 146–47, 193–94
Mnemonic devices, 151–52, 170.
   See also Aids to memory
Mood dependency of memories,
   144–45
Motivation, and memory, 131–32
Movement memory. See Kinesthetic
   memory
Muscle movements, memory of.
   See Kinesthetic memory
Music
    memory of
      emotional blocks affecting,
        5–6
      extraordinary, 131–32
      in idiot savants, 130–31
      rehearsals in, 247
      studying in, 179–80
    studying to, 180–81

N

Names and faces, memory of,
   129, 197, 200, 209–28
    in childhood, 216

emotions affecting, 5, 6, 8–9, 209–10, 217–18
episodic, 111
exercise on, 222–28
extraordinary, 131
for fictional characters, 218–19
Freud on, 67
imagery technique for, 212–13, 215–16
interpreted as slang words, 214
and misnaming, 217–18
in mixed nationalities, 213–14
and physical characteristics, 215–16, 217
for stage names, 219
and strategies for memory loss, 219–20, 221
Naming of items, as memory aid, 103, 111–15
Negative memories
duration of, 142
forgetting of, 49–50, 198–99
Freud on, 67
positive uses of, 51–52
Neocortex of brain, functions of, 72, 117
Neurons of brain, and memory, 74, 75, 117, 199
diet affecting, 27–28
Neurotransmitters in brain, and memory, 75–76
Niacin, affecting memory, 31
Nicotine, affecting memory, 43
Norepinephrine, and memory, 75, 76
Numbering systems, as memory aids, 152–56, 246–47
Number memory, 137, 156–57, 229–41
digit-span measurement of, 135–37
emotions affecting, 6–7, 229–30
exercise on, 235–41
extraordinary, 128–30
in formulas, 176–77
grouping for, 230
by idiot savants, 130, 131
imagery in, 234–35
peg system in, 233–35
photographic, 135
of pi, 130, 239–40
reciting for, 230

rhythm in, 146
short-term, 84
visual and verbal, 101, 135
word or letter equivalents for, 230–41
Nutrition, affecting memory, 27–35
animal research on, 27–28
in children, 29, 34
in weight loss diets, 34

O

Occupation, memory affecting success in, 53–55, 206–7, 209
Opinion pattern in nonfiction, 195, 197, 198–99
Organization for remembering, 142–44, 147–50
exercise on, 149–50
for facts, 188
in peg system, 158–66
problems in, 148–49
in reading, 194–200

P

Painful memories
duration of, 142
forgetting of, 49–50, 198–99
Freud on, 67
positive uses of, 51–52
Peg system as memory aid, 158–66
exercise on, 165–66
in history studies, 178
for numbers, 233–35
Perceptions
expectations affecting, 20–21
individual variations in, 19–20
and language, 21, 113, 114, 115
marijuana affecting, 41–42
sounds affecting, 21
Perfect memory, 128–33
Phone numbers, memory of, 230–31
emotional blocks affecting, 6–7
short-term, 84
system for improving, 156–57
Phosphatidylcholine intake, and memory, 27–29

Photo-fit system, for remembering names and faces, 217
Photographic memory, 102–3, 135
Physical memory blocks, 26–47, 81
    in alcohol use, 42–43
    in allergies, 39
    amnesia in, 36
    in arteriosclerosis, 37
    in cigarette smoking, 43
    diet affecting, 27–35
    drugs affecting, 40–41
    exercise affecting, 44
    in fatigue, 45
    in illnesses, 35–38, 124–25, 126–27
    in injuries, 36, 39
    in intensive care units, 37
    in marijuana use, 41–42
    in senility, 37–38, 124–25
    in tension and stress, 45–47
Physical skills, memory of. See Kinesthetic memory
Physostigmine, affecting memory, 40–41
Pi, memory of
    extraordinary, 130
    mnemonic for, 239–40
Picture-taking technique, as memory cue, 104–5
Pituitary gland, 72, 117
Plato, on memory, 62
Pleasant memories, 52
    duration of, 142
Poems
    memorization of, 129, 169, 244, 248
    as memory aid, 151, 152, 153, 154–55, 171–72
Potassium, affecting memory, 33
Potential for remembering, 73, 79–81. See also Capacity for remembering
Power sense, and emotional memory blocks, 7
Practise
    and rehearsal techniques, 242–48
    and skill in memorization, 244–45
Preoccupation, memory block in, 22
    for names, 211

Problem pattern in non-fiction, 195, 196–97, 198
Problem-solving, creativity in, 121
Prosopagnosia, 216
Protective mechanisms in emotional memory blocks, 5–13
Psychological aspects. See Emotions
Psychosis, in intensive care units, 37
Psychosomatic illnesses, 34–35
Public officials, memory for names of, 54, 55, 219–20
Pyridoxine, affecting memory, 30

Q

Quizzes and exercises
    on abnormal forgetfulness, 126–27
    on constructive forgetting, 57–59
    on easily remembered items, 133
    on emotional blocks, 17
    on enjoyment of memorizing, 248
    on episodic and semantic memory, 119
    on fact memory, 189–91
    on grouping to remember, 149–50
    on kinds of memory, 106–9
    on listening memory, 205–8
    on mechanical blocks, 25
    on names and faces, 222–28
    on number memory, 235–41
    on peg system, 165–66
    on physical blocks, 47
    on potential for remembering, 79–81
    on reading memory, 196–200
    on reasons for forgetting, 69
    on recall and recognition of information, 95–98
    on retrieval of information, 92
    on stages of memory, 87–89
    on studying techniques, 185

R

R-complex brain, 72
Readiness for learning, 181

Reading
emotional block to, 11–13
memory of, 173, 192–200
exercise on, 196–200
in information pattern, 195,
197, 199–200
in instruction pattern, 195,
197, 200
omissions and transfor-
mations in, 194
in opinion pattern, 195,
197, 198–99
in problem pattern, 195,
196–97, 198
structure and organization
affecting, 194–200
in studying, 167
in thesis pattern, 195, 197,
199
and misreading, 193–94
speed, 193
Reality, creation of, 20
Recall of information, 90, 91, 92,
93
compared to recognition,
95–98
duration of, 93
exercise on, 95–98
in hypnosis, 145–46
marijuana affecting, 42
Receptors in brain, in remembering,
75
Recognition of information, 90,
91–93
compared to recall, 95–98
duration of, 93
exercise on, 95–98
Redecision therapy, in emotional
memory blocks, 14–16
Registration of information, 90, 91
in childhood, 123
Rehearsal techniques, 144,
242–48
cues in, 243–44, 246–47
and memorization skills after
practise, 244-45
in movement memorization,
246–47
in music memorization, 247
in script memorization, 242–44
in speech memorization,
245–46

Reinforcement of memory, 103,
104–5, 108–9, 202
rehearsals in, 144, 242–48
writing in, 23, 144, 250
Relaxation
prior to tests, 181
in tension-induced memory
blocks, 46, 47
Remembering, 60–133
in ageing, 38, 120–27
aids for improvement of,
134–254
brain in, 70–81
capacity for, 73, 79–81, 83. *See
also* Capacity for
remembering
as hard work, 23–24
historical theories on, 61–69
kinds of memory in, 88–119
and misremembering, 146–47
perfect memory in, 128–33
process of, 82–98
Repetition, and memory, 140
of faces and names, 212
in rehearsals, 242–48
in studying, 173
Reptilian brain, 71–72, 117
Research on memory
animal models in. *See* Animal
models in memory
research
on brain, future areas of, 79
ethical considerations in,
183–84
historical, 65–66
practical implications of, 118
on study techniques, 172–73
Resentment, and emotional memory blocks, 6
Resolution of emotional memory
blocks, 10
professional help in, 13–16
Restudying forgotten information,
93, 94, 173–74
Retention of information, 90, 91
depth of processing affecting,
141
duration of, 83. *See also* Duration of memories
Retrieval of information, 90, 91–93
in ageing, 120
cues in, 140–41

Retrieval of information *(continued)*
depth of processing affecting,
141
distractions in, 23
emotions affecting, 111
improvement of, 140–41
misfiled, 22
recall in, 90, 91, 92, 93, 95–98
recognition in, 90, 91–93,
95–98
word associations in, 141
Rewards of remembering, 138–39,
143, 144, 182
exercise on, 248
of names and faces, 209
Rhymes, as memory aids, 151,
152, 153, 154–55, 171–72
Rhythm as memory aid, 146
Rooms in house, as memory pegs,
161–63, 165–66
Rote memorization, in studying,
168–72
aids for, 170–72
Rubber bands, as memory aids,
249–50

S

Safety pin, as memory aid, 249–50
Sedentary lifestyle, memory in, 44
Selective forgetting, 56
Self-evaluation
quizzes and exercises for. *See*
Quizzes and exercises
of reasons for forgetting, 68–69
Self-image, memory affecting, 24,
51, 139, 252–54
in emotional memory blocks,
15–16
Self-preservation, forgetting for,
11–13, 48–49, 198
Semantic memory, 110, 111–15
exercise on, 119
long-term, 86, 87–88
Senility, 37–38, 124–25
diet affecting, 28, 79
Sensory images enhancing
memory, 139. *See also* Imagery,
as memory aid
Sequencing, as memory aid, 147
Serotonin, and memory, 75, 76

Short-term memory, 66, 83, 84–95
exercise on, 87
transferred to long-term
memory, 85, 86
aids in, 137–40
Siamese twins trick, as memory aid,
251
Silence, listening to, 204
Skill memory, 116. *See also* Kines-
thetic memory
Sleep, affecting memory, 50
of dreams, 145
of thought just prior to falling
asleep, 250
Smoking, affecting memory, 43
Somatopsychic illnesses, 34–35
Songs. *See* Music
Sounds
affecting perceptions and expectations, 21
memory of. *See* Auditory
memory
Speech memorization, rehearsals
for, 245–46
Speed listening, 202–3
Speed reading, 193
Stage names, memory of, 219
Stages of memory, 82–90
Step-on-it-trick, as memory aid, 250
Stress, affecting memory, 45–47
Structures-for-remembering,
142–44, 147–50, 251
exercise on, 149–50
of facts, 188
in hearing and listening, 205
of names of faces, 212, 217
of numbers, 230
in peg system, 158–66
problems in, 148–49
in reading, 192–200
Studying, 167–85
aural repetition in, 173
concentration required for, 168
cramming in, 167
Darwin's law on, 184
exercise on, 185
fading of information learned
in, 174
of history, 171–72, 177–79
interferences affecting, 174–75
learning by understanding in,
168–69, 176, 177

of mathematical formulas, 176–77
of music, 179–80
music affecting, 180–81
negative feedback affecting, 183
predicting results of, 173
readiness affecting, 181
and restudying forgotten information, 93, 94, 173–74
rewards of, 182
rote memorization in, 168–72
aids for, 170–72
time spent in, and amount learned, 172–73
Swallowing of memories, animal research on, 77–78
Synapses in brain, in memory, 74, 75
age-related changes of, 123, 125
Synthesia, 129

T

Tension and stress, affecting memory, 45–47
Tests
predicting performance on, 173
for self-assessment. *See* Quizzes and exercises
study techniques in preparation for, 167–85
Therapy, for resolution of emotional memory blocks, 13–16
Thesis pattern in non-fiction, 195, 197, 199
Thiamine, affecting memory, 27, 30
Trace decay of memories, 65
Trauma
emotional memory blocks in, 36
of head, memory after, 36, 39, 73, 116
physical memory blocks in, 36, 39
Travel memories
emotional block of, 9–10
mechanical block of, 22–23
negative, 51, 52

U

Unconscious factors affecting memory, 49
in emotional memory blocks, 4–17
Freud on, 66–67
Understanding, and memory
of facts, 187–88
in hearing, 202
of scripts, 242–43
in studying, 168–69, 176, 177
Unpleasant memories
duration of, 142
forgetting of, 49–50, 198–99
Freud on, 67
positive uses of, 51–52

V

Vasopressin, enhancing memory, 78
Verbal memory, 99, 100–102, 135
counting system as aid for, 153–55
exercise on, 106–9
kinesthetic memory reinforcing, 104–5, 108–9
in studying, 172
visual memory reinforcing, 103, 108–9
Visual memory, 99, 100–102, 144
counting system as aid for, 153–55
exercise on, 106–9
of faces and names, 215
kinesthetic memory reinforcing, 104–5, 108–9
photographic, 102–3, 135
in reading, 192–200
reinforcing auditory memory, 202
in studying, 172, 173
verbal memory reinforcing, 103, 108–9
Vitamin B$_1$, affecting memory, 27, 30
Vitamin B$_6$, affecting memory, 30
Vitamin B$_{12}$, affecting memory, 30
Vitamin C, affecting memory, 31

W

Watch-on-wrong-wrist trick, as
memory aid, 249
Weight loss diets, affecting memory,
34
Word associations
of names, 213, 214, 215–16,
227
and retrieval of information, 141
Words and letters, as memory aid
for numbers, 230–41

Work, memory affecting success in,
53–55, 206–7, 209
Writing
and reading. See Reading
in reinforcement of memory,
23, 144, 250

Z

Zeigarnick effect on memory, 53
Zinc, affecting memory, 33

Other recommended reading . . .

IMPROVE YOUR CONFIDENCE QUOTIENT

Meryle Gellman Ph.D. and Diane Gage

★ Do you worry whether or not others like you?

★ Do you miss out on opportunities because you don't try?

★ Do you avoid getting into new relationships for fear of being rejected?

★Do you have trouble accepting compliments?

★ Do you eat, smoke or drink alcohol excessively?

If you are like most of us, you have probably experienced self-doubt that prevented you from doing what you wanted in business, social life or at school.

In ten easy steps the authors show how you can use your Confidence Quotient to conquer self-doubt and throw off the shackles that are hindering your life.

HOW TO BOOST YOUR BRAIN POWER

Roger B. Yepsen, Jr

Use the strategies in this book to sharpen your thinking skills, focus your powers of concentration, improve your memory and unlock your creativity.

The author presents the latest scientific research and current thinking on how mental ability is affected by food, medication, caffeine, alcohol, sleep, emotions, light, noise, pollution, time of day, stress, and ageing and tells you what you can do to keep your mental motor running in top gear.

- covers all aspects of mental activity: intelligence, reasoning ability, creativity, memory and ability to concentrate

- explodes common myths such as 'forgetfulness is part of growing older' and 'you're either born intelligent or you're not'

- presents the most up-to-date research findings alongside personal experience